THE BEAUTY
OF HOLINESS

A GUIDE TO BIBLICAL WORSHIP

MICHAEL P. V. BARRETT

AMBASSADOR INTERNATIONAL
GREENVILLE, SOUTH CAROLINA & BELFAST, NORTHERN IRELAND

The Beauty of Holiness
A Guide to Biblical Worship
Copyright © 2006 Michael P. V. Barrett

Cover Design and Internal Layout by A&E Media

ISBN 1 932307 62 1

Published by the Ambassador Group

Ambassador International
427 Wade Hampton Blvd.
Greenville, SC 29609
USA
www.emeraldhouse.com

and

Ambassador Publications Ltd.
Providence House
Ardenlee Street
Belfast BT6 8QJ
Northern Ireland
www.ambassador-productions.com

The colophon is a trademark of Ambassador

DEDICATION

To
Mary Evelyn Barrett
and
Mary Gladys Vowels
My mother and hers
Both of whom now worship their Lord in the perfect beauty of holiness

TABLE OF CONTENTS

PREFACE   vii

INTRODUCTION   1

1 THE DANGER OF WORSHIP   9
   A Warning from Isaiah   12
   A Warning from Jeremiah   23
   A Warning from Ezekiel   31

2 THE OBJECT OF WORSHIP   39
   Theocentric Worship   41
   Trinitarian Worship   54

3 THE SUBJECT OF WORSHIP   59
   The August Person of God   61
   The Attractive Perfections of God   65
   The Awesome Works of God   67

4 THE LITURGY OF WORSHIP   77
   Reading Scripture   78
   Praying   83
   Preaching   88
   Singing   96

5 AIDS FOR WORSHIP   103
   The Sabbath: A Time for Worship   104
   Sacraments: Tools for Worship   117

6 EXAMPLES OF WORSHIP   123
   The Example of Moses   124
   The Example of Isaiah   144
   The Example of John   154

7 PARADIGMS FOR WORSHIP   159
   Focus of the Psalms   161
   Formula in the Psalms   165
   Function of the Psalms   172

CONCLUSION   177

APPENDICES
   1 The Message of Malachi:
      An Analysis of Dead Religion   185
   2 Some Thoughts on Women in the Church   199
   3 Thoughts on Head Covering for Public Worship   205
   4 Some Thoughts on the Meaning of Music from a   215
      Christian World View by Paul Overly
   5 Contemporary Worship and the Next Generation   221
      of Fundamentalist Leaders by David L. Burggraff

ENDNOTES   250
SCRIPTURE INDEX   277

PREFACE

This has been a strange project. I usually stick at what I'm working on until I finish it, but for various reasons I've shifted this project between the proverbial front and back burners more often than I can remember. For me, writing is hard when there is no fire to keep the burners hot. My initial enthusiasm dwindled in the early stages because so many books began to appear on the theme of worship. Worship was a hot topic. Some of these books were well done and expressed many of my concerns, so I decided to abandon the undertaking and adapt what I had done to a couple of lectures. But then some of the books with their expressions of nonsense inflamed the passion once again, particularly when daily on my computer desktop I would see a folder labeled "Book Project 3." So I'd pick it up again. Then another issue commanded my attention, and I relabeled the folder "Book Project 4" while I wrote *God's Unfailing Purpose*. Then important issues in the work of the Geneva Reformed Seminary and my denomination, the Free Presbyterian Church of North America, took away whatever writing time I had. But finally, here is my "two-cents" added to the persistently hot topic. I say this for those who have been asking me for the last few years when this book would be finished.

Let me give a "heads-up" about the format. You will find that some chapters have endnotes. You should be able to follow what I'm saying without referring to them, but I hope you will take the time to wade or maybe plow through them. In these notes I offer corroborating evidence, more detailed explanations, or some digressions from the topic. Those that read them will be annoyed that they are endnotes rather than footnotes, but those that don't read them won't be intimated or distracted by their presence.

I want to acknowledge with thanksgiving those who have helped and supported me through this work. I express my thanks to Geneva Reformed Seminary and Faith Free Presbyterian Church for allowing me write some on "work time." I must thank Dr. Caren Silvester for her remarkable expertise in editing–for her willingness to let it alone unless it was really bad. I offer my special thanks to Sandra (my Sander) for her almost daily prayer that the Lord would give me time to write, for her being the first to read every chapter offering her sweet critique, for her collecting data for the Scripture index, and for checking the final format. I express my special thanks to Ambassador for its willingness to publish another of my works. And to the Lord I offer my praise and thanksgiving for His good providence in putting me in this place to serve Him. I trust that in some way He will use this effort to His glory.

Michael P. V. Barrett
President of Geneva Reformed Seminary
Associate Minister of Faith Free Presbyterian Church
Greenville, South Carolina

INTRODUCTION

Contemporary! Traditional! Divisive words–particularly when referring to methods of worship. Some churches commit themselves to one particular style while others divide themselves into distinct congregations with separate services to accommodate a mismatched membership with dissimilar preferences regarding music or dress. For some reason music always seems to be at the heart of the issue. Should the congregation find the words to hymns in hardback hymnals or the words to choruses projected on a screen? Should soloists sing to recorded music with microphone in hand or to organ accompaniment with arms passively at the side? Should the congregation applaud or whisper "amen" when blessed? Should drums and guitars be allowed in church? Should music styles reflect changing cultural models, or are some melodies and rhythms inherently inappropriate for worship? These are tough questions with answers that almost always fail to convince or change the other side.

Advocates of contemporary methods charge traditionalists with dead formalism, and traditionalists accuse those who use modern methods with appealing to the flesh. Unhappily, the whole controversy about worship style has degenerated into arguments based on personal preference. Far too frequently, advocates on both sides, while giving verbal testimony to their concern for God's glory, defend their positions with man-centered reasoning. Although proponents of neither position would admit it, what pleases the people often takes precedence over any consideration of what pleases the Lord. Worship as entertainment prevails over worship as service rendered to God.

The music controversy, however, is just a surface symptom of a far greater malady. That the modern church has lost "the art of worship" is a common lament. Whether or not it is proper to designate worship as an "art," it is the tragic truth that worship practices in many of today's evangelical, orthodox, and fundamentally conservative churches have departed from the precepts and patterns of worship set down in the Scripture. Some even question whether or not the Bible provides a mandatory guide for how to worship.

This question is not new to the church. Whether the church, tradition, or Scripture owns the right to direct methods of worship has been a matter of disputation for centuries. Theologians have debated the issue in terms of the regulative and normative principles. Simply defined, the regulative principle allows only such practices of worship as the Scripture sanctions, whereas the normative principle allows any practice that the Scripture does not expressly forbid. Extreme applications of both principles exist. Some who rigidly adhere to the letter of the law use the regulative principle to prohibit any expression of worship that is not on the inked surface of Scripture. On this basis, for instance, special services commemorating Christ's incarnation at Christmas or His resurrection at Easter would violate what the Bible prescribes and thus would be inappropriate. On the other hand, following the normative principle can lead to the extremes of rigid liturgical ritual established by years of tradition, or seeker-sensitive services flexibly designed to eliminate religious shock by infusing cultural norms into a bit of gospel.

Given the intensity of this worship controversy that is increasingly dividing professedly Bible-believing churches into distinctive camps, I have felt inclined to make my contribution to the concern. I am neither so naïve nor so arrogant to assume that what I offer here will answer all the questions definitively or satisfy those who may disagree with my conclusions. I am neither a church historian nor a musician, so I will not presume to venture into those areas of my incompetence, although they are ultimately relevant to the issue. I am thoroughly convinced, however, that the Bible does establish clear guidelines for both what we are to believe (issues of faith) and what we are to practice (issues of obedience) and that this direction includes matters of worship. In this regard I affirm and agree completely with the *Westminster Confession of Faith*.

> The whole counsel of God concerning all things necessary for His own glory, man's salvation, faith and life, is either expressly set down in Scripture, or by good and necessary consequence may be deduced from Scripture...and that there are some circumstances concerning the worship of God, and government of the Church, common to human actions and societies, which are to be ordered by the light of nature, and Christian prudence, according to the general rules of the Word, which are always to be observed. (Chapter 1, section 6)

> The light of nature sheweth that there is a God, who hath lordship and sovereignty over all, is good, and doth good unto all, and is therefore to be feared, loved, praised, called upon, trusted in, and served, with all the heart, and with all the soul, and with all the might. But the acceptable way of worshipping the true God is instituted by Himself, and so limited by His own revealed will, that He may not be worshipped according to the imaginations and devices of men, or the suggestions of Satan, under any visible representation, or any other way not prescribed in the holy Scripture. (Chapter 21, section 1)

If there is any overriding biblical truth that must circumscribe every worship practice, it is that worship is all about God and not about us. The inspired Preacher issues an imperative for worship that sums up our duty and should protect us from unduly elevating self and personal preference.

> Keep thy foot when thou goest to the house of God, and be more ready to hear, than to give the sacrifice of fools: for they consider not that they do evil. Be not rash with thy mouth, and let not thine heart be hasty to utter any thing before God: for God is in heaven, and thou upon earth: therefore let thy words be few. (Ecclesiastes 5:1-2)

God is in heaven, and we are on earth. But amazingly while we are on the earth, the Lord invites us into His presence. Being in the presence of God is a privilege that ought to overwhelm us and create within us a sense of caution and reverent submission. "Keeping the foot" simply means to guard the steps, to be careful about conduct, to exercise personal restraint. As Moses removed his shoes before the burning bush and Joshua his before the Captain of the Lord's host, so must every worshipper recognize that the place of worship is a holy place. As we become increasingly conscious that biblical worship brings us into the holy presence of God, we must become increasingly cautious that we do nothing to offend that holy presence.

How we act in God's presence is important. David's initial encounter with the Ark of the Covenant–the visible token of God's presence–remains a vivid lesson of this sobering fact (2 Samuel 6 and 1 Chronicles 13). David, the man after God's own heart, planned to retrieve the Ark from Kirjath-jearim, where it had been exiled for over fifty years, and to restore it to its deserved place of preeminence. Notwithstanding his concern for God's honor and glory, his fervent zeal succumbed to carelessness with tragic consequence. Although his desire was good and his motive was pure, his disregard of God's order displeased the Lord he thought he was honoring. It is not sufficient to claim a worthy purpose and proper spirit without conforming as well to the clear mandates of God's word. Many Christians desire the right things, but are lax in the modes used to achieve those desires. Methods of worship and service do indeed matter: Uzzah's corpse testifies to that.

Happily, David learned the lesson, and his second attempt to exalt the Lord's presence was "according to the word of the Lord" (1 Chronicles 15:15). The results were wonderfully different. My guess is that the lesson David learned early in his reign contributed at least in part to his becoming the sweet psalmist, whose inspired songs set the standard and provided so many patterns for proper worship. Significantly, one of the most sublime imperatives to worship that he issued links the logic and manner of worship: "Give unto the Lord the glory due unto his name; worship the Lord in the beauty of holiness" (Psalm 29:2). The logic of worship is simply that God deserves it. Attention belongs to all His infinite assets; His infinite worth is the mandate for worship. Bowing down before the Lord in the beauty of holiness is the manner in which worship must occur. The expression the *beauty of holiness* is certainly suggestive. Although its exact meaning can be debated, the sense differs little whether the word beauty is an abstract concept or a concrete thing. Whether we are to worship with holy splendor or to worship dressed in the holy attire befitting priests, it is obvious that behavior and appearance in the place of worship is to be holy, distinct from the normal and mundane. At the very least, bringing the world into the holy place defies what worship is all about. To recognize the Lord's infinitely august person, His infinitely attractive perfections, and His infinitely awesome works demands that the finite creature bow submissively. Acceptable worship flows from the true knowledge of God and follows His revealed will. Worship is holy service rendered to the Lord, not an occasion adapted to the likes and dislikes of would-be worshippers.

Not only must outward practices of worship follow the instruction of Scripture, but so must the attitude of the worshipper conform to God's demands. The Lord Jesus Himself highlighted this mandate when He unveiled the formula for worship during His encounter with the Samaritan woman at the well (John 4). Like so many before and since, she defined worship externally in terms of place. In essence, she said, "We do it here–they do it there; we're right–they're wrong." In a profoundly simple yet weighty response, Christ explained, "God is a Spirit: and they that worship him must worship him in spirit and in truth" (John 4:24). As simple as this statement is, it has been open to various interpretations. Although some argue that "spirit" refers to the Holy Spirit and that "spirit and truth" are independent elements of worship procedure, I would suggest that the reference is to man's spirit and that spirit and truth should be united to designate one essential thought. The Scripture makes it abundantly clear that worship must be both spiritual and according to truth, but Christ is teaching here that worship's sum and substance is internal, not external. Most likely the expression *in spirit and in truth* is a literary device called *hendiadys*. Literally meaning "one through two," this figure occurs when two words connected by the conjunction "and" refer to one principal idea. Although the English translation repeats the preposition before both words, it actually occurs only once in the Greek text (in spirit and truth). Taken together, the words imply the necessity of worshipping with a truthful spirit. In other words, biblical worship is directed to God with a sincere heart. Both elements are essential. Insincere worship directed to God is unacceptable. Sincere worship directed to any other than God is unacceptable. The "beauty of holiness" factor, however, means that even sincere worship directed to God in the wrong way is unacceptable.

In every way, worship is a serious matter. My concern, therefore, in this day of worship debate and perversion, is that we let the Bible be our guide. In this book I want simply to examine some of the Scripture's guidelines concerning the object, the manner, and the heart of worship. A biblical theology of worship is foundational to any formulation of worship practice. Too much of the debate concerning worship focuses on application issues without paying due attention to the central and essential truths from which the practices must flow. Rushing to relevancy and practical application without careful exposition and understanding of doctrine is the unhappy tendency of too many evangelicals and fundamentalists today. Perhaps the reason there is such variance in the application of worship principles among Bible-believing churches is the failure to start from the clear precepts of Scripture. There is little hope of worshipping in a manner that is pleasing to the Lord if we do not start with the Bible and stress what it stresses. Although I cannot begin to make all the necessary applications or to critique particular music styles or liturgies, I can highlight what the Bible accents. My desire is that we simply let the Bible guide us and not be afraid to obey it. We must not shy away from what it says regardless of how out of sync with culture it seems to be. God's Word, not culture–whether modern or medieval–defines the way of worship.

It is my prayer that the Holy Spirit will help us to see how big our God is and how small we are and to worship Him accordingly.

CHAPTER 1

THE DANGER OF WORSHIP

A guide has multiple responsibilities. Not only does he lead the way and explain points of interest along the way, but he also assumes responsibility for the safety and welfare of those he leads. Usually before the adventure begins, the guide briefs his soon-to-be followers about any pitfalls that may lie ahead or about potential dangers that may lurk in unexpected places. It is always good to know going into something what the risks and hazards are. The Bible is our guide to worship that is both acceptable and pleasing to the Lord. It is not surprising, then, that along with the instructions that we are to follow, there are also warnings that we are to heed. It makes sense to start with the warnings.

In one of His frequent exchanges with the Pharisees, the Lord Jesus said, "In vain they do worship me" (Matthew 15:9; Mark 7:7). The sad danger is that vain worship is possible. Worshipping in vain is worshipping without purpose or result, in emptiness and deception. Two factors mark this worthless worship. (1) It abandons God's directives in favor of man's

traditions: "Thus have ye made the commandment of God
of none effect by your traditions…teaching for doctrines the
commandments of men" (Matthew 15:6, 9; see also Mark 7:7-
8). (2) It is talk without heart: "This people draweth nigh unto
me with their mouth, and honoureth me with their lips; but
their heart is far from me" (Matthew 15:8; Mark 7:6). That
Christ quotes this indictment from Isaiah 29:13 indicates that it
was not just a Pharisaical flaw. Heartless religion was possible in
the Old Testament dispensation; it was rampant in the days of
Christ's earthly incarnation; unhappily, it pervades even the best
of churches today. If we can learn anything from Christ's appeal
to Isaiah in His exposé of first-century Pharisaical hypocrisy,
it is this: God has never been and will never be satisfied with
heartless worship. Heartless worship is a major pitfall to avoid.

Tragically, the notion seems to be deeply ingrained in man
that formal acts of worship–whatever form they take–constitute
legitimate worship that will by its very performance be accepted
by God. Men tend to form their opinions of God from their
estimations of themselves. Because they satisfy themselves with
outward acts of ritual, they assume that God must be satisfied
as well. Many people today who are without Christ assume that
going to church and keeping the golden rule will somehow
balance to their favor in the end. Even many who profess Christ
allow their pious religious routines to substitute for private
devotion and a sincere heart. To estimate God in this way is
either to question His omniscience–that he is able to see the
heart–or His moral perfection–that He cares about the heart. In
contrast to all this human reasoning is the divine preference for
heart obedience over manual religion: "Behold, to obey is better
than sacrifice" (1 Samuel 15:22).

Nonetheless, so convinced are some that their "worship"
works that they cannot fathom the notion it does not. The
Lord's incontestable indictment of Israel's heartless religion
recorded in Micah 6 illustrates this unfounded confidence. The

nation defended itself against God's accusation by arguing that if God was not satisfied with what they were doing, it was His fault for not making His expectations clear. They claimed that they were willing to offer any sacrifice He wanted; all He had to do was ask.

> Wherewith shall I come before the Lord, and bow myself before the high God? shall I come before him with burnt offerings, with calves of a year old? Will the Lord be pleased with thousands of rivers of oil? shall I give my firstborn for my transgression, the fruit of my body for the sin of my soul? (Micah 6:6-7)

Their self-justifying questions concerning how to approach and satisfy God reveal both the false conception that external religion is enough to please Him and the frustration as to how much is enough. This dilemma always plagues those who assume that outward displays of religion or personal deprivations please God. Since there can never be any certainty that enough has been done, the cyclic solution is to do more and more. Their quandary is evident in the intensification of their offers ranging from the best of the animal sacrifices (calves of a year old) to the exaggerated quantities of sacrifices (thousands of rams and ten thousand rivers of oil) to the desperate abomination of child sacrifice. Their willingness to stoop to heathen practice in order to reach the heights of God reveals their total ignorance not only of what God wants but of who God is. Ironically, rather than defending itself, Israel further incriminated itself by assuming God wanted things rather than hearts.

Because heartless worship is so offensive to God and constitutes such a dangerous impediment to biblical worship, I want to focus our attention on some significant texts dealing with the issue and simply let the Bible speak for itself. Although the warning occurs multiple times throughout Scripture, I am arbitrarily choosing three outstanding texts from the major prophets to make the point, and I trust that the Holy Spirit will make the point stick in our hearts.

A WARNING FROM ISAIAH

Isaiah elaborates on the danger of vain worship in the first chapter of his prophecy. His logic is faultless. This prince of old dispensation preachers addressed the visible covenant community, warning them that being Israelites–notwithstanding the privileges and advantages–was not sufficient to make them acceptable before God. Unhappily, Isaiah's message to the covenant sinners of his day has too much relevance to the churched sinners of our day. Now as then, would-be worshippers must learn the folly and danger of heartless religion and consider that the only cure to heartless religion is a spiritual relationship with God through faith in the Lord Jesus Christ. Nothing less or other will satisfy God. While exposing the deplorable spiritual condition of the people, Isaiah both reveals the problem of and offers the solution to heartless worship. Three themes are on the surface of his argument.

The Problem of Spiritual Insensitivity

External religion breeds spiritual insensitivity by making the "worshipper" oblivious to his real spiritual condition. The moral depravity of the nation magnified the worthlessness of their outward religion. In spite of the Lord's special interest in Israel– evident by His father-like care and provision for them– they rebelled against Him, defying and resisting His rightful authority (1:2). In order to demonstrate the absurdity of Israel's attitude and behavior and to highlight the degree of their spiritual stupidity and insensitivity, the prophet contrasted the people's irrational ignorance to the apparently rational behavior of dumb beasts: "The ox knoweth his owner, and the ass his master's crib: but Israel doth not know, my people doth not consider" (1:3).

Oxen and donkeys are not particularly bright animals, but they exercise better sense than thoughtless worshippers. The dullness of these animals in contrast to the special enlightenment of Israel makes the comparison extremely pointed. Whereas the dumb ox and donkey never fail to know their owner or the place of their sustenance, Israel failed to know. The Hebrew concept of knowing is much more than simple mental awareness or understanding. It conveys the notion of willful acknowledgment and recognition. Israel's ignorance consisted in the failure both to acknowledge the Lord as master and to recognize Him as the source and sustainer of life. The last verb of verse 3, *consider*, continues the condemnation by stressing the failure to give attention to what they should be thinking about. Unaware of their privilege, they were not worshipping perceptively or properly. Since true worship flows from the knowledge of God, it follows that improper thinking about God contaminates and invalidates any act of worship.

The Cause of Spiritual Insensitivity

Although Isaiah 1:4 is a worst-case scenario, it illustrates how far the distance can be between God and those who are professedly worshipping Him. The prophet expresses his grief (woe) over the lamentable state of the people by making it unmistakably clear that their spiritual ignorance and insensitivity was related to their depraved condition and behavior. Piling four unflattering epithets (sinful nation, a people laden with iniquity, a seed of evildoers, children that are corrupters) on top of three verbal clauses without using any conjunctions (forsaken, provoked, gone away backward), the prophet, in grammatical rapid-fire, depicts the nation's spiritual plight. All together, the sevenfold combination warns us that "worshippers" can in actuality be alienated from God, active in sin, and confirmed in guilt. Religion, ironically, can make a person oblivious to sin, but it cannot solve the problem of sin.

The three verbal clauses, particularly, address the root of the matter: alienation from God. Each of these verbs expresses what the people really thought about God. Although their involvement in ritual gave the impression that they were drawing near to the Lord, the opposite was in fact true. And God knew it. First, they forsook the Lord. In the Old Testament, *forsaking* the Lord is the comprehensive expression of apostasy: they abandoned Him. That the LORD is the stated object of this forsaking makes it even worse. This is the personal name of God associated inseparably with the covenant. Therefore, to abandon the LORD was to reject that special relationship with all of its corresponding responsibilities. Second, they provoked the Holy One of Israel to anger. More literally, they despised and irreverently disdained Him. This particular form of the verb (the iterative use of the *piel*) suggests this contempt to be deliberate and sustained. Again, the stated object of this disrespect–"the Holy One of Israel"–intensifies the violence of the act. Whereas His holiness demanded the reverent recognition of His unique distinction, they callously regarded Him as though He was nothing special at all. Third, they turned away backward. The verb is reflexive (*niphal*) and thus it underscores the self-determination and self-interest involved in this estrangement. They alienated themselves. Notwithstanding their religious routines, their heart and thoughts drew them away from the Lord.

Three of the four descriptive epithets synopsize the behavior of the nation that exhibited their alienation from God, and the remaining one pronounces the necessary consequence of such behavior. Significantly, the three statements describing the nation's sinful activity boldface the endlessness of the transgressions by using participles, grammatical forms that in Hebrew emphasize the habitual performance of the stated condition. Sin was a way of life. First, their behavior was marked by sin ("sinful nation"). Their purpose as a nation set apart as God's special possession was "to keep all his commandments" and to be "an holy people unto the LORD" (Deuteronomy 26:18-19). But tragically, they were constantly missing the mark or goal that God had set for them: they were habitually falling short of the glory of God (Romans 3:23). Second, they were a group whose common attribute was the doing of evil ("a seed of evildoers"). Outside of the moral and ethical sphere, the word "evil" refers to calamity or disaster, expressing a disorder in the regular arrangement of circumstances. In the moral sphere, it conveys the disruption or violation of the orderly standards and rules of God. They were guilty of disorderly conduct with calamitous consequence to both self and society at large. Third, they were a class of people whose behavior was ruinous, corrupt, and destructive ("children that are corrupters"). Perpetual sin against God, self, and society—not the behavior you might expect from those worshipping God.

The fourth unflattering caption of the nation declares the consequence of sinful practices: they were a people encumbered with guilt ("a people laden with iniquity"). The terseness of Isaiah's language paints a vivid picture of a people bowed down with a dreadful burden (literally, "a people heavy of iniquity"). The term "iniquity" simply means twisted or crooked and, when referring to sin, presents it as perverseness, a twisting away from the proper path. However, this word not only designates the act of sin but by metonymy also refers to sin's consequences, in terms of punishment or guilt. Indeed, it is the principal word used in the Old Testament to designate guilt as the consequence of sin. The fact that this epithet does not use a participle to express habitual behavior, as do the other three expressions, would suggest the consequence of guilt to be in view rather than the commission of some sort of perverse behavior. The Lord had them pegged for what they really were; the fact that they were in the church only intensified the guilt.

The Callousness of Spiritual Insensitivity

God always deals with sinners for their sin, and Israel was not exempt from chastisement. Although divine discipline is justly punitive, it should be remedial in its consequence. Good parents punish misbehaving children, inflicting discomfort both to warn of the more severe end of sin and to encourage proper behavior. Few things are more disappointing and frustrating to parents than unresponsive children. Some children seem never to learn regardless of the intensity or frequency of disciplinary measures. This is the analogy Isaiah uses to picture–and I speak here perhaps foolishly in human terms–God's "frustration" over the callousness of the nation's spiritual insensitivity. In verse 2, the Lord declared that He had "nourished and brought up children" and that they had rebelled against Him. Verses 5-9 describe a people who had already experienced some of the consequences of sin. They had been chastised but remained oblivious to what the Lord, as a father, was doing.

The prophet describes Israel's condition in terms of an individual whose entire body bears evidence of wounds.

> ...the whole head is sick, and the whole heart faint. From the sole of the foot even unto the head there is no soundness in it; but wounds, and bruises, and putrifying sores: they have not been closed, neither bound up, neither mollified with ointment. (1:5b-6)

Although these words vividly imply the total effects of sin and thus are often employed as biblical proof of the truth of man's total depravity, their principal focus points to wounds that have been inflicted externally either by the sword or by scourging rather than to sores that fester from internal and inherent corruption. That verses 7 and 8 detail the invasion of the land by foreigners confirms the imagery. Sadly, these are wounds to which there was no response; they were ignored and left untreated to putrefy through infection.

The question of verse 5 indicates that the Lord was the primary agent who inflicted the wounds and that in spite of the thoroughness with which He had punished, the nation continued in rebellion. There are two possible translations of this question, both of which engender amazement over the persistent rebellion: (1) "Why will you be stricken again?" or (2) "Where can you be stricken anymore?" The first suggests the foolishness of a people who continue to be beaten when repentance could remedy their condition. The second pictures a body that, having been beaten so repeatedly and extensively, has no unwounded area. It underscores the insensitive and obdurate character of the nation that remained contumacious despite multiplied efforts to arouse spiritual concern. Regardless of the translation, the significance is pretty much the same. It is as though the Lord is asking in "divine frustration" where He could smite them again to do any good. I can only wonder if Isaiah's morbid image does not mirror the detailed account of God's successive disciplinary acts that his contemporary Amos indexed, each with the tragic refrain, "yet have ye not returned unto me, saith the LORD" (4:6-12). Isaiah's description of this spiritual callousness soundly echoes the warning of Solomon: "He, that being often reproved hardeneth his neck, shall suddenly be destroyed, and that without remedy" (Proverbs 29:1). All the religion in the world is not the remedy. In fact, heartless religion was a chief contributor to the problem.

The Evaluation of Empty Worship

Outwardly religious people are often the most difficult to convince of their need for God. No doubt, the people responded to Isaiah's message of condemnation with skepticism and disbelief, claiming that their worship habits exempted them from any divine displeasure. False security seems always to accompany hypocritical worship (cf. Malachi 1:6-7; 3:8). With irrefutable argument, Isaiah levels God's complaint against these trained sinners by proving that their religion was inwardly wrong although it was outwardly right. Verses 10-15 record God's evaluation of empty worship.

Outwardly Right

A survey of this passage indicates that the people observed the letter of the law; they followed the Mosaic instructions according to rule, doing everything they were supposed to do. In terms of modern worship jargon, they adhered flawlessly to the regulative principle. The manner in which they multiplied sacrifices suggests that they were absolutely and indisputably orthodox (verse 11). The burnt offerings required the sacrificial victim to be burned completely on the altar—they held nothing back. The fat represented the best part of the sacrifice to be reserved for the Lord—they offered the fattest. The blood marked the most essential element of the sacrifice—from bulls to goats they shed it all. Not only were they orthodox in the manner of their worship, but they were consistent in observing all of the required feasts and ceremonies; they never missed an occasion for worship (verses 13-14). If the "church doors" were open, they were there: they had a perfect attendance record. Similarly, they prayed fervently. Spreading the hands was symbolic of fervor and zeal (verse 15). They were consistent in their "daily devotions." Since all of this was true, it never crossed their minds that God could be displeased with them. They were satisfied; they assumed God would be as well.

Inwardly Wrong

Although God was the author of Israel's system of worship, He categorically rejected its formalistic practice by a people whose behavior and character warranted the appellations "rulers of Sodom" and "people of Gomorrah" (verse 10). Given what He knew to be the condition of their hearts, the Lord's analysis of Israel's worship was justifiably harsh. How He saw their religion differed dramatically from how they perceived it. He saw their approach to Him as a treading of His courts (verse 12). Treading is an activity normally associated with beasts—a graphic image. Without regard for God's holiness, these worshippers lumbered ox-like in the delicate surroundings of the temple, like the proverbial bull in the china shop. He regarded their oblations as "vain" (verse 13). What should have been a sincere reflection of devoted hearts was in fact empty, unsubstantial, and worthless. The Lord also regarded their ineffectual offerings as an "abomination," something most disgusting and detestable (verse 13). Significantly, the Scripture frequently uses this term to describe God's attitude toward idolatry. It is sobering to realize that God regards hypocritical and heartless worship of Himself to be just as repugnant and loathsome as the worship of false gods. Even the hands spread so diligently in prayer only pretended piety because the Lord saw the hands as dripping with the guilt of violence (i.e., full of blood, verse 15). Orthodoxy (right doctrine) and orthopraxis (right practice)—though essential elements—are not the sum total of genuine religion and acceptable worship.

The Lord's assessment of empty religion accounts for His attitude and actions towards it. Several first person declarations express the divine repugnance and grief. The initial question of verse 11 sets the tone for the crescendo of disgust that follows: "To what purpose is the multitude of your sacrifices to me?" The terseness of the literal rendering suggests something of the disdain He had for every detail of their worship: "What to me is the abundance of your sacrifices?" Their worship meant nothing to Him; there was a total disconnect between the Lord and what they were doing. That the Lord asks those appearing before Him who had "required this" from them implies that He had no part in their pious masquerade (verse 12). In language that can only be classified as boldly anthropopathic (language expressing human feelings), the Lord declares that He has had enough of their burnt offerings (verse 11, "I am full"), that He has grown tired of their rituals (verse 14, "I am weary"), and that He just could not take it any more (verse 13, "I cannot away with"). For omnipotent Deity to confess such exhaustion puts in boldface how offensive heartless worship must be to the Lord. Given God's attitude about heartless religion, there can be no surprise that He declares His lack of pleasure in their sacrifices (verse 11, "I delight not"), His refusal to accept their observances as legitimate acts of worship (verse 14, "my soul hateth," i.e., rejects), and His repudiation of their prayers by shutting (literally, darkening) His eyes and closing His ears (verse 15, "I will hide" and "I will not hear").

The lesson is clear, and the application is encompassing—God is not satisfied with external religion. Even the right mechanics of worship are without merit. Worship must be the expression of faith.

The Corrective of Worthless Worship

As offensive as worthless worship is before the Lord, the offenders are not beyond the reach of His grace. There is hope for sinners, even for those who are highly trained in religion. Grace transforms sinners to saints, creating hearts capable of the purity required for true worship. And grace, once received, always shows itself in life, revealing the clean hands that are equally required for true worship. Psalm 24:3-4 states the inviolable law of worship: "Who shall ascend into the hill of the LORD? Or who shall stand in his holy place? He that hath clean hands, and a pure heart…." So to these wickedly religious people, whose hearts were corrupt and whose hands were dirty, the Lord extends hope by offering His grace and explaining what that grace demands.

The Demand of True Religion

God demands that the life of would-be worshippers correspond to the practice of their religion. Israel had made a mockery of their worship by the impiety of their lives, and things had to change. Verses 16 and 17 state both negatively and positively what God requires for a truly pious life–for those who would worship rightly. Simply stated, they had to stop sinning and start behaving well. Negatively, the Lord commanded the people to cleanse themselves, which could be accomplished by putting away the evil and ceasing to do it (verse 16). The principle is clear: fellowship with God demands purity. Positively, the Lord instructed them to "learn to do well" (verse 17). He followed that general requirement with specific examples of how that good behavior could show itself in life (e.g., kindness to widows and orphans). Interestingly, the New Testament defines true religion in almost the same terms. "Pure religion and undefiled before God and the Father is this, To visit the fatherless and widows in their affliction, and to keep himself unspotted from the world" (James 1:27). The point is that there is more to true piety than just talk. That is always true. What God demanded for those who approach Him in worship was a far cry from what they were. Repentance is essential to correcting worthless worship; without it true worship is impossible.

The Offer of Grace

Isaiah 1:18, one of those high water texts in the Bible, sets the course for the necessary repentance. Although it invites lengthy discourse, I must resist temptation and highlight just a couple of thoughts. First, the Lord issues a most gracious invitation:

"Come now, and let us reason together." We can't take this to mean that God is offering to make concessions to sinners through negotiation. God never makes deals or compromises His absolute requirements in order to entice worshippers. Rather, the invitation is to face the facts by grace-generated understanding and then to submit to the dictates that God establishes. The only saving way for a sinner to reason with God is to forsake his own thoughts, which are contrary to God's, and to agree with God's, which are infinitely superior to his (see Isaiah 55:7-9). Reasoning with God is submitting to Him; anything else is unreasonable. It is the response of faith.

Second, the Lord declares His willingness and ability to forgive. In spite of the indisputable evidence of guilt (sins like scarlet and crimson), the Lord pardons: He turns red to white. This color modification pictures the cleansing or pardon necessary for acceptance before the Lord. Again keep in mind the law of worship: only those with clean hands and pure hearts can approach His holy presence (Psalm 24:3-4). Contrarily, these people had been trying to worship the Lord with hands dripping in blood guiltiness (verse 15) and with hearts in rebellion (verse 2), so the Lord Himself makes them fit for worship by forgiving their transgressions. But that should not be surprising seeing that the Lord is good and "ready to forgive," abounding in mercy to all that call upon Him (Psalm 86:5). Although the Lord commands them to cleanse themselves (verse 16), He declares them clean. The link between the divine command and the divine operation is common (e.g., "sanctify yourselves...I am the Lord which sanctify you" in Leviticus 20:7-8). That is grace, and it is only way the necessary changes can occur.

If anything is obvious from Isaiah's indictment of Israel's vain worship, it is that God takes worship seriously. Isaiah's warning is clear enough.

A WARNING FROM JEREMIAH

Jeremiah concurs with Isaiah that religion without a saving relationship with the Lord is dangerous. Religion can be most deceptive. Exposing falsehood was an oft-occurring theme in Jeremiah's preaching. He mocked the absurdity of false gods, which were nothing but broken cisterns yet more attractive to Judah than the true God, who is the fountain of living water (see Jeremiah 2:13). He was in constant conflict with false prophets, who without divine authority or authorization preached peace without peace–a popular "feel good about yourself" religion, a message that resounds in so many modern pulpits (see Jeremiah 8:9-11). He also condemned the false security that characterized his day. Ironically, the very generation that was on the eve of national disaster felt insouciantly confident that religion would exempt them from judgment. External religion breeds a sense of safety; it is unfounded but nonetheless real. This kind of false security resting on a false hope is difficult for preachers to undermine, even for the inspired Jeremiah. Real hypocrites tend never to worry about their souls; they believe all is well. But feeling secure and being secure are two different things. The words of Bildad ring timelessly true: "and the hypocrite's hope shall perish: Whose hope shall be cut off, and whose trust shall be a spider's web" (Job 8:13-14). I want to reflect on this theme of religious hypocrisy from one of Jeremiah's great sermons. Often designated as the "Temple Sermon," this message in Jeremiah 7 cuts to the quick as it issues the warning against this serious danger of worship.

The Existence of Hypocrisy

Perhaps one of the most salient and sobering lessons from this Temple Sermon is that hypocrisy can exist in the best places. The Lord instructed Jeremiah to "stand in the gate of the LORD's house" (7:2). As his pulpit platform, Jeremiah most likely used the steps on the south side of the Temple leading up to one of the chief gates through which the people entered to worship. The point is sobering. This was not a message directed either to pagans or to the rabble of the back streets and alleys of Jerusalem or even to religious renegades. On the contrary, it was directed to the most outwardly religious segment of society. If I may put it in these terms, it was directed to respectable churchgoers who were members of the most conservative and orthodox church in town. Not only were these people going to the right place, but they were going for the right reason, too: "to worship the LORD" (7:2). They entered the Temple gates with the pretense of bowing down before the Lord, giving God His due. From the outside everything looked right: in the right place doing the right things. That Jeremiah exhorted these worshippers to repent (7:3) makes it all too clear that worship ritual does not guarantee that the worshipper is right with God. Mechanical worship is but a thin disguise for the hypocrite, and no church is exempt–no matter how right the rituals.

The Expression of Hypocrisy

With prophetic precision and inspired insight, Jeremiah identified two expressions of hypocrisy among his parishioners. First, the hypocritical worshippers affirmed a false creed. In other words, they believed the wrong thing–their theology was wrong. The threefold repetition of the phrase "the temple of the Lord" expresses the unorthodox confession of faith of the seemingly orthodox worshippers (7:4). The repetition of this "temple theology" may have had some superstitious significance, as though by their saying it over and over it would become true and ward off danger; or it may simply have signified the zeal and fervor with which they affirmed the creed. Regardless of why the statement was repeated, it evidences a misplaced confidence in the structure rather than the spiritual substance of the Temple. The Temple was the sign of God's presence, and there was a long history of God's protecting His dwelling place against every enemy. Even the inspired songs of worship celebrated the Lord's special love of Zion and the certain hope that He would protect it (see, for instance, Psalms 69:35; 74:2; 76:2; 78:68; 129:5). Seemingly against all odds, God preserved His dwelling place against the Assyrians (2 Kings 18-19), so there was no reason to assume He would not spare it from the Babylonians regardless of what Jeremiah threatened. The "temple theology" attributed something magical to the place where the Lord had chosen to dwell. They apparently assumed that if they could keep God "happy" by giving Him what they thought He wanted in the temple ceremonies, He would stay and all would be well. They expressed confidence in tradition, in location, and in practice, but not in the Lord Himself.

Second, the false creed gave expression to a false trust. Jeremiah declared that they were trusting "lying words, that cannot profit" (7:8; see also 7:4). The word "trust" implies a feeling of strong confidence and safety in its object. But regardless of how safe they felt, they were not safe at all because they were trusting, literally, "the words of the lie" (7:4, 8). Referring to something that is empty, worthless, and consequently futile, the word for "lie" underscores a vital lesson about faith and trust: the object of faith determines the value of faith. It is not the fact of faith that saves; it is the object of faith that saves. That is, the object of faith saves when and only if the object is the Lord, His Word and His Christ. These people trusted the temple with its external rituals without internalizing the divinely intended message of the rituals. That they trusted is without dispute; what they trusted was without power to save. There is always the danger of having a form of godliness without the experience of its power (see 2 Timothy 3:5). Religion, as I've said before, can be dangerously deceptive.

Exhibition of Hypocrisy

The disconnect between "religious life" and "real life" is a common mark of hypocrisy. Hypocrites tend to assume that religious activity earns them the freedom to live without restraint and with impunity. Jeremiah's temple congregation annunciated that assumption in these terms: "We are delivered to do all these abominations" (7:10). Notwithstanding their consistent worship in the temple, their lifestyle exhibited a disregard for God's law and a light regard for God's holiness. The list of crimes of which they were guilty violated both divisions of the Decalogue (7:9– theft, murder, adultery, false oaths, idolatry, and polytheism). True religion produces a desire in the heart to walk in holiness; life must correspond to profession. The apostle John concurs with the prophet Jeremiah in his assessment of those who live incongruously to their profession: "If we say that we have fellowship with him, and walk in darkness, we lie, and do not the truth" (1 John 1:6). How one views the law of God is always an index to the genuineness of his religion. Obedience will never be perfect, but it is always the outgrowth of true trust.

How one regards the law of God is a reflection of how one regards the Lord Himself. Coming to stand before the Lord in His holy temple and claiming deliverance or sanction to sin (7:10) exhibited a spiritual callousness and insensitivity to the holiness of God, a holiness which demands cleanness of hands and purity of heart for all who would approach the divine presence (Psalm 24:3-4). The very fact that they went through the motions of worship while at the same time blatantly transgressing God's law betrays a low estimation of who the Lord really is. Worshipping in the fear of God fosters daily living in the fear of God. True worship always connects with life.

Exposure of Hypocrisy

"The LORD is in his holy temple, the LORD's throne is in heaven: his eyelids try, the children of men" (Psalm 11:4). Indeed, "all things are naked and opened unto the eyes of him with whom we have to do" (Hebrews 4:13). Heartless, external, and hypocritical worship may satisfy the worshipper and impress the observer, but the Lord sees it for what it is and will deal with it according to His infallible knowledge and inflexible judgment.

Verse 11 records the some of the most sobering words of the passage. "Is this house, which is called by my name, become a den of robbers in your eyes? Behold, even I have seen it, saith the LORD." Although the temple should have been a most sacred place because it was hallowed by God's name, it had become a cave of thieves, a hideout for bandits. The imagery is telling. I must confess that every time I read this text I think of my youth when I would listen to the tales of the Lone Ranger. As I recall, the Butch Cavendesh gang caused constant havoc in the territory patrolled by the Lone Ranger and Tonto. Butch and his gang would rob a train or a bank or commit some other dastardly deed and then retreat to their secluded hideout for safety. So long as they could make it to the hideout, they were exempt from the arm of the law. Not even the Lone Ranger knew where the gang hid out. This is the analogy of the text. Israel would commit every conceivable crime on the outside (7:9) and then retreat to the temple claiming to be delivered (7:10). The temple was their place of refuge, their hideout, where they would be exempt from the demands and penalty of the law. But unlike the Lone Ranger, the Lord declared, "I have seen it" (7:11). He knew right where they were, and the temple was no place of safety for them. Sadly, Israel's notion persists. Many today have made church or the place of prayer to be a hideout, assuming that no matter what they do everything will be okay if they can just get to church or say sorry at bedtime prayer. But God is still incapable of being fooled; He still sees. Religion provides no refuge for hypocrites.

Not only does God know all about hypocritical worship, but He constantly warned against it and consistently judged it. The Lord reminded the people that He had spoken to them "rising up early and speaking" and that He had called to them without their hearing or answering (7:13). "Rising up early" is a Hebrew idiom that refers not to the time of action but rather to the zeal and fervency with which an action occurs. The divine warning against heartless religion was a high priority and a common component of inspired preaching from the days of Moses right through to the days of Jeremiah. The priority of the message has never diminished and therefore remains relevant. The hope is that those who hear the warning will heed it.

To illustrate His consistency in judging hypocrisy, the Lord gave a history lesson. Just as all of Israel's history serves as an example for us in this dispensation (see 1 Corinthians 10), so whatever amount of Israel's history existed at any given time served as an example for each succeeding generation in the old dispensation. The Lord told the temple worshippers in Jerusalem to remember what had happened to the tabernacle worshippers at Shiloh (7:12, 14). The tabernacle like the temple was a place of worship, sacrifice, and revelation. But when the previous generation turned it into a hideout for all their wickedness, God did not spare it. Shiloh was not a safe place just because the tabernacle was there (1 Samuel 4). The demise of Shiloh was concrete evidence of God's intolerance of talismanic religion. God asked the temple hypocrites of Jeremiah's day, "Where is the tabernacle?" God asks the church hypocrites of today, "Where is the tabernacle? Where is the temple?" History makes it clear that God is not satisfied with religion. It is folly to think that what was inexcusable then will be overlooked now.

The Excision of Hypocrisy

The only hope for the hypocrite is to quit his hypocrisy. The introduction to Jeremiah's Temple sermon was the command to repent: "Amend your ways and your doings" (7:3). Amending the ways required making good (the literal rendering of "amend") the whole course of life, including the inclinations, propensities, and desires of the heart as well as the habits of living. Making good the doings required the alteration of the specific deeds that were generated by the inner character. This was not a call for reformation or for resolution to do better but a call for the transformation of the heart, without which the hypocrisy would persist. Elsewhere Jeremiah made the appeal in terms of the circumcision of the heart (Jeremiah 4:4), a most fitting analogy for those who took pride and confidence in the circumcision of the flesh (cf. Romans 2:28-29). In verses 5 and 6 Jeremiah set down some specific guidelines for applying repentance to life. Interestingly, the specifics covered both divisions of the law, evidencing love for neighbor as well as love for God (kindness to orphans and widows, preservation of life, and ethical monotheism). It is always true that behavior toward men is an index of the extent of devotion to God. Regardless of the specific applications he made to the temple worshippers, Jeremiah's point is timelessly to the point: true religion always connects with behavior.

It is also invariably true that God accepts true repentance: "The sacrifices of God are a broken spirit: a broken and a contrite heart, O God, thou wilt not despise" (Psalm 51:17). If Jeremiah's generation persisted in their hypocritical worship, they would find no salvation in the temple. But if they repented, God promised to keep them in the land of promise (7:3, 7). There was a way to escape judgment. Although there are inherent dangers in religion, true religion in the heart is the sinner's only hope. The heart is the key.

Extent of Hypocrisy

Without genuine repentance, there is really no way of telling how far heartless, hypocritical worship can go in taking the worshipper away from God. Jeremiah's temple worshippers crossed the line of no return. So far gone were they that God forbade Jeremiah even to pray for them (7:16)–a sobering and fearful prohibition. Religious hypocrisy led to outright paganism. All the while that the people were entering the temple under the pretense of worshipping the one true and living God (7:2), they were worshipping the queen of heaven (7:18; 44:17). This is a reference to the Assyro-Babylonian Astarte or Ishtar. In Mesopotamian myth, this goddess was designated either queen or mistress and, as an astral deity, was commonly worshipped out in the open (Jeremiah 19:13; 32:29). The worship of this goddess along with all the host of heaven became popular in Judah during the wicked reign of Manasseh, who introduced all sorts of apostasy to the soon-to-be-doomed nation (2 Kings 21). It is as though in their religious ignorance and superstition they were trying to cover all the bases, giving to every deity they heard of what they thought would make that deity happy and earn them some relief.

But they were certainly not giving the true God what He wanted. There can be little wonder that this religious syncretism led to the dramatic indictment of the entire sacrificial system that was so integral to temple worship (7:21-28). Critics often cite this condemnation of sacrifices to demonstrate a contradiction in Scripture. They argue that since God instituted the Mosaic sacrificial system, it is odd that He would now reject it. Rather than seeing a contradiction between Moses and Jeremiah, we should recognize two significant facts about the Old Testament sacrifices, both of which are important and one of which has direct bearing on our topic. (1) The Old Testament sacrifices had no inherent efficacy (see Hebrews 10). If God had intended the animal sacrifices to be a way of salvation, He would not have condemned them. This involves far-reaching theology, but for now remains beside our point. (2) The sacrifices had to be offered from a proper heart relationship to God. Ritual without obedience and a heart alive to God is absolutely meaningless. External religion is nothing unless the heart is right. This is very much to our point. Jeremiah, therefore, is not contradicting Mosaic law; he is stressing the spirit of the law that was intended from the beginning.

I hope that the point is clear for us. Whatever the form worship takes—whether suited to the old or the new dispensations—it must be in spirit and truth or it is unacceptable to the God whom we profess to worship. Religious motion without heart devotion is an abomination to the Lord. Jeremiah is clear about that.

A WARNING FROM EZEKIEL

True and spiritual worship is a means of drawing near to God with the anticipation of His drawing near in return (see James 4:4). Significantly James, like David a millennium earlier, linked the command to approach God with the commands to cleanse the hands and purify the heart (James 4:4; cf. Psalm 24:3-4). Here are two different dispensations, but the same requirements for worship. The mechanical form of worship changed, but the sum and substance of truly spiritual worship remains constant. To be in the presence of God obliges the worshipper to comply with His demands.

Beyond doubt, one of the most pathetically poignant scenes in Scripture is that of Christ standing outside the door of the church in Laodicea knocking to enter (Revelation 3:20). Here was a prosperous church going through the motions of worship, all the while unconscious that the Christ it professed to worship was absent. I wonder how often this biblical scene is repeated in what appear to be the very best churches in our time. The place of public worship should be a holy place sanctified by the presence of the Lord. It is tragic when worship activity occurs without the divine presence.

If it is tragic when worship occurs without the presence of God, it is even more tragic when worship drives God away. Ezekiel 8 pictures such a sad state of affairs in the temple of Ezekiel's time. Filled with mysterious visions, confusing symbols, and seemingly irrelevant details, the book of Ezekiel is one of the most difficult Old Testament books to understand, and consequently it is often ignored. But Ezekiel provides almost unparalleled insight into the nature of God. The book throughout reveals God's gloriously holy presence with its corollary implications and demands. In the particular vision recorded in chapters 8 through 10, God's glorious presence is contrasted with Israel's perverse sinfulness. The vision progresses downward until "the glory of the LORD departed" from the very threshold of the temple (10:18). The Lord's departure from the place of worship is one of the dangers associated with worship. When Ichabod ("no glory") is written over the church entrance, it would be best to close the doors altogether. Ultimately, that is what God did to the temple.

In the part of the vision I want to consider, the Lord enabled Ezekiel to see worship in the temple as He saw it. Anyone else would have seen the rituals performed precisely as Moses had prescribed. But what would have been impressive to natural sight was an absolute abomination from God's perspective. The application extends to modern worship in the church as well. How the Lord sees the church is infinitely more important than what appears on the surface. What goes on in the heart is always more crucial than what goes on in the pew. I have to wonder, how much of what impresses us as legitimate worship is in reality loathsome to the Lord? Let me sum up the vision in Ezekiel 8 by noting why and when God's presence departs from the place of worship. It is a sobering message.

God Leaves When His Glory is Shared

Although Ezekiel remained bodily in Babylon, in this divinely revealed vision, the Spirit snatched him up by his hair and flew him to the temple in Jerusalem (8:3). He immediately saw two mutually exclusive things, and this was the problem. On the one hand, he saw the Lord: "And behold, the glory of the God of Israel was there" (8:4); it was the same manifestation of divine glory that previously had caused him to fall on his face (Ezekiel 1:28). Falling on his face was the right thing to do. Seeing the majestically holy, glorious, and sovereign Lord as He graciously reveals Himself should generate that submissive and humble response. The Lord is the only legitimate object of worship, and His glory belonged in the temple.

But sadly, Ezekiel saw something else in the temple, something that did not belong there: "the seat of the image of jealousy, which provoketh to jealousy" (8:3, 5). The exact identity of this image that incited carnal passion and provoked divine wrath is disputed. But its presence, not its precise identity, is the crucial issue. It is noteworthy, however, that during the wicked reign of Manasseh, such images were actually in the temple (2 Kings 21:3–7), and this may be an allusion to the pagan goddess Asherah (translated "grove" in the Authorized Version). During the righteous reign of Josiah, however, the images were removed (2 Kings 23:6). If this is the allusion, then Ezekiel's seeing the image there is all the more significant. God enabled the prophet to see through the religious sham. Although the material image was not there, the *spirit* of the image was there in the hearts of the worshippers. Josiah could reform the fashion of worship, but he could not transform the hearts of the idolaters.

Man is such a natural idolater that an image does not have to be materially in place for him to violate the first commandment: "Thou shalt have no other gods before me" (Exodus 20:3). The Lord demands total allegiance and will not tolerate divided worship or permit competition with Himself: "I am the LORD: that is my name: and my glory will I not give to another, neither my praise to graven images" (Isaiah 42:8). Whether images rest on pedestals or reside in hearts, God is infinitely jealous for His name and His glory, and He will leave a place before He shares His place with anything else. Ezekiel's x-ray vision exposed what was really happening in the minds and hearts of those going through the motions of worshipping Jehovah. The time had come for the Lord to "go far off" from the sanctuary (8:6). He had to leave. Years earlier the Philistines had stolen the ark, and the name *Ichabod* told the tale (1 Samuel 4:21–22). It was deplorable when the enemy held the ark hostage; it is far more calamitous when a people professedly worshipping the Lord actually drive Him away. The sad fact is that it happens.

God Leaves When His Gospel is Replaced

The principal lesson about true worship, pictured and prophesied by the temple ritual, is that God is approachable only through the blood of atonement. Without the shedding of blood there can be no forgiveness (see Leviticus 17:11; Hebrews 10:22), and without forgiveness there can be no fellowship with God (see Psalm 65:3–4). Therefore, any worship or religious routine that minimizes, denies, or distracts from the central truth of the atonement–the foundation of the gospel–is in jeopardy of missing the Lord. Of course, the ultimate reality is that Jesus Christ is the gospel. Apart from Christ and His atoning work, true worship is impossible. Any worship bypassing Christ is false worship.

Although the Old Testament revealed the person and work of Christ in many ways, the rituals of the tabernacle and temple vividly portrayed in particular His atoning work. Understanding this truth explains the shameful severity of what Ezekiel witnessed in his temple vision. The first thing he saw was the image of jealousy erected at the north entrance of the temple (8:3, 5). The mere presence of the image was bad enough, but the placement of the image exposed the depths of the people's ungodly folly. The northern gate was the altar gate, the place where sacrifices were offered (see Leviticus 1:11). By setting aside the sacrifice and finding a substitution for the blood, they assumed that God was different from what He is, that man is different from what he is, and that sin is less severe than it is.

When God's way of worship is set aside, men are left to their own devices and imaginations in their vain efforts to approach God. What Ezekiel saw was nothing more than "Cain" worship, worship that never works. Once the blood is rejected, hell is the only limit to what a base and unregenerate heart can contrive as worship (see Romans 1:18–32). As Ezekiel pushed forward through the temple (8:8), he saw the worship of animals (8:10), of Tammuz (8:14), and of the sun (8:16–18).

The images of the creeping things and abominable beasts plastered all over the walls vividly violated the second commandment (Exodus 20:4). The worship of Tammuz revealed a God-for-profit motive. Tammuz was a fertility god who in times of drought and famine was confined to the underworld. His escape from the underworld resulted in crops and prosperity. Since prosperity depended on the welfare of Tammuz, worship was a means of keeping him around. Even today many seek to worship God with Tammuz theology. To use worship as a means of manipulating God for personal interest or gain is a violation of the third commandment (Exodus 20:7). God will not be used. The sun worshippers represent the violation of the first commandment itself (Exodus 20:3). That they faced the rising sun with their backs to the temple (Ezekiel 8:16) is a graphic demonstration that true worship and false worship are mutually exclusive.

It is not surprising that the word *abomination* occurs repeatedly in this temple vision (8:6, 9, 10, 13, 15, 17). Referring to something disgusting, detestable, and unacceptable, this word often designates idolatry and false worship. It is not surprising that God's presence would leave such a place. The Lord promised to meet His people at the place of sacrifice (Exodus 29:42–43); there is, therefore, no hope of His presence apart from atonement. To replace the gospel with anything is to be left alone.

False worship always betrays a blindly ignorant misinterpretation and misrepresentation of the Lord. When men don't see the Lord for who He is, they convince themselves that God does not see them, either. Those committing the abominations convinced themselves in their supposedly dark and secret places that the "Lord seeth us not" (8:12). Ironically, while they were professing God's blindness to them and their behavior, the Lord was looking right at them, or, more precisely, right through them. And in view of what God saw, there was nothing He could do but leave (10:18) and declare His necessary judgment: "Therefore will I also deal in fury: mine eye shall not spare, neither will I have pity: and though they cry in mine ears with a loud voice, yet will I not hear them" (8:18). If the presence of God is fullness of joy (Psalm 16:11), then His absence is judgment. Ezekiel's warning is clear enough: men must worship God alone in His way alone—or else.

I have arbitrarily selected these three passages from the Major Prophets to establish the biblical warning against improper worship. Isaiah, Jeremiah, Ezekiel, and virtually every other inspired writer of Scripture concur that there are inherent dangers in worship. Religious practice that is pleasing and acceptable to God must not only conform to God's revelation, but must also flow from a heart that is alive with conscious devotion to the Lord. The object, mechanics, and motive of worship all matter.

Throughout these expositions, I have not made much specific or direct application to the modern issues or problems confronting the church. It has been my desire to allow the force of the Scripture to speak to the facts. But it does not require a great deal of spiritual acumen to see the many unfortunate parallels between the distant past of Israel's profane practices and what occurs in the modern church. The danger for us is to find the easy and legitimate application to Romanism and apostate Protestantism while failing to see the not-so-easy-to-swallow application to the most conservative, evangelical, and fundamental churches. May the Lord make us ever sensitive to the truth that while we are doing everything right on the outside, He is looking at our hearts.

CHAPTER 2

THE OBJECT OF WORSHIP

"Worship God" (Revelation 19:10). Nothing is more basic than this, and it seems simplistically and obviously clear. Yet so many of the indecorous methods of worship that plague the church flow from improper identification of or careless attention to who God really is. Defining God is impossible since definition sets borders for understanding, and God is infinite. At best, we can describe God according to the terms by which He has revealed Himself. Few statements are more to the point than the answer to the question "What is God?" given in the Shorter Catechism: "God is a Spirit, infinite, eternal, and unchangeable, in his being, wisdom, power, holiness, justice, goodness, and truth" (*Westminster Shorter Catechism*, 4). Although God cannot be defined in terms of His essential being, He can be defined functionally, that is, according to the attendant circumstances and actions that identify or accompany deity. Indeed, receiving worship is a component of the functional definition of "god." Worship pertains only to God. That was the point reinforced to John when he was told to worship God rather than his fellow servant who had given him such a glorious message (Revelation 19:10).

The problem, however, with this functional definition of "god" is the potential it creates for competing gods. If god is what is worshipped, the sad fact is that there are multiple gods. This polytheism is, of course, theoretical and not real. Regardless of what men worship or perceive to be deity, the unalterable fact is that there is but one true and living God. This one true God Himself declared, "I am the LORD, and there is none else, there is no God beside me" (Isaiah 45:5). Absolute monotheism is the very foundation of true religion and the logical ground of the greatest commandment God ever issued. "The Lord our God is one Lord: And thou shalt love the Lord thy God with all thy heart, and with all thy soul, and with all thy strength: this is the first commandment" (Jesus in Mark 12:29-30 quoting Moses in Deuteronomy 6:4-5). The logical corollary to absolute monotheism is the impossibility of polytheism. I'll say more about this later.

Although monotheism is absolute, the Scripture often addresses it on the ethical level. In other words, it makes it a matter of choice and behavior. God is one, but nonetheless He commands, "Thou shalt have no other gods before me" (Exodus 20:3). Ethical monotheism is a matter of both logic and obedience. Logically, it is a "no-brainer" since there is in fact only one real God. But obedience factors in the heart, which threatens logic. The problem, as Calvin said, is that human nature is "a perpetual factory of idols." He further said, "Man's mind, full as it is of pride and boldness, dares to imagine a god according to its own capacity; as it sluggishly plods, indeed is overwhelmed with the crassest ignorance, it conceives an unreality and an empty appearance as God."[1] Polytheism is possible after all.

The bottom line is that the activity of worship cannot be right if the object of worship is not right. So this is where we must focus. The *Westminster Confession of Faith* sums up the fundamental parameters for true worship and suggests the scope for our consideration.

> Religious worship is to be given to God, the Father, Son, and Holy Ghost; and to Him alone; not to angels, saints, or any other creature: and since the fall, not without a Mediator; nor in the mediation of any other but of Christ alone. (21.2)

It is important to worship the right God not only in name but also in the totality of His infinite worth as He has revealed Himself. We must avoid–even under the pretense of worshipping the one true and living God–the natural propensity to imagine Him according to our own capacity and thereby to conceive an unreality. True worship must give attention to God alone as He is in the Persons of the Holy Trinity in all of His infinite perfections.

THEOCENTRIC WORSHIP

Worship centers on God, not man: it is Theocentric, not anthropocentric. God is to be worshipped for what He is worth and not for what worshipping Him may gain for the worshipper. Worshipping God as a means to an end rather than as the end itself turns worship away from God to man. This brings us to the essence of what it is to worship. The Bible uses various terms that focus on different elements and factors of worship, but our word "worship" suggests a thought that supports the point of this chapter. The word "worship" is a compound of two Old English words *weorth* (value) and *scipe* (to ascribe); hence to worship is to ascribe value to something, at least according to etymology. The kind of value we ascribe to God determines whether our worship of Him remains theocentric or degenerates to self-motivated concerns. There are essentially two categories of value: intrinsic and instrumental.[2] Things of instrumental value are means to an end, and they lose their worth when they cease to function for their intended purpose. Things of intrinsic value have absolute worth independent of anything else.

Until we acknowledge that God is the only object of intrinsic value and that everything else and everybody else in existence has instrumental value, a consistently God-centered worship is going to be impossible. Herein lies the problem for so many Christians—the reason that so many are unhappy or discontented with their lives and envious of others. They tend to confuse things of instrumental value with the one thing of intrinsic value. Rather than glorifying and enjoying God as the chief end of their existence,[3] many perceive God to be the means of providing what they really want. They assume that God's chief end is to serve them. Delighting self in the Lord becomes the means to receiving whatever is the actual desire of their heart (the too-often carnal application of Psalm 37:4).[4] Then, when God does not act to achieve their desired end, they get upset with Him and begin to question either His goodness or greatness or both.[5] Or, when they do get what they think they wanted and inevitably discover its failure to satisfy, they end up disenchanted and disappointed. God is neither man's prize nor puppet; He is the absolutely independent One who is the Sovereign over all. Confessing and worshipping Him for His infinite and inherent worth is the only thing that can truly satisfy the soul and prevent disappointment, either with God or anything or anyone else. God-centered worship puts everything else in proper focus.

This theme and fundamental principle of worship permeates the Scripture: it is the principal commandment of the moral law and a major concern in Christ's exposition of the law.

The Statement of the Law

God's moral law, which is summarized in the Ten Commandments, is the capsule statement of God's requirements.

Indeed, the Lord Himself is at the heart and center of the moral law because it reflects and declares His very nature; hence, it is "holy, and just, and good" (Romans 7:12).[6] Although the commandments were central to the Israelite theocracy of the Old Testament dispensation, the Lord Jesus made it clear that the ancient code is equally valid for this dispensation as well (Matthew 5:17-37; 19:16-20). In addition to recognizing the timeless validity of the commandments, Christ also demonstrated the proper method of interpretation and application: the individual statements include within them all the degrees and forms of the represented prohibition or command. The surface requirements of the law are clear: what God forbids should never be done, and what God commands should be done. But the spirit of the law goes beyond the surface. Included in every prohibition is the demand for every converse duty. Included in a duty is the prohibition of every converse sin. Included in a duty or prohibition are not only all the "same-kind" issues but also the causes, means, and provocations associated with it. This hermeneutic that considers the spirit as well as the letter is essential and makes the application of the commandments to the Christian life profoundly simple.

The first division of the Decalogue concerns man's duty to God and begins with a preamble, which, though not one of the ten words, constitutes a vital part of the whole. God identified Himself as Jehovah, who redeemed the people from the bondage of Egypt (Exodus 20:2). By highlighting the covenant relationship that He had with His people, the Lord justified His right to make demands on them that governed their entire lives. Because of what God had done in redeeming them, they owed their existence to Him and were obligated to live a special way before Him. Remembering redemption creates an attitude toward the Lord that makes worship and obedience both necessary and pleasurable.[7] Sincere acknowledgment of God's saving and faithful acts must inspire obedience and total, humble devotion. This was Paul's argument when he testified of Christ's constraining love, evidenced by His atoning death (2 Corinthians 5:14-15). A saving, vital, personal relationship to God through the Lord Jesus Christ is the foundation for all proper living, including proper worship. Total devotion to God is the expression of a truly God-centered worship.

The Command

"Thou shalt have no other gods before me" (Exodus 20:3). The purpose of this first commandment is to identify the Lord as the sole object of legitimate worship, to demand exclusive allegiance to Jehovah. It obviously requires knowing and recognizing the Lord to be the one true and living God and to worship and glorify Him as He deserves. As the only real God and as the God of covenant grace and mercy, the Lord will not tolerate divided worship; He must be the lone object of devotion. This commandment addresses every manifestation of worship, obedience, and submission. Its inclusiveness should guard against any and all offensive behavior and motivate outward conduct and inward meditation pleasing to the Lord. The last two words, "before me," aid in understanding the full force of the commandment. The expression refers to personal presence but can also have overtones of hostility or defiance (e.g., Genesis 16:12; Psalm 21:12). Literally "to my face," the phrase is not unlike the similar statement in colloquial English: "in your face." Anything that distracts from or competes with the absolute devotion to God is a defiant insult to the great God who made us and the gracious God who saved us. In fact, the *Westminster Larger Catechism* marks it as "a most impudent provocation" (106). This commandment demands that everything else and everyone else be subservient to the Lord. It is only as He occupies His rightful place in the heart of His people that true worship is possible. This commandment teaches "the exclusive dignity of Jehovah" and "the essential duty of man" to worship Him.[8] In other words, only God owns the intrinsic worth that is deserving of worship.[9]

The Logic

Deuteronomy 6:4 asseverates the most fundamental fact of true religion: "Hear, O Israel: The LORD our God is one LORD." Known as the *Shema* (the Hebrew word translated "hear"), this declaration is the logic behind the first commandment. Because the Lord is who He is, He is the only legitimate object of worship, and all legitimate worship must center on Him alone. The Shema is one of those benchmark and pregnant statements in the Bible full of significance and implication. The proposition asserts both the uniqueness and the unity[10] of the Lord God. That Jehovah is uniquely God and that no other god should be worshipped constitute the surface meaning and application. The Scripture reiterates this truth often. Moses recognized it long before he wrote the *Shema*: "Who is like unto thee, O Lord, among the gods? who is like thee, glorious in holiness, fearful in praises, doing wonders?" (Exodus 15:11). Similarly David confessed, "Wherefore thou art great, O LORD God: for there is none like thee, neither is there any God beside thee..." (2 Samuel 7:22). So Solomon acknowledged in his great prayer, "LORD God of Israel, there is no God like thee, in heaven above, or on earth beneath..." (1 Kings 8:23). Likewise the prophet Jeremiah affirmed, "Forasmuch as there is none like unto thee, O LORD; thou art great...the LORD is the true God, he is the living God..." (Jeremiah 10:6, 10). Given the absolute uniqueness of God, it is not surprising that Moses warned the nation against worshipping other gods "lest the anger of the LORD thy God be kindled against thee" (Deuteronomy 6:15). God's inflexible intolerance of shared devotion or allegiance flows righteously from His fervent zeal for His own name: "For the LORD thy God is a jealous God among you" (Deuteronomy 6:15). The God of Israel is our God, and this fundamental fact of true religion is as weighty now as ever (see Mark 12:29). Given who the Lord is, God-centered worship is the only logical focus for all worship activity.

The Evidence

God-centered worship is, however, more than just a creedal affirmation of Jehovah's exclusiveness. It must express itself in total devotion to that One affirmed to be the one true and living God. There is more to worship than just talk or liturgy. Remember Christ's directive that proper worship must be "in spirit and in truth" (John 4:24; cf. Joshua 24:14), i.e., with a truthful spirit or sincere heart. Similarly and significantly, after declaring God's uniqueness and unity, the Shema issued the imperative of total devotion: "And thou shalt love the LORD thy God with all thine heart, and with all thy soul, and with all thy might" (Deuteronomy 6:5). The language is forceful and could well be translated "you must love the Lord." There is no other legitimate option; this is the obligatory response in light of God's uniqueness.

The command to love is itself significant. Love usually just happens; it is something that we have little control over. We tend to fall into it before we know what is happening. I still remember when I first fell in love with my wife; I just couldn't help myself. Nobody had to tell me to do it. But here we are told that we must love God. Loving God becomes a matter of obedience; it is something over which we have control. Although the Hebrew word for love used here includes emotion and affection, it is principally a volitional word requiring a conscious exercise of the will expressed in desire, inclination, preference, and choice for the loved object. It requires a conscious rejection of every competitor. This is, as well, the principal significance of the key New Testament word for love, *agape*– a Greek word that almost every Christian knows.

When I fell in love with my wife, I may have been temporarily out of control emotionally, but the time came when I made a conscious decision to choose her and reject every other woman on the face of the earth. That was love. So it is that loving God is a conscious choice of Him and a conscious rejection of anything and everybody else that compete for His rightful place. Loving God and loving anything else as God are mutually exclusive. Loving God does not preclude loving other things for what they are worth: it only precludes loving them for what God is worth. This is the significance of Christ's caveat that discipleship hinges on hating father, mother, wife, children, brothers, sisters, and self (Luke 14:26; Matthew 10:37). Similarly, Joshua made it clear that serving God "in sincerity and in truth" required putting away all other gods (Joshua 24:14). Therefore, he insisted, "choose you this day whom ye will serve" (Joshua 24:15).

This exclusive love for God is all encompassing: "And thou shalt love the LORD thy God with all thine heart, and with all thy soul, and with all thy might." The linking of heart, soul, and strength is a way of stressing the totality of commitment we owe the Lord. There is no part of our being untouched by grace, and there should be no part of our being exempt from worshipping and loving the God whose grace and first love enable us to love Him at all (1 John 4:19). "Heart" in the Bible refers to the entirety of the inner man: intellect, emotion, and will. "Soul" is the word in the Old Testament that designates the whole man, the totality of the person, everything that there is about him—outwardly and inwardly. Loving with the heart means that we think about God, desire God, and embrace God. Loving with the soul means that all of our inner faculties as well as outer deportment witness to our exclusive allegiance to God. Just in case we fail to grasp what it means to love God with everything in us and with everything we are, we are told to love with all our strength and energy. The point is that loving God is neither casual nor occasional; it is consuming. Loving God as specified in this greatest of all commandments will certainly insure the exclusivity of God-centered worship.

In his exposition of the *Shema*, Moses delineated the practical elements and exercise of total devotion to the Lord, all of which are essential components of true worship. First, we are *to fear the Lord* (Deuteronomy 6:1, 13, 24). Fearing God is the distinctive expression of true religion and of a right relationship to God. The essence of fearing God is awareness of God, a God-consciousness defined by knowledge of Him. Being aware of God will cause us to hold Him in utmost reverence and respect, to bow in absolute awe of His being. Being aware of God will move us to personal purity and piety. Fearing God is nothing more or less than living with the overwhelming awareness of the reality of God. The more we know Him the more we will fear Him, and the more we fear Him the more we will perform our duty to Him. Second, we are *to serve the Lord* (Deuteronomy 6:13). Serving God requires us to submit humbly to His lordship, ownership, and authority. By virtue of His creating us and especially in light of His redeeming us, He owns us and all of our rights. Worship, therefore, is service rendered to the Lord. Third, we are *to commit ourselves to the Lord* (Deuteronomy 6:13). This is the significance of swearing by His name. Swearing by His name is the oath or pledge of allegiance that we vow to the Lord. Committing to Him requires rejecting all other gods (Deuteronomy 6:14) and loyally affirming Him as the one and true God deserving of worship. Fourth, we are *to obey the Lord* (Deuteronomy 6:6, 17, 25). Loving the Lord, who is the lawgiver, produces love for the law itself. God's Word is the projection of His mind and will and is, therefore, linked inseparably to His person. How we view the law of God is a certain index to how we love the Lord: "For this is the love of God, that we keep his commandments: and his commandments are not grievous" (1 John 5:3). Christ also made the connection explicitly clear: "If ye love me, keep my commandments" (John 14:15). Truly worshipping God and blatantly disobeying God cannot coexist.

To put it simply, according to Deuteronomy 6:25, observing God's commandments is the right thing to do. Fifth, we are *to remember the Lord* (Deuteronomy 6:12, 6-9). Verse 12 states this element negatively by warning against forgetting the Lord. In the Old Testament, remembering and forgetting are always acts of the will, not involuntary impulses of the mind. To remember is to think about something on purpose; to forget is purposefully to refuse to think about something. Remembering God is factoring Him into all the issues of life. The instructions of verses 6-9 specify that no part of life is exempt. Home life, community life, and heart life are to be marked by thoughts of God.

It seems clear enough that true worship is not an hourly exercise once a week but a way of life. Proper public worship is the expression of a consciousness of God that must give Him the sole place He deserves by His infinite worth.

The Exposition of the Law

It is not surprising that the greatest Preacher in His greatest recorded sermon, the Sermon on the Mount (Matthew 5-7), deals with so many issues related to matters of worship. Nor is it surprising that so many of His themes develop as necessary applications of the moral law of God. I want to concentrate for a moment on a small section in the Sermon that I think is a practical exposition of the Shema and, therefore, an important lesson regarding God-centered worship. Christ teaches that total devotion to God is the essence of true religion and that God is the supreme satisfaction of the soul. Applying these truths will insure God's rightful place in worship practice as well as in all of life. Here's the text for consideration.

> Lay not up for yourselves treasures upon earth, where moth and
> rust doth corrupt, and where thieves break through and steal:
> But lay up for yourselves treasures in heaven, where neither

moth nor rust doth corrupt, and where thieves do not break through nor steal: For where your treasure is, there will your heart be also. The light of the body is the eye: if therefore thine eye be single, thy whole body shall be full of light. But if thine eye be evil, thy whole body shall be full of darkness. If therefore the light that is in thee be darkness, how great is that darkness!

No man can serve two masters: for either he will hate the one, and love the other; or else he will hold to the one, and despise the other. Ye cannot serve God and mammon. (Matthew 6:19-24)

The Lord Jesus wants us to consider this matter with focused vision. A single eye is one that focuses sharply and clearly; an evil eye is one that malfunctions, blurring reality. I want to comment on Christ's teaching under two heads to help focus sight on the mechanics and necessity of a God-centered life and worship.

The Imperatives of Ethical Monotheism

Remember that although monotheism is absolute, it functions on the ethical level. There is only one true and living God, but we must choose to acknowledge no other god except Him. Remember also that what we worship is what we ascribe value to. Worship must be reserved only for what has intrinsic value—in other words, only for God. Christ explains this in terms of treasure and makes it clear that the heart always stays where it perceives its treasure to be. Since, according to the Shema, the heart is essential for proper worship, it is imperative to deposit our treasures in the right place.

The first imperative leading to proper worship is simply not to value the wrong things: "Lay not up for yourselves treasures upon earth." The things of earth may have varying degrees of instrumental value, but none of them are worthy of the kind of heart devotion that must be reserved for the Lord alone.

We may love them and use them for all they are worth while never losing sight of their inability to bring ultimate and lasting satisfaction. *Everything on earth is subject to deterioration.* Moths refer to those insects that deposit their eggs in woolens, which eggs then hatch into that larval stage that gnaws away at the garment until it is "moth-eaten." Rust refers to that corrosive process that renders metal objects at worst unusable and at best unattractive. Together they represent all the processes and factors that cause the stuff of life to diminish in value and finally to cease to serve their instrumental function and purpose. Bread becomes moldy. Roofs cave in. Silver tarnishes. The vigor of youth dissipates (see Ecclesiastes 12:1-7 for biblical confirmation of what the mirror reflects and the bones feel). And so it goes. Similarly, *everything on earth is subject to defalcation* (i.e., the failure to meet expectations). Thieves easily break in and rob, taking away what was thought to be inviolable. Inflation, taxes, and stock-market slumps all steal away what we expected to be profit. If it is not one thing, it is something else that robs our plans and expectations. Christ's teaching here mirrors the common themes exhausted by the Preacher in Ecclesiastes. To devote life to the pursuit of pleasure, wealth, experience, or even wisdom with the hope of finding contentment is folly. All these things are gifts from God for us to enjoy, and we are to use them for their intended purposes. But they are not ends in themselves and will sooner or later fail.

The point is clear. Nothing on earth can ultimately satisfy, and certainly nothing on earth constitutes worthy objects of worship. Too often people, even Christians, treasure the things of life, ascribing intrinsic value to them, and then suffer disappointment and despair when those things inevitably deteriorate and fail to meet their expectations. The situation worsens when God is viewed as the instrument or means to supply what are perceived to be the real treasures. When that happens, on top of everything else, these people become disappointed with God.

Christ's second imperative leading to proper worship is simply to value the right thing: "But lay up for yourselves treasures in heaven." Treasure in heaven is moth-proof, rust-proof, and burglar-proof. In other words, treasure in heaven is exempt from decay and incapable of disappointing. The heavenly treasure is the Lord Himself. Paul's instructions reiterate the point: "If ye then be risen with Christ, seek those things which are above, where Christ sitteth on the right hand of God. Set your affection on things above, not on things on the earth" (Colossians 3:1-2). The triune God is the one and only absolutely intrinsically valuable entity worthy of worship. If the Lord is our treasure, we can never be disappointed because He will never–indeed, can never–fail. The bottom line is that Christ's treasure imperatives precisely follow the logic of the *Shema*. Since the Lord is unique, it makes sense to treasure Him for His infinite worth. Worshipping and loving God with all the heart, soul, and might is tantamount to having our hearts where our treasure is.

The Impossibility of Ethical Polytheism

Christ takes the prohibition against polytheism a step further. The First Commandment forbade the worship of any other gods, and that prohibition in one form or another is repeated regularly throughout the Old Testament. Christ cuts through and exposes the heart of the issue by declaring that consistent polytheism is impossible: "No man can serve two masters: for either he will hate the one, and love the other; or else he will hold to the one, and despise the other. Ye cannot serve God and mammon." Christ's declaration prompts two pertinent observations.

First, polytheism always creates conflict. The Lord self-proclaimed through Isaiah, "I am the LORD: that is my name: and my glory will I not give to another, neither my praise to graven images" (Isaiah 42:8). God is jealous and intolerant of divided allegiance or worship (see again Deuteronomy 6:15). Significantly, so is every other so-called god. It is beyond my scope to introduce a survey in comparative religion, but suffice it to say that the gods of paganism were in constant turf wars and their adherents were caught in the battles, trying by their worship to broker peace. For instance, Canaanite religion revolved around the conflicts among Baal Hadad, the god of the storms whose scepter was lightning, and Yam, the god of sea or river, and Mot, the god of the underworld, along with a whole cast of supporting deified characters. Since rain was essential for prosperity, whatever had to be done to insure Baal's supremacy was done. Greek mythology was no different. Think of how Odysseus, whose primary allegiance was to Zeus, found himself in Poseidon's turf (rather, surf) and experienced constant conflict. Polytheists use worship as a means of pacifying all the gods that they can concoct, giving them what they think they want so they can get on with life. Worship was a means of manipulating deities for personal concerns.

Polytheism doesn't work when the cast consists of nothing but imagined gods; it certainly doesn't work when the true God is factored in. This is what Israel often tried and consequently earned the wrath and condemnation of God (see, for instance, Jeremiah 7). I should add as well a caveat against worshipping God with the pagan mentality that uses worship as means of manipulating deity for personal interest. Too often, Christ is viewed as the solution to this or that problem of life. Getting problems fixed becomes the chief end of worshipping. Such worship reduces the Lord to merely instrumental significance, and that is unacceptable worship. You can't serve two masters; you can't serve God and mammon (money, but here a metonym for anything other than God).

Second, polytheism demands resolution. Sooner or later it requires a decision, a choice between the contestants. Christ says that those who try to serve both will ultimately hate and despise one and love and cleave to the another. In this sense, Demas, having loved the present world, did what he had to do (2 Timothy 4:10). If we are thinking and seeing clearing with that "single eye," the only logical choice to make is to love and cleave to the One who is truly God of gods and Lord of lords.

Any kind of worship, therefore, that is not theocentric is unacceptable to God and in reality impossible for man. Christ and the Law unmistakably and forcibly identify the exclusive object of genuine worship.

TRINITARIAN WORSHIP

"Religious worship is to be given to God, the Father, Son, and Holy Ghost" (*Westminster Confession of Faith*, 21.2). This statement marks the uniqueness of Christianity, the one and only true religion. Recall that the great statement of the Shema demanding exclusive worship of the Lord our God declares that the oneness of our God is not monolithic but rather a unity in one (see endnote 10). Although the Shema does not name Father, Son, and Holy Spirit as the persons of the unified one, it nonetheless assumes the dynamic existence. God is one in essence, yet three in persons. True monotheism is Trinitarian, and Trinitarian monotheism demands that each of the distinct persons of the Godhead is the proper and necessary object of worship. Remember also that receiving worship is a component of the functional definition of God. True worship can be rendered only to the true God and only as He reveals Himself to be. Since He reveals Himself to be One, yet Three, it is impossible to worship God in truth without that worship being received by the Father, by the Son, and by the Holy Spirit.[11]

Nonetheless, the Scripture warrants that worship be directed not only to the Godhead but also to each Divine Person specifically. It is not my purpose to explicate the doctrine of the

Trinity, to prove the deity of any one of the specific persons or to delineate either the common or distinctive aspects of their work.[12] For the context of our study, I want simply to illustrate that the biblical pattern identifies the Trinity as the proper object of worship. This illustration is in no way exhaustive of the biblical evidence and directives.

Worship of the Father

As the first Person of the Godhead, the Father is the proper object of worship. In His explanation of true and genuine worship to the Samaritan woman, the Lord Jesus made this explicit. "But the hour cometh, and now is, when the true worshippers shall worship the Father in spirit and in truth: for the Father seeketh such to worship him" (John 4:23). During His earthly incarnation, Christ illustrated by His own actions and by His teaching that worship was to be directed to the Father. As we will see in due course, prayer is an essential vehicle of worship. Significantly, then, when Christ prayed, He directed His prayers to the Father (e.g., Mark 14:36; John 17:1). When He gave prayer instructions, He taught His disciples to direct their petitions to the Father: "Our Father which are in heaven" (Matthew 6:9; John 15:16, etc.). Likewise, the apostles expressed their worship of the Father. In simple confession, Paul testified, "I bow my knees unto the Father of our Lord Jesus Christ" (Ephesians 3:14). He and Peter both invoked blessing toward the Father (an expression of worship): "Blessed be the God and Father of our Lord Jesus Christ" (1 Peter 1:3; see also 2 Corinthians 1:3; Ephesians 1:3). The evidence is clear enough.

Worship of the Son

As the second Person of the Godhead, the Son is the proper object of worship. Christ is the sole Mediator between God

and men (1 Timothy 2:5), and none may approach the Father
except through Him (John 14:6). The necessity and mechanics
of His mediation are essential dogmas of true religion and relate
directly to the matter of worship. Apart from Jesus Christ true
worship is impossible. But for now, the simple fact of the matter
is that Jesus Christ Himself is worthy of worship. The Scripture
thus directs that worship be given Him the same way it is given
to the Father: "That all men should honour the Son, even as
they honour the Father" (John 5:23). According to Paul, the
very name of Jesus is reason for "every knee to bow" and "for
every tongue" to confess that "Jesus Christ is Lord, to the glory
of God the Father" (Philippians 2:10-11). As an expression of
the highest adoration, all the angels, for whom Christ is not
a mediator, worship the Son (Hebrews 1:6). The Psalmist
commands that we "kiss the Son" (Psalm 2:6), an act of humble
homage. The New Testament offers doxologies to Christ (2
Timothy 4:18; 1 Peter 4:11; 2 Peter 3:18), and the book of the
Revelation records something of the ceaseless worship directed
to Christ in heaven itself. "Worthy is the Lamb that was slain....
Blessing, and honour, and glory, and power, be unto him that
sitteth upon the throne, and unto the Lamb for ever and ever"
(Revelation 5:12-13; see also 1:6; 7:10-12). Again, the evidence
is clear enough.

Worship of the Holy Spirit

As the third Person of the Godhead, the Holy Spirit is the
proper object of worship. It is the Holy Spirit who applies all the
benefits of grace, moving believers to worship in the first place.
Admittedly, the Scriptures say less about the worship of the
Spirit than of the Father or the Son. I think Shedd's statement
is noteworthy here:

> The reason why less is said in Scripture respecting the adoration and worship of the third person than of the others is, that in the economy of redemption it is the office of the Spirit to awaken feelings of worship, and naturally, therefore, he appears more as the author than the object of worship. But a person who by an internal operation can awaken feelings of worship is ipso facto God.[13]

Notwithstanding the smaller corpus of data, the Scripture unquestionably includes the Spirit in worship formulas. Again, as we will consider in due course, the sacraments–rightly administered–are integral elements in worship. The inclusion of the name of the Holy Spirit along with the Father and the Son in the baptismal formula testifies to His rightful place in the worship ceremony (Matthew 28:19). Paul's well-known Trinitarian benediction speaks to the issue as well with the Spirit's inclusion in the prayer petition (2 Corinthians 13:14). Comparing 1 Corinthians 6:19 with 6:20 suggests the proper worship of the Spirit. Verse 20 issues the imperative to glorify God in the body, which is significant in light of the identification of the body in verse 19 as the temple of the Holy Spirit. The bottom line is that because the Spirit is God, we owe Him as much respect, reverence, and worship as the Father and the Son. I would submit once again that the evidence is clear enough.

I finish this chapter where I started: "Worship God." There are many reasons that God deserves worship, all of which constitute themes for worship. However, the bottom line with which we started this particular study remains: the activity of worship cannot be right if the object of worship is not right. It is important to settle from the beginning that worship is about God and not about us. Attention to the object of worship is vitally more important than the subjective and personal preferences of the worshipper. But then again, nothing should make us happier than truly worshipping and loving God for all of His infinite and intrinsic worth. Glorifying Him and enjoying Him go hand in hand.

CHAPTER 3

THE SUBJECT OF WORSHIP

The level of genuine, heartfelt, and heart active worship will always be in proportion to how much we are impressed with the object of worship. True worship, therefore, arises from the knowledge of God. The greater the knowledge of God, the greater will be the exercise of true worship. I suppose this brings us back to a theme I developed in the last chapter. What we worship is what we ascribe value to, and only God has the infinite and intrinsic value to be the legitimate object of worship. In this regard we can take a clue from nature as to the focus and theme of worship.[1] The Psalmist acclaimed, "The heavens declare the glory of God" (Psalm 19:1). More literally, "The heavens are counting out the assets of God." The Hebrew word for "glory" refers to more than some halo-like aura that mysteriously marks the divine presence; it refers to something of weight, something that constitutes value.[2] The glory of God, therefore, refers to all the infinite assets of His intrinsic worth; God's glory makes Him worthy of worship. With ceaseless habit,[3] nature spends its time enumerating what it can of God's limitless riches.[4] That is what worship is about, and it is a good example for all worshippers to follow. After all, we are as much a part of God's creation as the sun, which with bridegroom eagerness and strongman vigor participates in declaring God's glory (Psalm 19:5). Identifying and reflecting on the infinite riches of His glory constitute important elements in worship.

If God is the sole object of true worship, He must also be the subject of worship. In other words, the Triune God must be the topic of worship. Worship is about God. Simple enough! Notwithstanding the logical transparency of this proposition, so much of what masquerades as worship today seems to have very little to do with the Lord. Too frequently, God is little more than a word that is dropped here and there and from time to time to legitimize whatever else has usurped attention—whether personal testimonies lauding accomplishments, pulpit tactics manipulating behavior (usually by guilt or shame), or pep talks encouraging good feelings about self. The spiritual lameness that characterizes so much of modern worship traces directly to inappropriate themes or topics addressed.

Ascribing infinite value to God—worshipping Him—requires giving attention to what He has revealed about His worth. Just like the heavens, we must count out the assets of God. Since His worth is infinite, we can never glorify Him for all that He is worth. But worship creates a happy circle. Contemplation of God generates worship; worship of God heightens contemplation of God. The more we contemplate Him, the more impressed we must be by Him, and consequently, the more we are moved to worship Him. Worship breeds worship.

There is an obvious sense in which enumerating God's assets is a daunting operation. I think that one of the reasons we don't worship as we should is that we are not overwhelmed with the absolute reality of God, with who He is, what He is like, and what He does. A sight of God always magnifies Him and reduces every sense of self. Consider how both Ezekiel and John could only fall on their faces when overtaken by the glory of their God (see Ezekiel 1:28 and Revelation 1:17). Until man admits God's infinite bigness and his own pathetically finite smallness, true worship is unlikely. Being overwhelmed with God engenders both worship and the question of where to begin. As we should expect, the Scripture guides us regarding the subject content of our worship. The Psalmist enjoined in the final of the inspired worship models, "Praise ye the LORD...Praise him for his mighty acts: praise him according to his excellent greatness" (Psalm 150:1-2). This suggests three themes about God that should be the subject matter of all proper worship: His august Person, His attractive perfections, and His awesome works.

I must exercise self-discipline. Each of these themes is a subject for in-depth analysis and lengthy discussion. It is not my purpose and it is way beyond my scope to develop a theology proper, that is, the doctrine of God. I want simply to make a few observations about each of these heads as it relates to our overall theme of worship. If these themes become the real focal points in the exercise of worship, the trivia and triteness of so much of modern worship will self-destruct.

THE AUGUST PERSON OF GOD

If believing that "God is" is essential to the kind of faith that pleases God (Hebrews 11:6), it follows that attention to His essential Being should constitute an essential component of worship if we want the meditations of our hearts to be acceptable in His sight (Psalm 19:14). The point very simply is that God deserves worship because of who He is.[5] That God is a person and not some abstract cosmic force or energy I am presupposing on the authority of His self-revelation in the Scripture. Believing the Bible requires believing in a real and personal God in holy Trinity. This personal God is both great and good. But even if we never experienced anything of His goodness, His personal greatness warrants our worship and our love. The infinite greatness of His person is enough reason to worship and provides ample cause to excite us to bow down before Him. When the inspired Psalmist directs us to "hallelujah" (praise the Lord), he is directing our worship attention to the person of the Lord Himself, Jehovah.

The titles and appellations of God in the Bible are wonderful expressions of God's revelation of Himself. In these appellations, God graciously condescends to our necessarily finite way of thinking, for each revelation limits our thoughts about Him to one or another of His perfections or works. So, for instance, *El Shaddai* (God Almighty) draws attention to His all-sufficiency and power, *El Elyon* (the Most High God) to His majesty, *El Olam* (the Everlasting God) to His eternity, *Adonai* (Lord) to His sovereignty, and on it goes. The personal name *Jehovah*[6] (LORD), however, is another matter. Although God identified Himself to His people by this name from the beginning of His gracious self-revelations,[7] Moses learned firsthand the most-to-the-point explanation of its significance at the burning bush. Not only is Jehovah the unique proper name of the one true and living God; in a wonderful sense it avers God's absolute independence, self-existence, and infinity–the fullness of His august person.[8]

I concur that Jehovah is the special covenant name of God so closely associated with His interest in, salvation of, and faithfulness to His people.[9] But even beyond these contextually generated conclusions that outline thoughts for worship, the name Jehovah–in and of itself–declares the fact of His person so simplistically yet so profoundly that it itself warrants consideration as a thought for worship. If we are going to understand the significance of what God reveals about Himself in this wonderful name, we should go to that place where He explains Himself–the bush where Moses was compelled to remove his shoes because God's presence made it a most holy place (Exodus 3:5).

Exodus 3:14-15 is the Lord's answer to Moses's question concerning the name of his divine commissioner and is the closest thing to a definition of the divine name that we have. "And God said unto Moses, I AM THAT I AM: and he said, Thus shalt thou say unto the children of Israel, I AM hath sent me unto you...this is my name for ever, and this is my memorial unto all generations." The logical link between the "I AM" declaration and the name Jehovah is indisputable although the level of linguistic or etymological connection is questionable.[10] I want to focus on the sense of the proposition. At first glance, there seems to be a difference in how the Lord identifies Himself. Is His name I AM THAT I AM or I AM? A brief consideration of the grammar of the statement should answer that question and justify my conclusion that the name indeed reveals the Lord as absolutely independent, self-existent, and infinite.

When I was a kid in elementary school, I spent a lot of time learning how to diagram sentences. There was good reason they called it grammar school back in those days. Bear with me a little. A simple diagram of the propositional statement "I AM THAT I AM" indicates that God's name is "I AM," which explains why He told Moses to tell the people I AM was sending him and not I AM THAT I AM. This is a simple sentence involving a subject and a subject complement. Hebrew syntax differs from English, but it is still clear enough. Let me illustrate using this statement: I am Michael P. V. Barrett. In the diagramming of this statement, "I" would be in the subject slot and Michael P. V. Barrett would be in the subject complement slot with the verb "am" as the copula, linking the two parts. Although in Hebrew the subject is morphologically a part of the verb, the logic of the diagram would be the same. In the Lord's statement, then, "I" would be in the subject slot, and the statement "I AM" would be in the subject complement slot. The Lord says I am "I am.[11]"

The word that the Authorized Version translates as "THAT" is simply a function word that marks subordination between words. Although this particle does not normally introduce subject complements in Hebrew, it is necessary here because of the unique syntax of having a verb "I AM" used substantively (i.e., with a noun function) as the complement of the verb "to be." So the "THAT" is simply an indication that what follows is grammatically subordinate to what precedes. I hope you have followed this. To me, what I have just said is crystal clear, but then I love diagramming sentences.[12]

The point of the proposition is not that the Lord will be whatever He will be in terms either of the progressive revelation of Himself[13] or of the people's peculiar needs emerging from changing circumstances. Those alternatives are true enough, but the proposition is, rather, a direct affirmation of essential being, unaffected by and independent of anything outside of self. This certainly seems to be the significance of Christ's declaration of His eternal self-existence when He uttered what the Jews correctly recognized as the equivalent of the divine name: "Before Abraham was, I am" (John 8:58).

If self-determination and self-consciousness are the defining elements of personality, then Jehovah, the great I AM, is truly an august person, who is most worthy of worship. There are many other evidences of a personal God throughout the Bible, but His amazing name Jehovah sums it all. The frequent worship directive to praise the LORD should not be surprising in light of whom the divine name reveals. Think of the lines from that old hymn *The God of Abraham Praise*: "Jehovah, great I AM, by earth and heaven confessed; I bow and bless the sacred Name, forever blest." I submit that our worship of God will be in proportion to our consciousness of His absolute reality. Not only will contemplating His person generate worship, but it will give us much to worship about.

THE ATTRACTIVE PERFECTIONS OF GOD

Although God deserves worship fundamentally because He is, it is impossible to separate His essential being from His perfections–who He is from what He is like. Consequently, God's perfections or attributes both motivate worship and constitute motifs for worship. We are to "praise him according to his excellent greatness" (Psalm 150:2). In other words, God's perfections give us something to worship about.

This section has the potential of being either very brief or very lengthy. Although the temptation is strong to transgress the bounds of my outline, I will keep it brief by avoiding a delineation and exposition of God's self-revealed attributes. Again, it is not my purpose to write a theology proper, but rather simply to remark how important it is to reflect on and extol the divine perfections when we worship the Lord. Charnock in his classic treatment of God's attributes argues the same: "As the Divine nature is the object of worship, so the Divine perfections are to be honored in worship; we do not honor God if we honor him not as he is." [14] If, by the way, you have never read Stephen Charnock's *The Existence and Attributes of God*, I recommend it to you. Charnock's thorough treatment of God's perfections illustrates why I can't venture into that study in this particular work if we are going to stay on track. So when you finish reading this book, read Charnock's. It will provoke serious thinking, and it will bless your heart.

That God's perfections should constitute themes for worship is a simple matter of logic as well as the prescription of Scripture. Logically, it makes sense to think about and then to extol the virtues that characterize the object of our devotion. We readily understand this in the sphere of human relationships. I love my wife, and she always seems to like it when I tell her the various things about her that are attractive to me–all the reasons I love her. Most of the time, however, I just assume she knows, and so I fail to mention all those things that please her so much when she hears them. Sensitivity is not one of my virtues, so perhaps the groom in the Song of Solomon would serve as a better example. He could not speak to his bride without saying something good about her (see for instance, Song of Solomon 4:1-7). But then again, his bride did the same to him (Song of Solomon 5:10-16). If this is the advisable way to express devotion to the people we love, how much more should it be the pattern for expressing our devotion to God, whose attributes are infinitely perfect and beautifully attractive to spiritual perception. If my insensitive negligence to my wife is shameful, how much more so our professions of love to God without reference to what He is like, since those attributes intensify the need to worship Him for who He is.

The prescriptions for worship found in the examples of Scripture also mark God's perfections as the subject matters of worship. Celebrating the victory at the Red Sea, Moses asked in veneration, "Who is like unto thee O LORD, among the gods? who is like thee, glorious in holiness, fearful in praises, doing wonders?" (Exodus 15:11). The divine perfection of holiness was just one glorious component of God's uniqueness that Moses singled out in his song of praise and thanksgiving. When Paul broke out in doxologies, he often specified some of God's infinite perfections as elements in his praise: "Now unto the King eternal, immortal, invisible, the only wise God, be honour and glory for ever and ever. Amen" (1 Timothy 1:17, for example). Open the Psalms at random, and you will find the psalmist making some attribute of God a theme of his praise. The Sabbath day Psalm, for instance, instructs, "It is a good thing to give thanks unto the LORD, and to sing praises unto thy name, O most High: To shew forth thy lovingkindness in the morning, and thy faithfulness every night" (Psalm 92:1-2). The righteous are to "give thanks at the remembrance of his holiness" (Psalm 97:12), and all people are to praise God's great and terrible name "for it is holy" (Psalm 99:3). In Psalm 136, the psalmist just could not get over the fact that God's "mercy endureth forever" (every verse, 1-26). This could go on a hundred and fifty times. So instructive are the Psalms for worship patterns that I am going to devote the final chapter of this book to their analysis. Similarly, if you read through the great prayers recorded in the Bible–which as we will see are expressions of worship–you will find constant attention focused on some aspect of God's character (see as examples 1 Kings 8, Nehemiah 9, and Daniel 9).

For now, these examples are sufficient for my point. Extolling God's character is a key element of worship, and the sum of His perfections provides ample particulars for such praise. Public praying, singing, and preaching should consistently address the divine attributes. Tragically, this logical and scriptural formula stands in stark contrast to what far too often marks these public expressions of worship. In public praying, it has almost become a badge of spiritual honor to rush into God's presence with casual familiarity rather than with careful reverence. The theme of song is too often personal experience rather than the person of God. Preaching deals more with horizontal relationships and issues than with the great themes of theology. If God is the object of worship, then He must be what worship is about. No one prayer or song or sermon can exhaust the vast database of worship topics, since God is infinite, eternal, and unchangeable in the totality of His being, wisdom, holiness, justice, goodness and truth. It is impossible to worship Him for all that He is worth.

THE AWESOME WORKS OF GOD

God is, but God is not passive. His amazing and awesome works are part of His glory and, therefore, fitting themes for worship. According to Psalm 150:2, we are to praise the Lord "for his mighty acts." To name all the specific acts of God is impossible–a truth admitted by the inspired Psalmist. "Many, O LORD my God, are thy wonderful works which thou hast done, and thy thoughts which are to us-ward: they cannot be reckoned up in order unto thee: if I would declare and speak of them, they are more than can be numbered" (Psalm 40:5). Similarly, the apostle John expressed the same incapacity in regard to the earthly works of Jesus: "And there are also many other things which Jesus did, the which, if they should be written every one, I suppose that even the world itself could not contain the books that should be written" (John 21:25). Needless to say, then, if the works of God supplied the only topics for worship, there would be an inexhaustible supply of themes to worship about. Indeed, there is. Although not even the Bible enumerates every work of God, it does outline the divine works according to major kinds and thus suggest guidelines and directives for worship. Three kinds in particular receive special and frequent emphasis in the biblical worship patterns: creation, providence, and redemption.

Worship about Creation

Calvin refers to creation as the "magnificent theater of heaven and earth, crammed with innumerable miracles."[15] The Scripture reveals creation to be the unique work of the Triune God. That God is the only Creator testifies to His power, ownership, and authority over all that He created and to His right to receive the worship of the creature. The representative worshippers that John saw in his heavenly vision illustrate this truth. They fell before the throne and worshipped God by saying, "Thou art worthy, O Lord, to receive glory and honour and power: for thou hast created all things, and for thy pleasure they are and were created" (Revelation 4:11). The theology of creation relates to the theology of worship in multiple ways.

First, one of the vital implications of God's work of creation is that we, as part of that creation, owe Him our worship: "Man's chief end is to glorify God" (*Westminster Shorter Catechism*, 1). More than once, the Psalms connect our being God's creation with our consequent duty to worship Him. For instance, Psalm 95:6 enjoins, "O come, let us worship and bow down: let us kneel before the LORD our maker." In the famous 100th Psalm, serving the Lord with gladness and coming before His presence with singing are linked to the knowledge that God is "he that hath made us" (Psalm 100:2-3). The *Belgic Confession of Faith* of 1561 elaborates on this obligation when it says that God "created of nothing the heaven, the earth, and all creatures, as it seemed good unto him, giving unto every creature its being, shape, form, and several offices to serve its Creator" (Article 12). Failing to worship God is defaulting on the debt that we owe by virtue of His being Creator and our being creature.

Second, God's work of creation fosters a God-centered worship. The vastness of creation testifies to the infinity of the Creator. Of necessity, the Maker is greater than what He makes. This is biblical logic: "He who hath builded the house hath more honour than the house. For every house is builded by some man; but he that built all things is God" (Hebrews 3:3b-4). Creation, the spectacular theater of God's glory, declares how big God is and how small man is. Creation's sermon should prevent any temptation to make man's accomplishments or experiences subjects for worship. One thing is certain in the light of creation's vastness: man is not the center of the universe. Creation's vastness extends to things so huge and distant as to be beyond our reach, and things so small and even invisible as to escape our knowledge. But all these things, whether visible or invisible, "were created by him, and for him" (Colossians 1:16). I recall some years ago seeing a nature program about life in the unlighted depths of the ocean. When the lights from the unmanned submarine shone, they made public a previously secret society of creatures. I was absolutely fascinated with what I was seeing on this screen of God's theater; likewise, it was simply pleasurable to look at and reflect on. There was a whole world of stuff going on that I had known nothing about, and nobody else did, either, before the technology of light-shining submarines. But what man did not discover until some time in the twentieth century had, of course, been performing on the underwater stage since Day 5 of creation, and every day the Creator who made that distant underwater world sees it and is pleased, for He made it for His glory and pleasure.

Job's reaction after God's initial speech from the whirlwind illustrates the kind of response to creation that generates the God-centered worship that I am suggesting. Understandably, Job was somewhat self-focused in the throes of his suffering. But when God directed his thoughts away from himself to the wonders of both inanimate and animate creation that were far beyond man's control and understanding, Job was brought to humble and reverent silence before the Creator (Job 38:1-40:5). Reflecting on God's power and glory evinced by creation ought always to take our thoughts away from self and fix them on Him. How absolutely great He is!

Third, God's work of creation constitutes a theme for worship. What God created is certainly not the object of worship: orthodoxy is not pantheism. That God created, however, is a scripturally warranted subject for worship. The inspired Psalms, which prescribe so many worship patterns for us to follow, frequently include references to God's work in creation. My Bible is still open to Psalm 100 with its reference to God's making us. Psalm 102 reflects on God's creation as evidence of awesome power: "Of old hast thou laid the foundation of the earth: and the heavens are the work of thy hands" (verse 25). Psalm 104 begins by declaring the greatness of God, and then the rest of the Psalm develops the creation theme as evidence of that greatness. In the middle of his reflection, the Psalmist avers, "O LORD, how manifold are thy works! in wisdom hast thou made them all: the earth is full of thy riches" (verse 24). I had to turn only one page in the Bible to find these examples; there are certainly more. In addition to the Psalms, some of the most instructive prayers recorded in the Bible include references to creation. This is significant because prayer is an integral component of true worship. For instance, when Jeremiah prayed for God to do what seemed to be impossible, he reasoned from God's creative work that nothing was impossible for God: "Ah Lord GOD! behold, thou hast made the heaven and the earth by thy great power and stretched out arm, and there is nothing too hard for thee" (Jeremiah 32:17; see also Nehemiah 9:6). Similarly, the preaching of the prophets often appealed to God's creative activity as incentive to repentance. Amos provides a classic example. "For, lo, he that formeth the mountains, and createth the wind...The LORD, The God of hosts, is his name" (Amos 4:13). He also implored, "Seek him that maketh the seven stars and Orion...that calleth for the waters of the sea, and poureth them out upon the face of the earth: The LORD is his name" (Amos 5:8).

So in singing,[16] praying, and preaching–all essential components in worship[17]–God's work of creation is something to worship about.

Worship about Providence

Both in Scripture and in theological logic, creation and providence go together. Therefore, if creation is a reason for worship as well as a theme in worship, providence should be, too. Providence is the temporal operation of the eternal God, through which He accomplishes His unfailing purpose. Whereas creation is an extraordinary work of God, providence is His constant and ordinary work whereby He preserves and governs His creation to the designed end of His glory, which includes the corollary end of the good of His people. Since the aim of providence is God's glory, it follows that worship–ascribing worth or glory to Him–is itself a means to achieve that end. Since providence is the continuous activity of God, there will always be plenty of specific topics to worship about.

I need only to be suggestive at this point since it is not my purpose to develop the doctrine of God's providence with its implications and applications. I have done that already in another book, *God's Unfailing Purpose*.[18] Here I just want to mark and recommend it as a subject for worship. God's unfailing preservation and government of His creation testifies to His absolute power and authority. As the Psalmist declares, "the LORD sitteth King for ever" (Psalm 29:10). Recognizing and acknowledging the absolute sovereignty of God demands submissive and humble adoration. Any king deserves honor: how much more so the one who is the supreme King whose domain is all-inclusive. Especially those who by grace are willing subjects in His kingdom should reverently lift their voices and hearts in praise of the God who reigns. Indeed, as the hymn admonishes, "Sing praise to God who reigns above." I don't want to break into song here, but the second verse of that hymn is very relevant to our point: "What God's almighty power hath made, His gracious mercy keepeth…to God all praise and glory." That is providence, and that is a fitting subject of worshipful song.

Although the church owns many great hymns that extol God's providence and celebrate His protection, provision, and care, it is the Bible that leads the way in showing how to reference God's sovereign providence in expressions of worship. Here are a few examples. Psalm 104 praises God for all of His manifold works in making the necessary provisions to sustain man and beast in their varied existences. Significantly, the synopsis statement in my Oxford wide-margin Bible for this Psalm is "a meditation upon the power and providence of God." Similarly, the summary of Psalm 107 describes this poem as "praising God, to observe his manifold providence…in divers varieties of life." The refrain is fitting: "O that men would praise the LORD for his goodness, and for his wonderful works to the children of men" (Psalm 107:8, 15, 21, and 31). In prayer, Ezra acknowledged that it was God's mercy and intervention that caused the kings of Persia to grant the nation favor (Ezra 9:9). Similarly, Nehemiah linked God's providence to creation: "Thou, even thou, art LORD alone; thou hast made heaven, the heaven of heavens, with all their host, the earth, and all things that are therein, the seas, and all that is therein, and thou preservest them all; and the host of heaven worshippeth thee" (Nehemiah 9:6). As he continued to pray, he enumerated multiple examples of divine care and concern in Israel's checkered history. Nehemiah 9 is a classic prayer that deserves careful mediation and considered imitation in both public and private worship. The prophets often appealed to the operations of God's providence in their preaching. Amos, for instance, identified times of famine, drought, and pestilence as instances of God's government designed to incite repentance from a spiritually insensitive people (Amos 4).

So in singing, praying, and preaching–all essential components in worship–God's work of providence, just like His work of creation, is something to worship about.

Worship about Redemption

"Let the redeemed of the LORD say so" (Psalm 107:2). The very existence of a redeemed people is the subject of worshipful praise. Those redeemed by the blood of Christ according to the riches of divine grace exist as witnesses to the praise of God's glory (see Ephesians 1:7, 12). According to Peter, the purpose of God's calling a people out of darkness and making them "a chosen generation, a royal priesthood, an holy nation, a peculiar people" was to "shew forth the praises" of God (1 Peter 2:9).

The redeemed not only have a special and happy duty to worship the Lord; they alone worship on the ground of the fundamental criterion for true and acceptable worship–the mediation of Jesus Christ. The *Westminster Confession of Faith* sums up this biblically stressed requisite with forthright clarity: "Religious worship is to be given to God…and to Him alone… and, since the fall, not without a Mediator; nor in the mediation of any other but of Christ alone" (21. 2). Notwithstanding the trends toward generic religion that are so commonly touted as religious freedom and charity in our society, any attempt to approach God apart from Jesus Christ is an affront against the one and only true and living God. True religion with its corresponding true worship is exclusively narrow. Redemption ground is the only ground on which and from which true worship can be offered.

The apostle Peter expressly said that the offering up of spiritual sacrifices is "acceptable to God by Jesus Christ" (1 Peter 2:5). Two obvious thoughts arise from this statement: (1) any worship without Christ is unacceptable, and (2) worship through Jesus Christ is acceptable. Although this declaration is an indictment against false worship, it is also an encouragement to those desiring to worship the Lord according to the precepts of Scripture, for it assures them that it is the mediation of Christ that makes worship acceptable, not how well they offer it.

The exclusiveness of Christianity and the efficacy of Christ's mediation are topics that deserve detailed development, but as I reluctantly restrict myself to the subject of this chapter, all I can say for now is that redemption is something to worship about. Even providing biblical illustrations of how this theme was preached and prayed and sung is too extensive for my point now, although we will in a later chapter examine in detail examples of worship from Scripture (see Chapter 6). Suffice it now to observe the perfectly offered worship of the saints and angels in heaven. In vision John sees the four living creatures and the twenty-four elders prostrate before the Lamb and hears them singing this song: "Thou art worthy…for thou wast slain, and hast redeemed us to God by thy blood out of every kindred, and tongue, and people, and nation" (Revelation 5:9). After that stanza, he heard an innumerable choir joining in reiterating the same theme: "Worthy is the Lamb that was slain to receive power, and riches, and wisdom, and strength, and honour, and glory, and blessing" (Revelation 5:12). And then all creation joined in chorus, "Blessing and honour, and glory, and power, be unto him that sitteth upon the throne, and unto the Lamb for ever and ever" (Revelation 5:13). If Christ and His redeeming work are the subject of eternal worship, it certainly makes sense that they ought to be the subject of worship in time. What will be on our lips forever should be in our hearts and on our lips now.

Following the Bible will insure that the Lord alone will receive the attention in worship. He alone has the intrinsic worth to warrant worship, and He alone has the infinite assets (glory) to keep us busy in worship. We will never run out of things to worship about when the Triune God is the object and subject of worship. Even all the horizontal issues, which are admittedly important in Christian relationships but unfortunately consume so much focus in modern "worship services," will find their appropriate place when the vertical attention is maintained. Right thinking about God and the gospel of grace will produce right behavior.

CHAPTER 4

THE LITURGY OF WORSHIP

There is something risky about the title of this chapter. The very mention of the word "liturgy" conjures up notions of canned prayers, recited creeds, and chanting choirs. I suppose that if this were the first chapter, many readers, offended by the title, would immediately close the book with the suspicion that this Presbyterian was up to something Reformed. The fact of the matter is that whether formal or informal, planned or spontaneous, public worship begins and ends with things happening in between. Very simply, liturgy refers to what happens from that beginning to that end; it denotes the elements or components of public worship. It refers to the service[1] that is supposed to be rendered to the Lord—what we should do when worshipping Him.

Although the Scripture does not prescribe any specific order of service for Christian worship—when to stand or sit, sing or pray—it does reveal the essential components that constitute a divinely ordered service.[2] The worship patterns of the Old Testament dispensation, evinced in the tabernacle/temple economy, indicate that formal procedures were essential and integral to God-ordered and God-pleasing worship. Biblical worship in the New Testament dispensation is distinctively and starkly simple in its constituent parts but not without formal process.[3] Imperative to this formal agendum of corporate worship is the realization of the special presence of Christ: "For where two or three have gathered together in My name, I am there in their midst" (Matthew 18:20). Although this assurance is particularly applicable to church courts (Matthew 18:17-20), Revelation's description of Christ's being in the midst of the candlesticks (1:13) warrants extending the promise to the gathered church. Consciousness of that promised and therefore certain presence coupled with the care for God's glory should foster a sobriety that effects the biblically required decency and order that must mark public worship (1 Corinthians 14:40). So with the understanding that the process of implementing and incorporating the constituent elements of worship into the service or liturgy must be according to ordered decency, my delimitation for now is simply to identify the biblically mandated elements of worship without suggesting any sequence of events.

The *Westminster Confession of Faith* highlights the regular parts of ordinary religious worship as prayer, the reading of the Scripture, preaching, singing of psalms, and the sacraments.[4] Excluding the sacraments, which I will address in a separate chapter, and altering the order in which the Confession mentions these elements, I will use this summary of biblical data for my outline.

READING SCRIPTURE

I want to start with the reading of Scripture, not because it is necessarily the first order of business in public worship, but because of its place in contributing to the submissive heart that is so vital in true worship. The Scripture is a means of grace whereby the Lord reveals Himself to us, and thus it serves to establish the mindset necessary for worship.[5] The Preacher's admonition is apropos: "Keep thy foot when thou goest to the house of God, and be more ready to hear, than to give the sacrifice of fools..." (Ecclesiastes 5:1). He goes on to warn, "Be not rash with thy mouth, and let not thine heart be hasty to utter any thing before God: for God is in heaven, and thou upon earth: therefore let thy words be few" (Ecclesiastes 5:2). Although worship is active service rendered to God, part of that rendered service is receptive. But receiving does not equate with passivity. No part of worship is passive, and no participant in worship is a passive spectator. Both the reading and the hearing of the Scripture require activity. Proper hearing requires attention–a most strenuous activity: hearing and listening are not always the same thing.[6] If the public reading of Scripture is going to be an effective component of worship, both its reading and its hearing must give deference to it, as it is in truth the Lord Himself speaking.

To the Reader

At the end of his career, Moses gave the Law to the priests, instructing them to "read this law before all Israel in their hearing" so "that they may hear, and that they may learn, and fear the LORD your God, and observe to do all the words of this law" (Deuteronomy 31:9-12). About a thousand years later, Ezra, the priest and Torah scribe, read the book of Moses to the gathered people, who in turn paid attention, said their "Amen," and worshipped the Lord (Nehemiah 8:1-8). It was the habit of Jesus, the Ideal Priest and Prophet, to read the Scriptures publicly in the synagogues (Luke 4:16). Near the end of his apostolic ministry, Paul admonished Timothy, his ministerial protégé, to give attention to the public reading[38] of Scripture (1 Timothy 4:13). Significantly, Revelation 1:3 distinguishes between the singular reader and plural hearers, promising blessing to both. By command and by example, both the Old and New Testaments make the public reading of Scripture a ministerial obligation.

This ministerial public reading does not preclude the personal and private reading and meditation of Scripture nor the corporate, responsive, or occasional lay participation in public reading.[8] Indeed, the Lord instructs all His people to give continuous attention to His Word. This has been true for as long as there has been a "Bible." The first generation of God's people to receive the inscripturated Word was commanded to make it a daily part of their lives. The written Word was to have a prominent place in the home, not for decoration but for instruction (Deuteronomy 6:7-9). In David's day, the positive mark of the godly man was delighting in the law of the LORD and habitually meditating on it (Psalm 1:2). Likewise, the New Testament salutes those in Berea for searching the Scriptures daily, suggesting that they set an example that should be followed (Acts 17:11). A daily diet of Scripture is needful for every Christian, since "Man shall not live by bread alone, but by every word that proceedeth out the mouth of God" (Matthew 4:4, citing Deuteronomy 8:3).

Significantly, this biblically mandated ministerial reading became an integral part of the kind of worship regulated in the post-Reformation creeds and directories. The *Westminster Larger Catechism* in response to the question "Is the word of God to be read by all?" says, "Although all are not to be permitted to read the word publickly to the congregation, yet all sorts of people are bound to read it apart by themselves, and with their families..." (Q/A, 156). Similarly, The *Directory for the Publick Worship of God*, adopted by the Church of Scotland in 1645, detailed specifically how the Scriptures were to be read. "Reading of the word in the congregation, being part of the publick worship of God, (wherein we acknowledge our dependence upon him, and subjection to him,) and one mean sanctified by him for the edifying of his people, is to be performed by the pastors and teachers." In the section "Of Publick Reading of the Holy Scriptures,"[9] it further recommends a systematic reading of all the canonical books from the "best allowed translation" so that all can understand. So important was the reading of the Scripture that the minister who felt inclined to comment on the text was to desist until the text was read. Such a single focus on the Scripture without exposition or explanation emphasizes the inherent power of God's Word as a means of grace.

Whether privately or publicly, the "holy scriptures are to be read with an high and reverent esteem of them," with the "firm persuasion that they are the very word of God" (*Westminster Larger Catechism*, 157). Making the public reading an official ministerial function is an effective way to elevate the Word of God to a special place in the service of worship.[10] Too frequently in modern worship services the use of the Scripture is minimized. Preachers either apologize for reading extended texts, or "for the sake of time" they condense the reading to a fraction of the portion from which they are going to preach. Such practice conveys the message, even if unintentionally, that man's words and thoughts are more important than God's.[11]

To the Listener

Reading the Scripture publicly assumes a public hearing–an obvious assumption. If the "holy scriptures are to be read with an high and reverent esteem of them," with the "firm persuasion that they are the very word of God," they are to be heard the same way. Being conscious that what is being heard is indeed the word of God must create reverence and foster a spirit of worship. Israel's hearing the very voice of God at Sinai is paradigmatic of how the Lord's Word should be received: they responded with fear and reverent worship just as God had intended. The Lord had told Moses, "I will make them hear my words, that they may learn to fear me all the days that they shall live upon the earth" (Deuteronomy 4:10; see Exodus 19:9-25). Indeed the nation's immediately audible encounter with God, whose voice that day shook the earth (Hebrews 12:26), was so awesome that they could not endure to hear it that way again (Hebrews 12:19-20). There was no doubt that what they heard was God's Word, and hearing it made an impression.

And that's the point. Too frequently, we read or hear without being impressed. As I have already said, there is a lamentable difference between hearing and listening. Even in worship services in which proper time is assigned for the reading of Scripture, that reading is often heard with same attention as the announcements. The separate and singular reading of Scripture, if it has a place at all in the "order of service," is just a preliminary exercise to whatever is perceived to be the real business of the meeting. I emphasize that reading the Scripture is not a perfunctory preliminary to worship; it is worship. Again, I would suggest that ancient Israel set a good example for the modern church to follow when it comes to listening and responding to the Word's being read. A literal translation of Nehemiah 8:3 says that when Ezra read the Scripture "from the light until the half of the day...the ears of all the people (were) to the book of the law"–a vividly terse way of saying that they paid attention. In respect for the Word, they stood while Ezra read (Nehemiah 8:5; c.f. 9:3). In response to the Word, the entire congregation said, "Amen, Amen, with lifting up their hands: and they bowed their heads, and worshipped the LORD with their faces to the ground" (Nehemiah 8:6). It was obvious that hearing the Word made an impression on them that they demonstrated by worship. Although their posture and precise verbal expressions may not qualify as mandatory, the attitude expressed by their deportment and affirmation should. Reverently paying attention to the Bible is a part of worship.[12]

PRAYING

Prayer, another essential component of public worship, shares a special relationship with Scripture reading, and former theologians have aptly termed them the devotional services of the sanctuary. There is always a connection between God's Word and prayer–between God's speaking to us and our speaking to Him. Scriptural praying flows from and reasons according to the Scripture. Prayer is a vital vehicle for worshipping God, whether in private or in public. But there is a particular sense in which public praying–as part of corporate worship–contributes to and helps to foster a spirit of genuine worship.

I can't help thinking of the lessons about worship that God illustrated for Israel in the old Tabernacle. So vivid and timelessly relevant were those lessons that I will devote some attention to them in a later chapter. But without getting too far ahead of myself, I would have you consider the lesson from the altar of incense. This was the last item in the holy place, right up against the veil separating the holy place from the most holy. Significantly, this altar was fueled by coals from the altar of sacrifice in the outer court, and the priests would offer incense every morning and evening. As the smoke ascended from the altar, its fragrance would waft over the veil into the most holy place that kept the ark, the climactic symbol of God's presence. This offering of incense was a symbol of prayer. David obviously alluded to this altar when he prayed, "Let my prayer be set forth before thee as incense; and the lifting up of my hands as the evening sacrifice" (Psalm 141:2). Two significant truths stand out: (1) prayer takes us as close as possible to the holy presence of God without our actually being there in person; and (2) prayer works only because of the blood of the sacrifice, which opened up the way to God. More about this later, but the point for now is clear: prayer is an essential means of worship.

Its Place

That prayer has a place in the gathered church should go without saying. "Prayer, with thanksgiving, being one special part of religious worship, is by God required of all men... "(*Westminster Confession of Faith*, 21.3). Yet the unhappy fact of the matter is that prayer from both the pulpit and the pew suffers in the modern church. One of the most lamentable traits of today's churches is the demise of church-wide prayer meetings. What used to be midweek prayer meetings have become occasions for Bible study, youth activities, fellowship meals, or business meetings—all of which are legitimate but none of which are substitutes for corporate prayer. There is nothing sacrosanct about the midweek, but there is something sacrosanct about the church prayer meeting. This demise is too bad because, as surmised from the Tabernacle lesson, the sad truth is that the neglect of prayer keeps us from experiencing what is perhaps the closest communion with the presence of God that is possible to experience.

The practice of the first-century church should be the standard for every true church of Jesus Christ. It seems that every time they met, they spent time praying together with significant consequences for the expansion of Christ's kingdom (for examples, see Acts 1:14, 24; 4:23-24, 31; 12:5, etc.). It was evidently clear that praying time was not wasted time. Rather, recognizing their total dependence on God for protection and power, they prayed. Prayer is always in proportion to the consciousness of divine dependence. The more we recognize our need for God, the more we pray; the less we recognize that need, the less we pray. That's the bottom line.

As much as the modern church needs to return to the first-century practice of corporate prayer and as much as I am tempted to address this need, my principal concern for now is to focus on the pulpit rather than the pew. The pastoral prayer has a special place in corporate worship. It is a means both of glorifying God and of edifying the people.[13] It is the means of leading the congregation into the presence of the Lord, and the pulpit is the place of leading. The pastoral prayer has rightly been called a "kind of pulpit speech" and in the biblical and Protestant tradition is the special province of those God has called to the ministry of the gospel.[14] According to The Form of Presbyterial Church-Government of 1645, the first duty of the pastor is "to pray for and with his flock, as the mouth of the people unto God." As evidence that this is not just a Presbyterian notion, appeal is made to Acts 6:2-4 and 20:36, "where preaching and prayer are joined as several parts of the same office."

Placing prayer in the pulpit as part of official ministerial duty is not to dissuade or discourage the people from praying as something only preachers can do, but rather to underscore the place of prayer as a vital component of worship. It is incumbent, then, upon ministers to take seriously the obligation to pray in such a manner as to direct their people to God and to teach them by example how to approach God reverently.[15] To that end, it would be good for ministers to think about what they are going to pray before they lead their congregations in such a sacred exercise. I give you Dabney's thoughts.

> I deem that the minister is as much bound to prepare himself for praying in public as for preaching. The negligence with which many preachers leave their prayers to accident, while they lay out all their strength on their sermons, is most painfully suggestive of unbelief toward God and indifference to the edification of their brethren.[16]

These are sobering and convicting words for every minister—myself included.

Its Pattern

My temptation here is to develop a biblical theology of prayer and to expound some of the inspired prayers recorded in Scripture,[17] but both are beyond the present scope. The temptation, however, does suggest the point I need to make: the patterns for prayer are found in Scripture. In His Word, the Lord invites His people to pray, exhorts them to pray, teaches them to pray, and illustrates for them how to pray. Part of the minister's thoughtful preparation for prayer should be with a view to incorporate the language of Scripture into the pulpit prayers[18] and to shape those prayers according to biblical models. Since it is the minister's responsibility to lead the people in worship through praying and to teach them by example how to pray, there is no better way to achieve this dual purpose than to saturate the pulpit prayer with scriptural phraseology and petition. It is imperative, however, that the pulpit prayer does not become just a recital of Bible verses or phrases but that it is truly prayer offered unto God. There must be relevant needs and actual desires that are being addressed with scriptural warrant and language. Whereas pulpit prayer should be edifying and instructive to those in the pew, it should never be offered with the intent of impressing people.

In order to resist the temptation before me, I am only going to be suggestive in what I say regarding the patterns for public and pulpit prayer, which principles are relevant for private prayer as well. First, I would suggest that the recorded prayers of Scripture receive serious study. Not all are public prayers, but all are instructive and tend to expose the triteness and triviality that mark so much of modern praying. What follows is by no means exhaustive, but it identifies some of the classic prayers of Scripture that deserve careful consideration and imitation. The first extended example of prayer in Scripture is Abraham's intercession for Sodom (Genesis 18:16-33). It evidences persistence, humility, selflessness, and recognition of God's holiness, righteousness, and mercy. Moses's song of praise in deliverance from Egypt is a prayer directed to God in the hearing of the people, extolling God's unique perfections and recounting His many specific mercies (Exodus 15:1-18). Moses's prayer of intercession for Israel expresses reliance on God's covenant faithfulness and concern for God's reputation in the world (Exodus 32:11-32; Deuteronomy 9:18-20). Hannah's prayer for a son illustrates the power of petition (1 Samuel 1:8-12), and her prayer of praise and thanksgiving the proper response to answered prayer (2 Samuel 2:1-10). Solomon's prayer at the dedication of the Temple includes praise for God's covenant faithfulness in the past and petitions for God's continuing faithfulness to His promises, with consistent recognition of both God's justice and His mercy (1 Kings 8:22-61). Hezekiah's prayer for deliverance expresses the urgency of heart that seeks divine intervention for life's problems (2 Kings 19:14-18). The prayers of Daniel (Daniel 9:3-19), Ezra (Ezra 9:5-15), and Nehemiah (Nehemiah 1:4-11) demonstrate the genuine sorrow over national sin and desire for God's glory that mark corporate confession. These are just a few, and when you include the New Testament examples of Mary (Luke 1:46-55), Paul (Ephesians 1:15-23, etc.) and Christ Himself (Matthew 6:9-13; John 17), there is ample precedent to study and to imitate.

Second, I would suggest including in public praying the principal parts or kinds of prayer that the Scripture either enjoins or illustrates. Paul demanded this principle when he exhorted Timothy that "supplications, prayers, intercessions, and giving of thanks, be made for all men" (1 Timothy 2:1). Again, being governed by my own delimitation to avoid a biblical theology of prayer, I will only list the key types of prayer that ought to constitute part of public worship without exposition or detailed explanation. Not every prayer must include every element, and there is no particular sequence in which the elements must occur. But public prayer should involve the following: (1) *invocations* that call upon God, hallow His name, claim Him in the trinity of His sacred Persons to be the one true, living, and personal God, and appeal both to the blood and merits of Christ as the basis for approaching the throne of grace and to the Holy Spirit as necessary aid to worship, (2) *confessions* that focus on the corporate failures and sins of both church and state, (3) *intercessions* that appeal to God's intervention for others, (4) *petitions* that supplicate God for special needs–particularly those of the body as a whole–and especially for illumination to be granted for the ministry of the Word, (5) *imprecations* that seek divine intervention against those who hinder and oppose the work of the Christ, and (6) *praise* and *thanksgiving* that bring to focus and memory God's past blessings and faithfulness.

All prayer and especially public prayer should be marked by reverence, humility, sincerity, trust, earnestness, and purity. In addressing the Lord, those leading in public prayer should be careful to include the listening participants; and in expressing petitions, they should avoid personal references and use plural pronouns. That is courtesy, if nothing else. The bottom line is simply to remember that public and ministerial praying is an essential element in worship, and it's okay to think about what to pray for and how to pray. It may be humbling, but it would not be a bad idea to read some of the pastoral prayers of past preachers. I admit when I read something like Spurgeon's *The Pastor in Prayer* or *The Valley of Vision: A Collection of Puritan Prayers and Devotions,* or Matthew Henry's *A Method for Prayer,* I feel a sharp sense of inadequacy.

PREACHING

The central and preeminent component in Protestant and therefore biblical worship is the preaching of the Word of God. Dabney pointedly stated the difference between a Romanist and a Protestant: "The Papist says: 'I go to mass;' the Protestant, 'I go to preaching.'" [19] There is today on many fronts a tragic and religiously dangerous reversal of both Reformation theology and practice. Certainly, not the least tragic step back to the Dark Ages of religion is the demise of preaching. Right across the spectrum of evangelicalism and even fundamentalism is the collapse of the pulpit. Pulpit platforms have been replaced with stages featuring state-of-the-art lighting and sound systems for dramas, videos, concerts, and worship leaders to do their thing. Pastors have done more to cultivate their administrative skills as though they were CEOs of some corporation, or to refine their counseling techniques as though they were psychologists looking for a place to hang their shingle, than develop their sermon skills as though they really were preachers of the gospel. Sadly, programs take precedence over preaching on too many checklists used to identify "good" churches. People seem to tolerate incompetence in the pulpit if the church has all the programs and structure to provide something "Christian" for their families to do. Sadly, I know of those who have left ministries whose pulpits have confessedly fed their souls but were not able to cater to their other needs that were perceived as more important. To be sure, churches are organizations that must function according to order, and people have needs that require personal pastoral attention; I'm all in favor of Christian life revolving around the Church. But preaching must be the main business of preachers. It is not surprising that the modern church is engaged in such intense "worship wars" when the central component of worship has been relegated to secondary significance. Apart from the power and presence of God, what the church needs more than anything else–if I can borrow Haggai's epithet–is the Lord's messengers in the Lord's message (Haggai 1:13). My guess is that if the church has that kind of messenger, it will also have something of that divine power and presence.

The Mandate for Preaching

The mandate for preaching comes from both the commands and the examples of Scripture. Paul's command to Timothy is clear, concise, and uncontestable: "Preach the word; be instant in season, out of season; reprove, rebuke, exhort with all longsuffering and doctrine" (2 Timothy 4:2). Before this, he had already instructed Timothy to remind the brethren about false teachers and to give attention to exhortation, both of which would involve preaching (1 Timothy 4:6, 13). Timothy's being a good minister depended on this. Paul's instruction to Timothy was not uniquely applicable to Timothy; rather, it applies universally to all ministers who would rightly fulfill their office. This certainly was the understanding of the 17th century post-Reformation church. The section "Of the Preaching of the Word" in *The Directory for the Publick Worship of God* begins with this statement: "Preaching of the word, being the power of God unto salvation, and one of the greatest and most excellent works belonging to the ministry of the gospel, should be so performed, that the workman need not be ashamed, but may save himself, and those that hear him." Similarly, in detailing the duties of the pastor, *The Form of Presbyterial Church-Government* of 1645 addresses the pastor's mandate to preach by declaring "that the ministers of the gospel have as ample a charge and commission to dispense the word, as well as other ordinances, as the priests and Levites had under the law" and that it is their duty "to feed the flock, by preaching of the word, according to which he is to teach, convince, reprove, exhort, and comfort."

Examples of preaching abound in both the Old and the New Testaments. The Old Testament prophets were primarily preachers whose duty was to proclaim "Thus saith the Lord GOD" (see, for instance, Ezekiel 2:4). Ezra and his fellow Levites, having read the Scripture in the hearing of the people, "gave the sense, and caused them to understand the reading" (Nehemiah

8:8). That, by the way, is a classic pattern for pulpit ministry. John the Baptist preached in the Judean wilderness (Matthew 3:1). Jesus Himself went all over Galilee "preaching the gospel of the kingdom" (Matthew 4:23); indeed, it was one of the proofs of His being Messiah that He preached the gospel to the poor (Isaiah 61:1; Matthew 11:5). Preaching Christ was the habitual practice of the apostles (Acts 5:42), none of whom did so more diligently than Paul, whose testimony to the Ephesians that he did not shun declaring the whole counsel of God (Acts 20:27) could well sum up his entire ministry.

Obviously, not all the preaching referred to in Scripture took place in gatherings designated for worship. Open-air preaching was a common tactic in declaring God's Word—witness Jeremiah on the steps of the Temple declaiming to religious hypocrites on their way to worship (Jeremiah 7) or Paul on Mars Hill preaching to the agnostics of his day (Acts 17). But nonetheless, there is sufficient evidence in the New Testament that verbal proclamation of the Word (i.e., preaching)[20] was a key element in public meetings for worship. It was part of synagogue worship, and Jesus went all over Judea preaching in these public forums (Luke 4:44). Later, Paul did the same thing in his missionary endeavors (Acts 13:14-41; 14:1, etc.). Even if the practice of the synagogues may be arguably irrelevant as a guide to proper Christian worship, the custom of the newly constituted church was the same and should be regulative and therefore normative for the church today. Every day in the temple and in every house in which they met together, the apostles "ceased not to teach and preach Jesus Christ" (Acts 5:42). When Paul met with the group of disciples at Troas on the first day of the week, he "preached unto them…and continued his speech until midnight" (Acts 20:7). It would appear that the sermon was the principal part of the meeting.

The Magnitude of Preaching

God has assigned significant importance to preaching; that's why I refer to its magnitude. The magnitude of biblical preaching is inherent in its content and executed through its delivery. Needless to say, what I am about to discuss is true only for Bible preaching. The preacher has neither authority nor right to use the pulpit as a place to express his own opinions on anything: the pulpit is not a soapbox. Too many preachers have exaggerated, arrogant, and unscriptural notions of their office whereby they assume the prerogative of dictating the consciences of their people in every sphere of life. That is popery, and there is no place for it in the Church of Christ. So understand that when I address the inherent importance of preaching, I am excluding what takes place in many pulpits and am referring only to the declarations of "Thus saith the Lord." It is too bad that I have to say what should be needless to say.

The magnitude of preaching rests first of all in its content, the message being preached. The Scripture defines the content of preaching in different terms: the Word, the whole counsel of God, Christ, the gospel, etc. But each term is inclusive of the others, and each shares the same divinely set significance. A couple of Paul's inspired remarks about the content of preaching speak for themselves, but I will make some brief comments nonetheless to emphasize the point. First Corinthians 1:18 says, "For the preaching of the cross is to them that perish foolishness; but unto us which are saved it is the power of God." The word translated "preaching" is actually the word "word" (*logos*), which here refers to the message about the cross rather than to its proclamation. Paul continues in 1 Corinthians 1:21 by saying, "For after that in the wisdom of God the world by wisdom knew not God, it pleased God by the foolishness of preaching to save them that believe." The word for preaching here (*kerugma*) again refers to the substance of what is preached rather than the act of preaching it. Notwithstanding how foolish preaching may seem or how foolishly some preachers may actually preach, it is the gospel itself that unbelievers regard as foolish and that believers receive as the power of God unto their salvation. Because of the inherent importance of the message with its life and death implications, Paul resolved that he would not be like others who corrupted the Word of God or handled it deceitfully (2 Corinthians 2:17). That is a good example for every minister to follow.

Second, the magnitude of the act of preaching is the corollary to the message being preached. Preaching is a chief means that God has ordained to communicate His Word, and He has especially ordained preachers to do it. Romans 10:13-17 explains the link between God's purpose to save and the means He has determined to accomplish that purpose.

> For whosoever shall call upon the name of the Lord shall be saved. How then shall they call on him in whom they have not believed? and how shall they believe in him of whom they have not heard? and how shall they hear without a preacher? And how shall they preach, except they be sent? as it is written, How beautiful are the feet of them that preach the gospel of peace, and bring glad tidings of good things! But they have not all obeyed the gospel. For Esaias saith, Lord, who hath believed our report? So then faith cometh by hearing, and hearing by the word of God.

This text makes it clear that preaching is the means of evangelizing. That God gave to the church apostles, prophets, evangelists, and pastors/teachers, whose principal duties involved communicating God's Word "for the perfecting of the saints, for the work of the ministry, for the edifying of the body of Christ" (Ephesians 4:11-12), indicates the vital function preaching played in the whole operation of the church and continues to play, since He continues to supply His church with essential ministers whose duties remain the same. The fact that biblical preaching is a means of glorifying God as well as evangelizing the lost and edifying saints increases its vital significance. Here's how Peter put it: "If any man speak, let him speak as the oracles of God; if any man minister, let him do it as of the ability which God giveth: that God in all things may be glorified through Jesus Christ, to whom be praise and dominion for ever and ever. Amen" (1 Peter 4:11).

The *Westminster Larger Catechism* aptly sums up the importance of preaching as one of the "outward and ordinary means whereby Christ communicates to his church the benefits of his mediation" (154). This Reformation creed provides a fitting conclusion to this section, highlighting the vital place of preaching in the church.

> The Spirit of God maketh the reading, but especially the preaching of the word, and effectual means of enlightening, convincing, and humbling sinners; of driving them out of themselves, and drawing them unto Christ; of conforming them to his image, and subduing them to his will; of strengthening them against temptations and corruptions; of building them up in grace, and establishing their hearts in holiness and comfort through faith unto salvation. (155)

Given the emphasis on preaching in the Bible, the status to which it was restored during the Reformation (evident in the catechism) and the place to which it must be restored in the modern church, Mohler's statement is appropriate: "The heart of Christian worship is the authentic preaching of the word of God....More specifically, preaching is indispensable to Christian worship–and not only indispensable, but central."[21]

The Method of Preaching

It is not my purpose to define, evaluate, or recommend any particular homiletic style. There are plenty of available books that do that, and I would certainly recommend all preachers to study homiletics. Regardless of the sermon style, the proper method of preaching is inseparably linked to the message. Again, the only thing that I'm talking about is preaching the Bible, and conveying its message as honestly and accurately as possible is of prime importance. Preaching is not just talking about something in the Bible, and the Bible is certainly not a platform for diving into some stream of self-interest. Preaching is the means of declaring the timeless and consequently contemporary relevance of God's Word to a particular people. The method of all message-based preaching is expositional. Exposition is the process of getting from the text of Scripture to the pulpit. It couples the explanation of the text with the appropriate application of the text to the lives of those hearing the sermon. A sermon without application is just a book report; a sermon without the explanation of the biblical text is just opinion.

Exposition requires that the preacher study and determine the meaning of the text, that he should expect the text to address current needs, and that he must settle on how best to communicate the timeless truths of the ancient text to his contemporary audience. Establishing and communicating the relevancy of the Scripture are crucial to the ministerial obligation to "reprove, rebuke, exhort with all longsuffering and doctrine" (2 Timothy 4:2). Without biblical basis, the preacher has no right or authority to do any of that. So given the fearful duty to preach the Word, ministers must themselves seek for guidance and illumination from the Holy Spirit as they pray for a message from God for the people to whom they will minister.[22] There can be something quite mechanical about sermon preparation; there is something quite spiritual about communicating the message of God via the prepared sermon. The sermon is the structured means of communicating the message.

Communication presupposes two parties. Somebody gives, and somebody receives the message. If there is a method for preparing and preaching the message, there is also a method for receiving it. Preaching will accomplish its purpose in the place of worship when it is received with obedient faith and reverence. Hebrews 4:2 mentions those to whom the gospel was preached without profit because it was "not being mixed with faith in them that heard it." In contrast, Paul rejoiced in the Thessalonians because when they received the Word of God, they "received it not as the word of men, but as it is in truth, the word of God" (1 Thessalonians 2:13). Therefore, it behooves those who sit in pews to pray that those who stand in the pulpit will have a word from the Lord and the spiritual power to communicate it, and to pray for themselves that God will open their ears and their eyes to behold the wondrous things out of God's law (see Psalm 119:18). When done right and put in its proper and prominent place, the preaching of the Word will contribute much to the true and spiritual worship that is ultimately glorifying to God.

SINGING

The final routine element in the liturgy of worship that I will discuss is singing. I deal with it last not because it is the most or least important; singing occupies its own special and essential place in worship. Ironically, although singing's place in worship is indisputable, the number and variety of differing opinions as to how to sing are staggering. Controversies rage over music styles, the use or non-use of musical instruments, what kinds of instruments are permissible if instruments are in fact permissible (piano and organ vs. guitars, drums, and saxophones), the legitimacy of "special music" and choirs, and whether the inspired Psalms should be sung exclusively or not at all. So intense are some of the debates and so discordant are interpretations that music has often become a litmus test for fellowship or separation.

I do not minimize the importance of these issues, but a thorough analysis of each problem is outside the scope of my purpose for now.[23] Consequently, my delimitations may exceed my actual comments. Although I am musically incompetent,[24] I have my views and interpretations on all the controversial issues: I oppose CCM[25] (Contemporary Christian Music); I do not oppose the use of instruments; I do not oppose choirs or special music presentations so long as they are not showcases for talent or entertainment interludes (I abhor it when congregations applaud musicians); I oppose exclusive Psalmody, but do favor the regular singing of Psalms. My objective now is simply to observe singing's proper place in the service of worship. Singing may well be preliminary and preparatory for preaching, but it is not a prelude to worship. It is a means of worship.

Biblical Warrant

If the Scripture is the guide to worship, then singing is part of worship. Both by command and by example, the Bible warrants the song service. I love the words of Psalm 98, particularly as translated in the Scottish Psalter, that give express command.

> *Sing a new song to Jehovah; For he wondrous things hath wrought;*
> *His right hand and arm most holy Victory to him have brought.*
> *All the earth sing to Jehovah! Shout aloud! Sing and rejoice!*
> *With the harp sing to Jehovah! With the harp and tuneful voice.*
> *Sound the trumpet and the cornet, Shout before the Lord and King;*
> *Sea, and all its fullness, thunder; Earth, and all its people, sing.*
> (verses 1, 4, 5)

I found myself singing these words as I typed them on screen, but that's beside the point. The command is clear and repeated similarly and regularly throughout the Psalms. Likewise the New Testament commands worshipful singing. Paul's instructions are well-known:

And be not drunk with wine, wherein is excess; but be filled with the Spirit; Speaking to yourselves in psalms and hymns and spiritual songs, singing and making melody in your heart to the Lord. (Ephesians 5:18-19)

Let the word of Christ dwell in you richly in all wisdom; teaching and admonishing one another in psalms and hymns and spiritual songs, singing with grace in your hearts to the Lord. (Colossians 3:16)[26]

In both of these texts, singing is the consequence or expression of an inward spiritual experience. Singing is the expression of a heart affected by truth, not a manipulating technique to generate a spiritual euphoria that is nothing more than an emotional counterfeit of the real thing.

In addition to specific commands and instructions to sing, the Scripture provides many examples of singing as a means of worshipping the Lord. Significantly, Moses, the great lawgiver, was the first hymnologist as well. Immediately after safe passage from Egypt through the Red Sea, Moses sang a song of victory celebration unto the Lord and led Israel to sing with him (Exodus 15). He closed his ministry with the song of witness, which Israel was supposed to learn and sing by heart (Deuteronomy 31:19-32:44). Deborah's song of victory (Judges 5), Solomon's thousand-plus songs (1 Kings 4:32), Isaiah's use of prophetic songs (Isaiah 5, 26-27), as well as Habakkuk's prayer (Habakkuk 3) are all examples of the frequent use of song in Israel's liturgical history. When the Book of Psalms is factored in, it is overwhelmingly clear how integral singing was to worship. The pattern did not change in the New Testament. In fact, the events surrounding the birth of Christ occasioned the singing of some songs the Old Testament could only anticipate: the song of Mary (Luke 1:46-55), the song of Zacharias (Luke 1:67-79), the song of Simeon (Luke 2:29-32). Christ is certainly a reason to sing. The final book of the Bible with its unique focus on heavenly praise and worship reveals that singing will forever be part of worship (Revelation 4:8-11; 5:9-13). It may very well be that the New Testament records some of the first hymns that were sung by the infant church (perhaps Philippians 2:6-11; 1 Timothy 3:16). The bottom line is that the church has sufficient biblical warrant for singing. In fact, a church that doesn't sing defies the biblical patterns.

Musical Focus

The focus of worship music must be consonant with every other aspect of biblical and spiritual worship. The focus must be God–His person, perfections, and works. Worship is about God and for God. That certainly includes what He has graciously done for us and what should be our appropriate response to Him, but still the focus is on God. Too often, this fundamental of worship is set aside for the song service. Too easily, singing degenerates to entertainment, and what pleases the senses takes precedence over what pleases the Lord. This entertainment factor generally but not uniquely involves the music rather than the message of the song. Many regard the music as irrelevant or indifferent, so long as the message is sound. But ironically, it is the music that they will hold on to tenaciously and argue for vociferously. Some on the other extreme seem to conclude that any tune that they like must be unacceptable to God–the more doleful the melody, the more spiritual it must be.

Again, I would be most foolish to discuss composition theory or to weigh in on the virtues or vices of syncopation. But the theology of worship music suggests to me what should be obvious. There must be such a wedding of tunes with words that the message is conveyed without distraction. If the conveying of the message is the preeminent purpose, there are certain music forms that will be automatically precluded. Tunes and types of music that identify with worldly environments have no place in the worship of God even if the number of notes and syllables match. The consciousness of God's holiness–that is, His absolute separation from the common and mundane–should strongly influence the kind of melodies we bring into His presence in our worship to praise Him and offer Him the thanksgiving He so infinitely deserves. That does not mean that we can't enjoy the tunes, for what pleases Him ought to please us as well.

The worship focus for singing will be safeguarded the more we adhere to the Scripture's patterns for singing. This is one reason that the singing of the inspired Psalms should be a regular practice. They teach that praising, praying, and proclaiming truth through singing are divinely defined and sanctioned elements of God-glorifying worship. Singing the Psalms is proper since the God revealed in the Old Testament is still our God. But thoroughly Christian worship must include the specifics of Christian religion. As we have already seen, the Incarnation caused God's people to break forth in new songs. Remember the declaration of the *Westminster Confession of Faith* that "Religious worship is to be given to God, the Father, Son, and Holy Ghost...and since the fall, not without a Mediator; nor in the mediation of any other but of Christ alone" (21.2). Since singing is an element in the acceptable way of worshipping God, it must be governed by this caveat. Perhaps I'm being a bit simplistic or even naïve, but I believe if the purpose of worship and the focus of worship are in view, singing will take its proper place in the service of worship and will be offered reverently and soberly in the fear of the Lord.

Admittedly, I have not answered all the questions and disputes about worship that ultimately need to be answered and resolved. But I have more or less kept to the scope of this chapter, which is to identify the biblically mandated elements of worship, the liturgy of service. Reading Scripture, praying, singing, and preaching are the essential and indispensable elements that must be sequenced in public worship. The Bible does not specify the order of service, but it does identify the components. If we are to worship the Lord in the beauty of holiness, it is imperative that we follow His instructions on how to do it. We cannot leave out any pieces.

CHAPTER 5

AIDS FOR WORSHIP

Worship without hindrance or help marks the perfect worship of heaven, where sooner or later every believer will perform his service unto God. The sin-free environment (Revelation 22:3) in the immediate presence of God coupled with the actual sight of Christ in all of His exalted glory will be so overwhelming that worship will be our natural response and occupation. Heaven is not only sin-free, but also Temple-free, "for the Lord God Almighty and the Lamb are the temple of it" (Revelation 21:22). God had ordered the service of the Tabernacle/Temple to teach vital lessons about worship. If sin is the earthly hindrance to worship, then the Temple represents the earthly aids to worship that will be eternally obsolete. The time is coming when without any distraction or prompting, worship will occur in the perfect beauty of holiness.

But in the meantime, hindrances to worship abound. Even in the most spiritual of pursuits, we are prone to botch things up. We need all the help we can get. Knowing our frame and propensities, God who always meets our needs, has graciously given some aids to worship; and we, in order to worship biblically and acceptably, must use those means of assistance. Left to self, man tends to devise such elaborate and ornate aids to worship that the aids themselves potentially become the objects of worship. The golden calf syndrome recurs regularly because, according to Calvin's often referred to analogy, the heart of man is a factory for idols. In contrast, the God-given aids to worship are simple, and they require faith. Indeed, the spiritual and faithful use of these aids on the one hand prevents abuses in worship and on the other promotes proper and worshipful thoughts of God. The principal aids to worship that God has given are the Sabbath and the Sacraments. Admittedly, outside the Reformed tradition these words are not happily used. They have been abused, misunderstood, and hijacked by false religions and cults, but they are good words when properly defined and applied. So stay with me and let me use them (besides, they are nicely alliterated).

THE SABBATH: A TIME FOR WORSHIP

I am well aware that the very thought of keeping the Sabbath is foreign to most Christians today whether they are Reformed or dispensational. Opinions differ in terms of both its legitimate relevance for Christians or its specific practices if relevant. Interestingly, I have known Reformed men who, contrary to their creed,[1] deny its relevance by their practice, and I have known dispensationalists who were convinced Sabbatarians. Charges of legalism are often filed against those who seek to maintain any kind of standard on the Lord's Day. Tragically, it is all too common that the only difference in practice between Christians and the ungodly on Sunday is the couple of hours spent in church. I am neither so naïve nor so arrogant as to assume that I will shed any new light on the issue that will persuade any to my views, recognizing that some of the objections to what I am going to say are rooted in fundamental hermeneutical differences. It is my purpose to examine the Scripture's logic in commanding the spiritual observance of the Sabbath as a safeguard for spiritual worship. Admittedly, some issues concerning the Sabbath warrant consideration but are outside the perimeters of my purpose, and I am even now debating with myself how far to stray off course. I am going to resist discussing some significant matters,[2] but nonetheless I must address a few concerns outside the scope of my purpose in order to say what I really want to say. Otherwise, I fear some will not give what I want to say a fair hearing.

Standard Objections

I suppose that the often-asserted conflict between law and grace tops the list of objections, since keeping the Sabbath is mandated in the Decalogue. This conflict exists only when law is put on the wrong side of grace. When law replaces grace or assumes priority, there is conflict indeed.[3] In its proper place, the law serves many functions. Not only does its demand for perfect obedience condemn sinners before the righteous God, but it also is the schoolmaster that leads men to Christ, whose perfect active and passive obedience is the only ground for a sinner's acceptance before God. This evangelistic function, however, does not exhaust the law's purpose. Once delivered from the penalty of the broken law and the requirements of the law for spiritual life, the believer, whom the Lord has called to holiness (1 Peter 1:15-16), must live within the sphere of the law. The grace of the gospel does not give the Christian the right to whatever he desires. To come to Christ is to be under a yoke. It is an easy yoke, but it is nonetheless a yoke (Matthew 11:28-29). The gospel has loving boundaries (2 Corinthians 5:14), and to the genuine believer, living within those boundaries is pleasurable (1 John 5:3). The liberty of the gospel involves freedom from the law as the means of gaining divine favor, freedom from the law's penalty and guilt, and freedom to be holy. Holiness is not some abstract, indefinable virtue. Holiness is living according to the precepts of God's law. Nothing should be more desirable for a Christian than to do those things that are pleasing unto the Lord, and God's law defines the sphere of pleasing behavior. Christians should endeavor to keep the law, not because they could thereby gain divine favor or salvation (that would be legalism), but because they have received divine grace (that would be sanctification). Those in Christ are free from the law as a means of life, but they are not free from the law as a way of life. Grace always puts law in its proper place. This certainly applies to the practice of worship. If we are to worship in the beauty of holiness, we must worship according to what God defines as holiness. Grace gives us the desire and the ability to do it. Nothing is more "anti-grace" than disregarding God's law.

Two more specific objections to the Sabbath's applicability to Christians flow from the general notion of the law's current irrelevance: (1) the New Testament's failure to repeat the fourth commandment as it does the others, and (2) the New Testament's forthright condemnation of the practice of keeping the Sabbath. I can only state the basis of my objection to these objections. My first objection is based on my hermeneutical framework of covenant theology. I believe that there is such continuity between the Old and The New Testaments that the validity and authority of the Old does not depend on confirmation or reaffirmation by the New. The New Testament does not replace the Old; it continues and completes God's inspired revelation. Truth established is truth established. Having said that, I cannot concede that the New Testament addresses the Sabbath principle unfavorably. According to the Book of Hebrews, for instance, the prophetic ceremonies under the old covenant have been fulfilled, and they are consequently no longer operative in this dispensation; yet the keeping of the Sabbath continues and remains for God's people: "There remaineth therefore a rest [keeping of Sabbath] to the people of God" (Hebrews 4:9). Even if this refers specifically to eternity, it would be strange for a practice that started at creation,[4] continued through the whole course of redemptive history until the beginning of the organized church, and continues into eternity, to be temporarily set aside in this dispensation.

My second objection concerns what are misunderstandings and misinterpretations of some New Testament passages and statements that allegedly condemn the keeping of the Sabbath. Let me refer to some words of Jesus to illustrate my concern.[5] The Lord Jesus answered the Pharisees' accusation that He had broken the Sabbath: "The sabbath was made for man, and not man for the sabbath: Therefore the Son of man is Lord also of the sabbath" (Mark 2:27-28). Some would conclude that Christ here liberates man from the bondage of keeping the sabbath by declaring His authority to abrogate it. Amazingly, some modern interpreters actually concur with the Pharisaical assessment of Christ's behavior, that He broke God's law. It is a serious error with dangerous hermeneutical implications to equate Pharisaical theology with Old Testament theology. The Pharisees with all of their manmade traditions perverted rather than preserved the truth.[6] It is true enough that Jesus was constantly violating the traditions of the Pharisees, but in so doing He was obeying God's law perfectly. Christ's statement does not repeal the Sabbath but rather declares that it exists for man's benefit and not man's bondage. He affirmed God's intent. How either Christ's statement or His practice can be construed as His abolishing the Sabbath defies my understanding.

Summary of the Law

> Remember the sabbath day, to keep it holy. Six days shalt
> thou labour, and do all thy work: But the seventh day is the

sabbath of the LORD thy God: in it thou shalt not do any work, thou, nor thy son, nor thy daughter, thy manservant, nor thy maidservant, nor thy cattle, nor thy stranger that is within thy gates: For in six days the LORD made heaven and earth, the sea, and all that in them is, and rested the seventh day: wherefore the LORD blessed the sabbath day, and hallowed it. (Exodus 20:8-11)

Keep the sabbath day to sanctify it, as the LORD thy God hath commanded thee. Six days thou shalt labour, and do all thy work: But the seventh day is the sabbath of the LORD thy God: in it thou shalt not do any work, thou, nor thy son, nor thy daughter, nor thy manservant, nor thy maidservant, nor thine ox, nor thine ass, nor any of thy cattle, nor thy stranger that is within thy gates; that thy manservant and thy maidservant may rest as well as thou. And remember that thou wast a servant in the land of Egypt, and that the LORD thy God brought thee out thence through a mighty hand and by a stretched out arm: therefore the LORD thy God commanded thee to keep the sabbath day. (Deuteronomy 5:12-15)

This fourth commandment, recorded on stone in Exodus 20 and expounded by Moses in Deuteronomy 5, requires the keeping of the Sabbath. The inspired inscription of Exodus together with the inspired interpretation and application of Deuteronomy give clear direction for using the Sabbath as an aid to worship.

A proper definition of terms is critical to any discussion, and this is certainly the case for any discussion of the Sabbath since so much of the misunderstanding about the Sabbath stems from improper definitions. Let's start at the beginning. The verb "remember" in the Exodus statement suggests awareness of the Sabbath prior to Sinai, a knowledge that is assumed in the narrative in Exodus 16, where the Lord sets down the rules for gathering manna. Remembering does denote a mental recall, but it involves much more. Too often remembering, and its counterpart forgetting, are mental operations over which we have little control. It is a common human malady to forget what we should remember and to remember what we would like to forget. But the Hebrew terms for these mental maneuvers express willful, voluntary acts rather than uncontrollable, involuntary processes. In other words, to remember is to think about something on purpose; to forget is to refuse to think about something on purpose. Consequently, the Exodus exhortation requires conscious reflection and equates with Deuteronomy's command to keep or observe the Sabbath day, an action which in turn requires attentive and careful obedience.

Perhaps the biggest misconception involving the fourth commandment concerns the meaning of the term "Sabbath," which is basically a transliteration of the Hebrew word. In spite of its association in this context with the seventh day, the term does not inherently refer to the seventh day, nor does it have any connection to the number seven at all. The Sabbath designates the seventh day of the week only when the context specifies it as the seventh day. The word comes from a verbal root meaning "to cease." Simply, the Sabbath is a day that stops or a day that marks or sets a limit. It is a day of cessation, regardless of what day of the week it is. In fact, in the Old Testament's calendar, there were any number of days designated Sabbath that would not have fallen on the last day of the week.[7] The undeniable fact that the term Sabbath does not uniquely designate the seventh day of the week ought to remove any objections to referring to the first day of the week as the Christian Sabbath. It is crucial to note that the law's imperative required keeping the Sabbath day holy without specifying what that day was. The principle was that one day in seven was to be a Sabbath day, a day of rest. Inherent in the statement was a built-in provision for a dispensational shift of days but not for a dispensational subtraction from the Ten Commandments.

The infinitive expression "to keep it holy" or "to sanctify it" (the Hebrew text is the same in both Exodus and Deuteronomy) explains what remembering or keeping the Sabbath entails. This infinitive, the *factitive* form of the verb "to be holy"—grammatical jargon for putting something in a given state or condition—means simply that the Sabbath day is to be put into a state of holiness. Since the basic idea of holiness is separation, the idea is that the Sabbath must be made separate or distinct. Sanctifying the Sabbath requires setting it apart, making it different from all the other days of the week. Clear enough!

The Logic of the Sabbath

When the Exodus and Deuteronomy passages are considered together, there emerge two significant and related reasons that the Sabbath is required. According to Exodus, the Sabbath day is to be free from all labor because of the example God established at creation: He rested. God rested, and we as well must rest in imitation of Him.[8] His holiness is the perfect standard of ours: we must be holy because He is holy. Imitating His rest is tantamount to experiencing His presence. Scripture consistently presents a theology of rest of which the Sabbath principle is a key component. Theologically or spiritually, to be in the place of rest is to be where God is.[9] Being in the presence of God is an objective in worship, and remembering the Sabbath helps to accomplish that objective. According to Deuteronomy, the Sabbath is to be observed because God delivered His people from bondage. Resting in His presence and remembering His grace go hand in hand. Relief from the quotidian affairs of life allows time for proper reflection and worship of the Lord for who He is and what He has done. It takes time and a proper frame of mind to worship, and the Sabbath provides for both.

This is good logic. A scriptural keeping of the Sabbath is a means of shelving legitimate but mundane concerns and blocking out distractions that compete with spiritual matters for attention. The Christian must set himself apart from everyday labors and activities in order to worship the Lord effectively. By setting aside those things that are lawful and necessary on other days and making it the delight of the heart to spend time in public and private worship and in performing works of necessity and mercy with a true heart, the Christian will enjoy His God and find the necessary impetus to serve His God with fervent zeal. Suffice it to say that God deserves constant worship and praise. However, in His providence He has given us other things to do that demand our time and attention. He has given us six days to accomplish all that we must legitimately accomplish. In His law, He has set aside a time when we can and must give our full attention to Him. Without such a day, that kind of worship is impossible, so He has set one aside when giving full time and full attention to Him is possible. That is a demonstration of His goodness to us to aid us in both our work and our worship. I like the way Oehler summed it up when he called the Sabbath "a gift of Divine grace for the sanctification of the people."[10] Or even better, as Christ put it, "The Sabbath was made for man" (Mark 2:27).

A Safeguard of Worship

Contrary to common notions that link keeping the Sabbath to legalism, God's logic is that keeping the Sabbath is a safeguard to spiritual worship and a protection against a selfish formalism that is so deleterious to true worship. A proper observing of the Sabbath promotes a selflessness that is necessary for biblical worship. This humility is vital when we remember that worship is about God and not about us. The prophet Isaiah issues a statement about the Sabbath that makes this point clearly. Throughout his ministry, Isaiah evaluated the religion of his people in terms of God's law and their practice. With inspired insight, he exposed hypocrisy and mere outward ritual as offensive to God (see chapter 1). Whereas he consistently condemned heartless ceremonies of religion, he commanded the spiritual observance of the Sabbath. His argument is simple enough: keeping the Sabbath fosters true and spiritual worship. His evaluation of selfish worship in chapter 58 concludes with one of the most outstanding texts about the Sabbath in the entire Bible.

Without expounding the entire chapter,[11] I will simply suggest the following outline of Isaiah's argument and then say a few things about the climactic text. In verses 1-5, he proves that selfish worship is worthless, earning God's indictment. Even though the outward acts of devotion and piety appeared to be in order, the motives of heart were not right, and consequently the Israelites' fasting was unacceptable before God. It seems as though the people were fasting to merit some favor from the Lord, and when they did not get what they were after, they concluded that God was blind and unaware of their efforts. The Lord made it clear that spiritual fasting is not the deprivation of the body for material gain but the moving of the soul for spiritual profit. It is tragic that man can turn legitimate religious rituals designed to foster a spiritual relationship with God into mechanical and mercantile maneuvers intending to manipulate God for personal advantage. A relationship with God is more important than religion, and it is ultimately something that religious ritual cannot achieve.

In verses 6-12, Isaiah shows that selfless worship is worthwhile, receiving God's blessing. The prophet's assessment of true religion parallels the apostle's: "Pure religion and undefiled before God and the Father is this, To visit the fatherless and widows in their affliction, and to keep himself unspotted from the world" (James 1:27). Selflessness evidences true religion, and concern for others is a revealing gauge of that selflessness. Isaiah shows that God's favor attends true worship with spiritual illumination ("light shall break forth as the morning"), soundness of soul ("thine health shall spring forth speedily"), divine protection and guidance ("the glory of the LORD shall be thy rereward...and the LORD shall guide thee continually"), answered prayer ("then shalt thou call, and the LORD shall answer"), and fruitfulness ("thou shalt be like a watered garden"). All this illustrates the inseparable connection between man's relationship with God and his relationship with his fellowman. Proper horizontal relationships develop from a proper vertical relationship, and skewed horizontal relationships betray a relationship with God that is not right regardless of profession or ritual. True and spiritual worship is never about self.

All of this invites the questions of how to avoid the selfish motives and interests that preclude God's blessing and how to attain the essential selflessness that God requires. In verses 13-14, Isaiah answers these questions by showing that keeping the Sabbath promotes true worship, situating the worshipper for blessing. This significant text sets the spiritual framework for observing the Sabbath while protecting that observance from formal and legalistic do's and don'ts. Here's what Isaiah said:

> If thou turn away thy foot from the sabbath, from doing thy pleasure on my holy day; and call the sabbath a delight, the holy of the LORD, honourable; and shalt honour him, not doing thine own ways, nor finding thine own pleasure, nor speaking thine own words: Then shalt thou delight thyself in the LORD; and I will cause thee to ride upon the high places of the earth, and feed thee with the heritage of Jacob thy father: for the mouth of the LORD hath spoken it.

Three thoughts sum up the prophet's formula for keeping the Sabbath. For the sake of maintaining a parallel structure, I'll state them as imperatives. First, recognize the holiness of the day. In keeping with the law's requirement to keep the Sabbath day holy or distinct from other days, Isaiah said to "turn away thy foot from the sabbath." There are a couple of legitimate ways to translate this opening conditional statement, both of which lead to the same bottom line. One translation enjoins the recommended behavior: "if you turn your foot *because* of the Sabbath *from* doing your pleasure on my holy day...*and* call the sabbath a delight...." Turning away the foot is an expression of cautious reverence. The Preacher used similar imagery when he said to keep the foot when entering God's house (Ecclesiastes 5:1). So, because the Sabbath is a holy day, it requires guarded behavior. As Moses removed his shoes when standing on holy ground, so must we when stepping into the Sabbath. The other translation contrasts the breach of the sabbath with what ought to be the proper behavior: "if you turn your foot *away from* the Sabbath *by* doing your pleasure...*but rather* call the Sabbath a delight...." In other words, doing your own thing on the Sabbath equates with ignoring the day. In contrast, keeping the day should be a delightful experience. But as I've indicated, the bottom line is clear: the Sabbath is a day that must be treated differently from every other day.

Second, observe the requirements of the day. The genius of Isaiah is that he makes observing the Sabbath a spiritual issue, a matter of heart discernment. Keeping the Sabbath holy involves much more than ticking off do's or don'ts from a check list. In fact, it is possible to follow rigidly a list of rules, keeping what may appear to be the letter of the law, and still miss the meaning and purpose of the Sabbath. Christ's repeated contest with the Pharisees over Sabbath practices is a case in point. Although the members of this religious sect adhered unyieldingly to a set of prescribed behaviors, they were clueless concerning the spiritual purpose of the day divinely designed to direct man's heart and mind to God and away from self; one's own self tends to be the focus when measuring religious reality by human performance. So without prescribing a code of conduct, Isaiah delineates the kind of spirit with which to enter the Sabbath. He advises that the day be observed with a spirit of self-renunciation (refraining from doing one's own thing, seeking one's own pleasure, or speaking about whatever comes to mind), a spirit of devotion (honoring God by regarding Him as the only worthy object of worship), and a spirit of joy (calling the Sabbath a delight). The Sabbath is not a dull day just to "get through"; the Sabbath will not be a holy day unless it is a happy day.

Following Isaiah's guidelines for how to observe the Sabbath should answer all the specific questions concerning what behavior is permitted or not permitted. It will prevent mindless legalism and promote spiritual worship. Over the years when I have expounded the Scripture's teaching about the Sabbath in either a seminary or a church setting, the response has frequently been "just tell me what to do." Resisting the temptation to tell somebody what to do, I always direct the inquirers to Isaiah 58. Evaluating behavior in the light of Isaiah's recommendation helps to establish the convictions that will give the desired directions. For instance, if watching a football game all Sunday afternoon is contrary to one's own pleasure and contributes to thoughts worthy of worshipping God, then I suppose it would be legitimate. But given the mindset and emotional enthusiasm that mark the typical spectator watching a game on Saturday, it is not likely that the same spectating activity on Sunday would somehow be conducive to worshipping God in spirit and truth. I could multiply scenarios, and each in the light of Isaiah 58 would prove to be equally absurd. The bottom line is very simply whether or not any particular behavior contributes to thoughts of God. That should answer a lot of questions.

Third, get ready for blessing: "Then shalt thou delight thyself in the LORD; and I will cause thee to ride upon the high places of the earth, and feed thee with the heritage of Jacob thy father: for the mouth of the LORD hath spoken it" (58:14). The spiritual keeping of the Sabbath is an integral part of the Bible's theology of rest, and thus it significantly contributes to our ability to glorify God and enjoy Him both now and forever. Its rest from labor gives a temporary reprieve from the curse of sin and so anticipates heaven itself where we will be forever curse-free. It brings us through worship into the place of the divine presence where we can find immediate enjoyment and satisfaction in the Lord, true spiritual prosperity. The right use of the Sabbath will help form habits of devotion that will make selfless, spiritual religion a joy.

It has not been my intent to develop a complete theology of the Sabbath or to answer all the questions regarding the relevance of the Sabbath (or the day of the week to be so designated in this dispensation); good and helpful treatments dealing with these issues are available. My concern has simply been to consider the logic of the Sabbath principle as an aid to worship. Even apart from the biblical mandate for keeping the Sabbath, it just plain makes sense. Worship takes time and requires attentive concentration, both of which the Sabbath facilitates. By setting aside the ordinary business of life, it is possible to enjoy a frame of mind that allows unhindered thoughts of God. Too often Christians enter the sanctuary with a million different things on their minds, converse with fellow worshippers about anything and everything under the sun before the service begins, and then seemingly with a push of a "worship button" sing the doxology. It is not surprising that the church today is experiencing so many worship problems. I will be so bold as to suggest that many of today's worship woes can be resolved by a faithful and spiritual keeping of the Lord's Day, the Christian Sabbath. I would suggest to all who have a genuine desire to worship the Lord to sanctify the Sabbath day. Even if you disagree with my exegetical and theological analysis regarding the Sabbath, try it–you'll like it. The Sabbath is an aid to worship that the Lord has given us; it would be good to use it for what it's worth.[12]

SACRAMENTS: TOOLS FOR WORSHIP

The service of the sacraments, the Christ-ordained ordinances for the church, is an integral part of biblical worship. The regulative principle commonly employed in reformed worship and prescribed by the *Westminster Confession of Faith* includes the sacraments of baptism and the Lord's supper as regular parts of ordinary worship along with reading the Scripture, preaching, praying, and singing psalms (see chapter 4).[13] Although I could have appropriately addressed them in the previous chapter, I have chosen to deal with them here because as sensible signs of gospel truths, they function—much like the Tabernacle of the old dispensation—as visible aids to spiritual worship. Very simply, they are designed to help us worship.

However, I must emphasize at the outset that their use is never in isolation or independent from the Scripture. God's Word is a means of grace, and the sacraments, as visible portrayers of the Word, owe their significance to that Word, and consequently their legitimate use rests in company with the written Word.[14] It is the inherent connection to the Word of God that constitutes the sacraments as means of grace. I know that bothers some, but please don't misunderstand what I'm saying here. I am not implying that either baptism or the Lord's Supper effects salvation: there is no power or ability in water, wine, or bread to infuse saving grace into anybody.[15] But let's face it. Whenever God communicates to us—whether through the written or the visible Word—that is a most gracious act. Just as preaching audibly conveys the message of grace without the inherent power to confirm grace to the listening soul, so the sacraments visually convey the message of grace without any power to confirm grace to the seeing soul. Not to be conscious of God's grace when observing the sacraments is to be spiritually oblivious. To be spiritually oblivious when observing the sacraments—particularly the Lord's Supper–has serious repercussions (1 Corinthians 11: 29). My point in this section is to encourage a right and spiritual use of the sacraments or ordinances of the church (if that is a more comfortable designation) by using them for what they are worth as tools or aids for true and spiritual worship.

Many things that require consideration in any discussion of baptism or the Lord's Supper must remain outside the scope of this chapter. Disputes regarding these rites choke the annals of church history. Differences of opinion about whom to baptize and how to do it have separated brethren who otherwise agree on all the essential doctrines of orthodoxy, as though the subjects and mode of baptism constitute the one united fundamental component of Christianity. I do not minimize the importance of having strong convictions and being dogmatic about the correctness of one's interpretation. After all, I am thoroughly convinced that my views are correct. But without addressing all the issues of controversy or attempting to argue for my particular interpretations, I want to highlight the place and use that the baptism and communion services should have in the public worship of the church. The tragic thing is that too often a defense of position distracts from a worshipful practice of the rite. Many vehemently defend their view, belligerently attacking those who disagree with them (which, by the way, I know from the receiving end to be true by personal experience); yet these same persons reduce the actual practice to a perfunctory performance with admittedly correct mechanics but without any real thought about the message that is supposed to be conveyed. I have too often been in churches where both baptisms and the communion services have been tacked-on additions accompanied by such congregational commotion and inattention that worshipping the Lord was impossible. This ought not to be. The Lord has given the church these visible sermons to help us worship Him, so let's use them as He has intended.

Resisting the temptation to deal with baptism and the Lord's Supper separately and theologically, I want very briefly to state why they are so important and helpful for public worship.[16] The following statement from the *Westminster Confession of Faith* suggests three points I want to make about the sacraments.

> Sacraments are holy signs and seals of the covenant of grace, immediately instituted by God, to represent Christ and His benefits: and to confirm our interest in Him: as also, to put a visible difference between those that belong unto the Church and the rest of the world; and solemnly to engage them to the service of God in Christ, according to His Word. (27.1)

The Mandate

The first thing to note is that God has instituted and ordered baptism and the Lord's Supper; therefore, there is a divine mandate for their observance. Baptism was part of Christ's great commission to the church (Matthew 28:19), and thus its practice must accompany the expansion of the church. Paul, in his great exposition on the Lord's Supper, made it clear that he had received his instructions from the Lord and that the Lord Himself had given the command to eat and drink in remembrance of Him (1 Corinthians 11:23-26).

Therefore, incorporating the sacraments into the ministry of the church and observing them according to biblical instructions are mandatory in Christian worship. Although neither baptism nor the Lord's Supper is necessary for salvation, neither is optional. The privilege of participation is also a duty. Neglecting these divinely ordained ordinances is *de facto* disobedience. For a Christian not to be baptized or habitually to refrain from coming to the Lord's Table is incongruous with what it means to be a Christian. This disobedience defies the divine intent of the sacraments to mark a visible difference between Christians and the world. Neglecting the sacraments is unchristian.

So if, as we have argued, the how of worshipping God is biblically ordered, then the two visible signs that God has set in place to aid in worshipping Him must be a part of that worship. By divine mandate, we can look upon them and worship.

The Message

With remarkable simplicity these divinely defined symbols signify remarkably profound truths. Whereas man, using his own imagination, tends to devise ornate art and elaborately rich decoration to create atmospheres conducive for worship, God points to water, wine, and bread to help us to focus our gaze on Him and what He has done in demonstration of His grace. Although baptism and the Lord's Supper respectively represent different aspects of grace, in their own ways they both represent Christ and speak to the interest that we have in Him.

Baptism marks membership in the visible church and represents union and identification with Christ, a spiritual reality which involves the necessary regeneration, remission of sins, and consequent consecration to walk in newness of life in and through Jesus Christ. That is quite a sermon. Look and worship.

According to Paul, the bread and wine are visible sermons of the gospel: "For as often as ye eat this bread, and drink this cup, ye do shew the Lord's death till he come" (1 Corinthians 11:26). The word "shew" literally means to proclaim or declare. In other words, the communion is not a reenactment of the sacrifice of Christ; it is a sermon proclaiming the gospel. Look at the bread and worship Christ for His incarnation, His perfect obedience rendered to God's law for our justification, and His enduring all the afflictions and miseries of our sin and guilt imputed to Him. His was a body broken for us. Look at the wine whose rich red color represents the blood that He so freely shed for us in a sacrifice that so exactly satisfied and quenched God's wrath against us and washed away our sins. The bread and wine give us something to see, to feel, to taste as aids to jog our minds into thinking about Christ. The communion service is a time for thinking. It is quite a sermon. Look and worship.

The Meaning

The message of baptism and the Lord's Supper is objectively constant and clear; the meaning must be subjectively personal. The significance lies not in thoughtless or faithless form and ritual but in the believing appropriation of the truths portrayed. The sacraments are aids to worship only when accompanied by faith. It is faith that looks beyond the sign and the symbol to the reality signified. Failing to see the reality renders the signs without significance and potentially reduces them to idols. Paul's caveat against eating without discerning the Lord's body (1 Corinthians 11:29)–that is, eating without faith in what is symbolized–in principle applies also to baptism. Thoughtless and faithless participation is not only without spiritual profit; it is spiritually dangerous as well.

Every observance of the Lord's Supper or of a baptism ought to generate worship, praise, and thanksgiving in the heart. The communion service is occasional, and therefore it provides repeated opportunities for participants to engage actively in personal worship, gratefully acknowledging their place in Christ and enjoyment of all the benefits of grace purchased by His atonement. Although individual participation in baptism occurs only once, every observation of another's baptism ought to cause the Christian to remember his own baptism and thus contemplate God's specific mercy to him, renew his personal commitment to God, and repent of his sins against God's goodness and grace. The meaning must always be personal.

I have been intentionally broad and brief in my comments on the sacraments, because any more would necessarily lead to much more.[17] My point has simply been to see the sacraments as marvelous tools God has given to help us worship Him. They show us some important truths to think about, and true worship always requires thinking. It is a scriptural principle that we are to walk by faith and not by sight. But God, knowing our frame and weakness, graciously gives us some things to look at to aid our faith in worshipping Him. Don't rush through them or tack them on to other elements in the service. It would not be a bad idea to devote specific services just to the observance of baptism or the Lord's Supper. Remember that these are not independent of the written Word. But in connection with the Scripture and prayer, they can be wonderfully used by God to create within us a worshipful heart. Remember as well that the day will come when no helps will be necessary to worship as we ought. Partly for this reason, Christ said that we are to remember Him by eating and drinking until He comes. When He does come and we see Him face to face, there will be no hindrances to our worship, and no helps will be required. But until then, let's use the helps God gives.

CHAPTER 6

EXAMPLES OF WORSHIP

My ineptness regarding things mechanical is no secret, particularly within my family. The only thing that excels my ineptness is my impatience. Occasionally over the years, we have had to purchase items that require assembly. This often creates tension, and before the assembling project is over, something triggers that dreaded wifely comment, "If only your students or the people at church could see you now." But that's a whole different issue. The point for now is that included in the boxes with the unassembled product are all the necessary components and detailed instructions–often in multiple languages–that explain step by step how everything is supposed to fit together. Sometimes there are even "helpful" diagrams. In theory, everything necessary for the job is there; it is supposed to be as easy as one, two, three. But notwithstanding the advertised simplicity designed to make the task look enjoyable, my wife learned long ago that rather than making these projects occasions for family bonding, it would be best for me to leave until the job is done. Sometimes, however, I will just watch her while she puts the pieces together, and she makes it look easy. Watching her sheds light on the instructions. It often helps to see somebody do something in order to see how something should be done.

Now here's my transition to topic. God's Word, as our only guide and rule for faith and practice, sets down clear instructions as to what worshipping God means and how we are to worship Him. But in addition to the commands and precepts of His law, the Lord has given us many examples to help us actually see what worshipping Him looks like. In this chapter, I want to look at some of those examples. This survey cannot be exhaustive, but I trust it will be sufficient to demonstrate that we can truly worship Him as He instructs.

THE EXAMPLE OF MOSES

The Mosaic administration of the covenant of grace was marked by patterns and blueprints designed to teach, illustrate, and predict important principles of spiritual worship. Before Moses the essential components of worship were operative. But beginning with Moses God provided, for the pedagogic benefit of the covenant nation in its infancy, precisely defined pictures to portray how a redeemed people were to worship and serve Him. (Pictures and activities, after all, always help toddlers in the learning process.) Over time the complex and external symbols have given way to simplicity with the progression of divine revelation and the fulfillment of God's redemptive purpose in Christ, but the lessons about worship illustrated in the old dispensation's ritual structures are valid still. The manner and attendant circumstances have changed, but the essence has not. True worship was as much a heart issue then as it is now. Again we should look and learn.

The problem for me at this point is that there are so many things to look at and learn from; once more, I must be selective.

The Lord used people, times, places, and things to teach about both the mechanics and the themes of worship. The priesthood, for instance, taught that man's access to the holy God was only through a mediator. And all the problems and imperfections plaguing those priests pointed to the necessity of the Ideal Priest, the Messiah/Christ, who could and would perform the mediation perfectly. That was a vital lesson, the truth of which still governs true worship: it is only through the Lord Jesus Christ that man can dare approach God in worship. It was fearfully clear in the Mosaic economy that even priests could die for trying to worship in an unprescribed way. Remember what happened to Korah (Numbers 16), as well as Nadab and Abihu (Leviticus 10).

The designated times for special services, for another instance, identified significant themes for worship. In addition to the weekly Sabbath mandated by God's unchanging moral code and therefore necessarily incorporated into Israel's ceremonial routines, the Lord marked other times for His people to observe and to reflect on some of the particulars of His redeeming activities in their behalf. In one way or another, each of the feasts (the Passover and Feast of Unleavened Bread, the Feast of Weeks, the Feast of Tabernacles, the Feast of Trumpets) and the single day of fasting (the Day of Atonement) highlighted special and paradigmatic demonstrations of God's grace, goodness, and greatness in all His works of salvation and providence. Each occasion focused on reasons to worship. The ceremonies of the special times are no longer appropriate for this dispensation, but the reasons for the ancient holidays remain for us reasons to worship. So we should look and learn.

If one element more than anything else was a showcase for worship, it would be the place for worship that God ordained for the covenant nation. Through Moses, the Lord revealed that He would govern the place for corporate worship, the place where He would cause His name to dwell and thus signify His unique ownership of and presence in the place (see Exodus 20:24; Deuteronomy 12). In the visually oriented Old Testament, that centralized place of worship moved with the wanderings in the wilderness, settled temporarily in Gilgal, Shiloh, and Gibeon, and finally rested in Jerusalem where tent gave way to temple. But since our attention is on the example of Moses, the tent of worship is our concern.

If any one thing was central to the ceremonial laws defined in the Mosaic covenant, it was the Tabernacle. It was a simple yet complex structure that foreshadowed Christ and the gospel from every angle and from every action associated with it. The Tabernacle with its constituent parts was a picture prophecy that found fulfillment not only in the person and work of Christ but also in the benefits, blessings, and obligations attendant to and flowing from Him. The Tabernacle with its rituals taught by object lesson how to worship the holy God and how to experience the covenant promise of life and fellowship with God.

As we try to figure out all the salient points about worship from the Tabernacle, it is easy for us to get lost, bogged down, overly imaginative, or discouraged in all the details. Notwithstanding the abundance of details, there are some key lessons from the Tabernacle that picture gospel truths, point to Christ, and instruct us about spiritual worship. Volumes have been written and long series of sermons have been preached on the Tabernacle, so obviously I can touch only on the surface but salient lessons here.

Lessons from the New Testament

I think that Exodus 25:8 provides the main clue for ascertaining the primary message of the Tabernacle in God's statement of His intent: "Let them make me a sanctuary that I may dwell among them." Leviticus 26:11-12 expands on that statement of divine purpose in terms of covenant relationship and fellowship: "And

I will set my tabernacle among you....And I will walk among you, and will be your God, and ye shall be my people." The New Testament identifies the ultimate message by drawing four lines from the Tabernacle's rich symbolism to its richer realities.

First, it draws a line to the *Incarnation of Christ*. John unquestionably plays on Tabernacle prophecy when he declares, "The Word was made flesh, and dwelt among us" (John 1:14). The word "dwell" could well be translated "tabernacled." It teaches, therefore, that Christ is at the heart of all true worship.

Second, it draws a line to heaven, the principal dwelling place and throne of God. Hebrews settles this. "It was therefore necessary that the patterns of things in the heavens should be purified...for Christ is not entered into the holy places made with hands, which are the figures of the true; but into heaven itself, now to appear in the presence of God for us" (Hebrews 9:23-24). Not only does the Tabernacle proclaim that God is present with His people on earth, but it also pictures the final destination of His people who will dwell with Him in heaven. It teaches, therefore, that worship on earth is to mirror that in heaven.

Third, the Tabernacle draws a line to the church corporately. Paul warned ministers to guard their ministry lest they defile the temple of God, and then he reminded the Corinthian church that they were indeed that temple in which the Holy Spirit dwells (1 Corinthians 3:16-17). Using Tabernacle language, John identified the seven churches as golden candlesticks and declared that Christ was walking in the midst of them (Revelation 1:13, 20; 2:1). The Tabernacle teaches, therefore, that worship is to be a spiritual exercise in the Lord's immediate presence.

Fourth, it draws a line to believers individually. Paul's argument for individual purity and separation included the fact that God regarded believers as His temple: "Ye are the temple of the living God; as God hath said, I will dwell in them, and walk in them; and I will be their God, and they shall be my people" (2 Corinthians 6:16). It teaches that corporate worship consists of individual participation. Thus, the Tabernacle declares both God's purpose to dwell with His people and His plan whereby that goal of fellowship is achieved.

Lessons from the Details

The divine intent of the Tabernacle as an object lesson of truth is clear from all the specific instructions that God gave to guide its erection (Exodus 25-31) and from the detailed record of those instructions' being carried out (Exodus 35-40). Page after page of Exodus records the minutiae of the heavenly blueprint for the Tabernacle and then the execution of that plan by Moses and his construction crew. The Tabernacle section begins with God's command to Moses to follow the pattern that was revealed to him on the mount (Exodus 25:9, 40). The book ends with frequent testimony that Israel had followed the divinely given blueprints: they made it "according to all that the Lord commanded Moses" (Exodus 39:42; note that at least eight times in Exodus 40 Moses did as the Lord commanded). The details were obviously important.

Nevertheless, this plethora of detail makes for considerable repetition and causes some to skim hurriedly through the section, perhaps pausing momentarily with astonishment at the golden calf incident (Exodus 32) but then continuing the hasty perusal for something more edifying. Others tend to squeeze out from every detail a latent gospel truth. I am not inclined to find a gospel sermon in every thread or socket, but I am equally disinclined to regard the details as insignificant. God did reveal every detail on purpose–some for beauty, some for utility, some for sermons. Together the details underscore the important truth that God orders the way of worship, and man cannot and must not alter that way. His instructions to make the Tabernacle so long and no longer, so wide and no wider, with this material and no other warn that He is concerned and takes notice of every facet and dynamic of worship. It is important not only that we worship the right God but that we worship the right God in the right way. The Tabernacle stood as constant visible witness that worship was God's way or no way. Or to use our theological jargon, the details of the Tabernacle illustrate the regulative principle of worship.

Lessons from the Nomenclature

Many lessons derive from the names of the Tabernacle. The word translated "tabernacle" simply means "the place of dwelling" (*mishkan*). Although it is not a biblical word, we often speak of the Shekinah Glory to designate the manifest demonstrations of God's presence, the theophanies associated with both Tabernacle and Temple. For instance, at the end of Exodus the cloud covers the tent and the "glory of the Lord" fills the Tabernacle (Exodus 40:34-38). To label that manifestation the *Shekinah* Glory is appropriate because "*shekinah*" means "dwelling." *Shekinah* and *mishkan* derive from the same verbal root that means "to dwell or to inhabit." The word "Tabernacle," then, declares that God takes up residence with His people. He does not simply drop in from time to time; He lives with them. The Tabernacle pictured the constant abiding presence of God with His people. Certainly God, being omnipresent, fills all space immediately, but He dwells with His people in a most special and intimate way. That truth has never changed, and it never will change. Let's remember not to confuse the object lesson with the reality. God's presence with His people was not literally confined to the Tabernacle; it was a visible reminder and declaration that God was with them. What the name "Immanuel" declares, the Tabernacle illustrated and Christ fulfilled. The key lesson here is that God's special presence is in the place of worship. That knowledge ought to dictate what happens in that special place.

Sometimes the Tabernacle is called the Tent (*'ohel*). As a portable structure, it testified to the Lord's identification with His people in their circumstances. They were living in tents;

He dwelt in a tent. Again, it would be theologically ludicrous to conclude that the tent localized or limited His presence and ministry to the people. The tent illustrated what Isaiah later said concerning the Lord during Israel's wanderings: "In all their affliction he was afflicted, and the angel of his presence saved them" (Isaiah 63:9). Christ most vividly fulfilled the Tent prophecy as He came in the very likeness of sinful flesh (Romans 8:3); He is able, therefore, because of His personal experience, to be touched with the feeling of all our infirmities (Hebrews 4:15). That the Temple ultimately replaced the Tent testifies to the same truth. The people were living in houses; He dwelt in a house. This suggests that some aspects of worship are temporally and culturally elastic. That is not to say, however, that time, culture, or personal preference dictate worship practice; rather, it says that God is sensitive to our circumstances, and His truth is pragmatically relevant and applicable to every circumstance. In other words, the regulative principle is intact.

Two other names of the Tabernacle build on the Tent idea: the Tent of Testimony (*'ohel ha'eduth*) and the Tent of Meeting (*'ohel mo'ed*). These underscore particular benefits and blessings that derive from God's dwelling so intimately with them. The Tent of Testimony identifies the Tabernacle as a place of revelation. God would communicate, explain, and reveal Himself at this designated place. All of the rituals that occurred at the Tabernacle were points that the Lord made in this visible sermon. It prophesies Christ who dwelled among men as the perfect and Ideal Prophet, revealing God in person. The Tent of Meeting certainly suggests meeting together in communion and fellowship, but it also includes the important idea of meeting by appointment. Meeting with God is not haphazard, casual, or accidental. God sets the terms of meeting; He makes the appointment and guarantees His presence at those meetings. Follow the statements in Exodus 25-30 where the Lord says, "There I will meet with thee" (25:22; 29:42; 30:6), and you will learn three important truths concerning where God meets His people. At the ark, God meets His people at the place of propitiation. At the altar of burnt offering, God meets His people at the place of consecration. At the altar of incense, God meets His people at the place of prayer. Each of these places finds ultimate significance in Christ, the only place sinners can ever meet God in peace. These names highlight the function of Scripture, prayer, preaching, and spiritual communion in the place of worship.

The final common designation of the Tabernacle is Sanctuary (*miqdash*), literally "the place of holiness." The core component of holiness is separateness or otherness. Although including the notion of separation from sin, the concept of holiness goes far beyond that. Interestingly, the antonym to holiness in the Old Testament is not that which is sinful but that which is common, mundane, or ordinary. The Tabernacle was no ordinary tent; it announced its distinction from every other place. The Sanctuary declared that being in God's presence is special and that it therefore requires reverent caution. There is no barging into God's presence. The Sanctuary stood as witness to the truth that although He was near, access to Him was restricted. Approaching God requires clean hands and pure heart (Psalm 24:3-4). The Sanctuary declared loudly the need for an absolutely clean and pure Mediator who could approach the most holy God, taking those He represented with Him. That is exactly what Christ did and does. Although the Tent transitioned to the Temple, suggesting temporal adjustments, the designation "Sanctuary" refers to both structures. The fact that the place of worship is a holy place overshadows every other notion and precludes any attempt to introduce worldly and mundane elements into worship. That fact is a key lesson about worship.

Lessons from the Configuration

The structure and floor plan of the Tabernacle impart some lessons also. The Tabernacle was divided into three distinct sections: the outer court, the holy place, and the most holy place. The outer court was under the open sky and accessible to the covenant community. The holy place was veiled but lighted, and accessible only to the priests. The Holy of Holies (a superlative statement meaning "the most holy place") was completely veiled, dark, and accessible only to the high priest, only once a year, and never without blood. One of the most important lessons conveyed by the floor plan was the safeguard it provided against confusing the object lesson with the reality above and beyond it. Hebrews says that by these increasing restrictions, the Holy Spirit was "signifying that the way into the holiest of all was not yet made manifest, while as the first tabernacle was yet standing: which was a figure for the time then present..." (Hebrews 9:8, 9). Any Israelite with the slightest spiritual perception would conclude that the Tabernacle economy was not working if it was meant to bring people personally into the presence of God. But it was not supposed to. This was the built-in obsolescence that demanded and increased the hope for Christ who by His own blood would enter in once into the holy place, having obtained eternal redemption (Hebrews 9:12).

But apart from the important dispensational lesson, the structure conveyed a vital lesson about worship. Vividly, the floor plan declared that the closer to God one approaches, the greater the restrictions or requirements for holiness. The greater the awareness of God's holiness, the greater will be the consciousness of personal unholiness and of the need for a perfect Mediator. The greater that awareness, the greater will be fearful reverence as worship unfolds.

Lessons from the Furniture

The furniture in the Tabernacle carries instructional benefit for us as well. Each of these items, rich with spiritual symbolism, deserves much more attention that I can give here. But let's note some of the more salient lessons.

The Altar

Just inside the outer court was the altar. Right up front the Lord made it clear that the only way to get to Him was through the blood of the sacrifice. The altar, the foundation of which was constructed of the raw materials of earth and unhewn stones, testified to the inability of man to contribute any part or effort toward the work of salvation (Exodus 20:24-25). Thinking of the altar makes me recall Bonar's great hymn: "Not what these hands have done, can save this guilty soul....Thy work alone, my Savior, can ease this weight of sin; Thy blood alone, O Lamb of God, can give me peace within." The altar itself, made of shittim wood (acacia) overlaid with brass, suggests that it was the place of righteous judgment. That, in a nutshell, was the message of the altar. It points to the place of sacrifice and shedding of blood, without which there can be no forgiveness of sin. At the place of sacrifice, justice was served and pardon was won. There can be no genuine worship without the consciousness that Christ's sacrifice has opened the way for the believer to come into God's holy presence.

The Laver

Also in the outer court just past the altar was the laver, the wash basin. Its very position communicated a vital part of its message. On the other side of the altar, the laver symbolized the purity and cleanness required for fellowship with and service of God and the means whereby the sanctifying cleansing was achieved. The sinner did not clean himself up before approaching the altar; he came to the place of sacrifice with his sins. Then, as the sinner's representative, the priest ritually washed. That the laver was made from donated mirrors (Exodus 38:8) helps to identify the antitype. The New Testament more than once compares the Word of God to a glass that reveals the blemishes and guides in the cleansing process (2 Corinthians 3:18; James 1:23-25). The Lord Jesus, the Word of God, declared, "Ye are clean through the word which I have spoken unto you" (John 15:3). Paul seemed undoubtedly to have laver theology in mind when he said that Christ gave Himself for His church "that He might sanctify and cleanse it with the washing of water by the word, that He might present it to Himself a glorious church ... holy and without blemish" (Ephesians 5:26-27). Similarly, Titus 3:5 speaks of "the washing of regeneration." The laver represents an essential means of grace. Approaching God requires cleanness of hands and purity of heart–the lesson of the laver.

The Shewbread

There were three items inside the holy place. On one side was a table with the *shewbread*, literally, the "bread of faces" or "presentation." Leviticus 24:8 indicates that Israel presented this as a pledge of the covenant. The bread was something they had made from the grain God had supplied. The regular presentation of the bread acknowledged that they owed everything to the goodness of the Lord. It stood as testimony to their pledged consecration and dedication to the Lord and taught that praise and thanksgiving were an essential part of worship. Presenting oneself to the Lord for His praise and purpose is always the necessary corollary to and consequence of having been saved by the blood (see Romans 12:1). It certainly points to Christ who in every way dedicated Himself completely to the glory of the Father, presenting His work as a perfect fulfillment of the covenant.

The Lampstand

On the other side stood the lampstand, constructed of a single piece of gold with a predominant center shaft having six branches, three on each side. A regular supply of oil fueled the lamps. The light represents the spiritual enlightenment God gives His people through His revelation. David later noted the link between light and life: "For with thee is the fountain of life: in thy light shall we see light" (Psalm 36:9). The New Testament suggests the same when it speaks of the light of the gospel (2 Corinthians 4:4). If the light represents the gospel, the lampstand is a prophecy of both Christ and the church, corporately and individually. The Lord Jesus identified Himself and believers as the light of the world (Matthew 5:14; John 8:12). That the seven churches in the book of the Revelation are designated as seven lampstands confirms the corporate relevance.

All of this is most wonderfully suggestive. I would infer from it that the predominantly higher center shaft points to Christ, who as the Ideal Prophet reveals God and truth. The branches with their lamps directing light to the center shaft picture the function of the church to bear witness to Christ, "the true Light, which lighteth every man that cometh into the world" (John 1:9). Indeed, every believer ought to emulate the Baptist, who was "to bear witness of the Light, that all men through him might believe" (John 1:7). Because the lampstand was a single piece of gold, the branches could not be separated from the center shaft. Just so are believers inseparably united to Christ. As the oil was the energy source for the lamps, so the Holy Spirit empowered Christ and continues to empower and enable believers for their service. Christ had the Spirit without measure; we have the Spirit not only dwelling within us, but enabling us every time we ask for His gracious power (Luke 11:13). The light cannot shine without the oil. Worship never breeds passivity but always stimulates active service for the Lord.

The Altar of Incense

The last item in the holy place was the *altar of incense*, right up against the veil separating the holy place from the most holy.

Significantly, this altar was fueled by coals from the altar of sacrifice in the outer court, and the priests would offer incense every morning and evening. As the smoke ascended from the altar, its fragrance would waft over the veil into the most holy place. The offering of incense was a symbol of prayer, an integral component of worship, as we have already seen. David obviously alluded to this altar when he prayed, "Let my prayer be set forth before thee as incense; and the lifting up of my hands as the evening sacrifice" (Psalm 141:2). Two significant truths stand out: (1) prayer takes us as close as possible to the holy presence of God without our actually being there in person; and (2) prayer works only because of the blood of Christ's sacrifice, which opened up the way to God.

The Ark of the Covenant

The Holy of Holies had one item: the *ark of the covenant*. Without question, the ark was the climactic and central piece of all the Tabernacle furniture. The ark was simply a box that symbolized the presence of the Lord with His people. Although the ark was just an object lesson, the restrictions guiding its construction, content, location, and transportation were rigid and inflexible. By the box, God was declaring that there is something wonderfully fearful about His presence; man cannot trifle with the Most Holy God. Although manifold spiritual are lessons taught by the ark, I want to isolate five key lessons that I think are very much on the surface of the ark symbolism, all of which relate to worship.

(1) Its being overlaid with gold declares the sovereign majesty of God. To be in the presence of God is to be in presence of the King, and consequently it requires humble submission to His authority. This element of ark theology was prominent in later inspired writers who referred to the ark as the throne and

footstool of God (Jeremiah 3:16-17; 1 Chronicles 28:2; Psalms 99:1-5; 132:7-8).

(2) Its being overshadowed by the cherubim declares the holiness of God. Of the entire angelic host, the cherubim seem to be the guardians and heralds of divine holiness and glory. Their first appearance was at the gate of Eden, where the angels stood wielding swords to prevent fallen man from entering paradise and reaching the tree of life (Genesis 3:24). Years later, Ezekiel identified the four living creatures which attended the majestic and holy throne of God in his mysterious vision as the cherubim (Ezekiel 1, 10). Stationed over the ark, they silently proclaimed to unholy sinners that approach to the holy God was prohibited so long as they were unholy. Those who approach God must do so with clean hands and pure heart (Psalm 24:3-4). Worship and fellowship with God demand purity. At first sight, the cherubim do not extend much hope.

(3) Its containing a pot of manna (Exodus 16:33-34) and Aaron's rod (Numbers 17:10) testifies to God's gracious provision for His people. The manna was evidence of the Lord's faithfulness in sustaining His people and a reminder that man does not live by bread alone but by every word that proceeds from the mouth of the Lord. As they trusted God's promise for a new supply of the daily bread, so God's people of every generation can and should trust His every promise. He is faithful. Aaron's rod that budded confirmed that man could approach God only through mediation and only through the mediator of His choice. God set the terms: the way to His presence is His way or no way. But the grace of it is that there is a way.

(4) Its containing the tablets of the law, the Decalogue, speaks of God's righteousness and His inflexible demand for righteousness ("For the righteous Lord loveth righteousness"– Psalm 11:7). The law testified to God's covenant will toward His people yet stood as witness against them. To be righteous in terms of the law required absolute obedience both to the letter and to

the spirit. From the open box, the laws cried for righteousness and demanded condemnation for unrighteousness. If the box were left open, man had no hope.

(5) Its being covered with the mercy seat proclaims hope. The mercy seat symbolized the essence of the gospel: there is a way into the presence of the sovereign, holy, and righteous God. The mercy seat is simply the "atoning lid." If the open box demanded the sinner's condemnation, the closed box declared the sinner's salvation. The mercy seat was God's visible pledge that He will be satisfied with the atonement and will by virtue of that atonement dwell with men. When the blood was sprinkled on the atoning lid, the impediments to fellowship with God were removed. The blood was a propitiation or satisfaction of God's just wrath against the sinner. The blood was placed over the demands of the law and all was well. As clear a picture of the gospel that the ark was, it was only a picture. All that the ancient box pictured, Jesus Christ is.

I think that Jeremiah evidenced his understanding of the messianic reality conveyed by the ark when he prophesied that the day would come when no ark of the covenant of the Lord would be necessary (Jeremiah 3:16). There would be no need for the shadow when the reality was present. The apostle Paul in one of his great expositions on justification explained that we are "justified freely by his grace through the redemption that is in Christ Jesus: whom God hath set forth to be a propitiation through faith in his blood" (Romans 3:24-25). Significantly, the word translated "propitiation" is the same word the Septuagint, the Greek translation of the Old Testament, used to translate the "mercy seat." I submit that Paul knew that and made an intentional link between Christ and the ark, between antitype and type. Although the prophecy of the ark has been fulfilled, its message is still the glorious gospel and the only hope for sinners. The old hymn says it well: "There is a place where mercy sheds the oil of gladness on our heads, a place than all beside more sweet–it is the blood stained mercy seat."

Lessons from the Rituals

Pre-eminently, the Tabernacle was the place where the rituals and ceremonies of worship occurred. The sacrificial system that was so specifically defined under the Mosaic administration was a graphic but intentionally imperfect picture of the work of Christ. In part the sacrifices were typical events, but they were such an integral part of the Tabernacle economy that any consideration of Tabernacle theology necessitates an explication of them. In every way these sacrifices were types prophesying of Christ, "the Lamb slain from the foundation of the world" (Revelation 13:8). Since these sacrifices had no independent significance apart from what they pictured about Christ, to obey the ritual, in faith looking beyond the visible, was tantamount to obeying the gospel. The sacrifices were picture sermons of the gospel. The general and regular sacrifices fell into two broad categories: sweet savor offerings and guilt offerings. Leviticus 1-7 records the most detailed instructions about the sacrifices.

Burnt Offering

The burnt offering, the most general of the sacrifices, was a sweet savor offering. It shared some common features with the other sacrifices and taught key lessons about the atonement. (1) The animal selected for this offering had to be a "male without blemish" (Leviticus 1:3, 10). Symbolically, this taught that the only acceptable sacrifice had to be pure, perfect, and blameless. Since the offerer was guilty of sin, this strict requirement made it clear that atonement had to come from a source outside the self. Typically, this pure victim was a picture of Christ, the "lamb without blemish and without spot" (1 Peter 1:19). The lamb without blemish points to the whole active obedience of Christ, which offered to God a perfect righteousness and demonstrated to the world His absolute perfection and sinlessness.

(2) The offerer leaned on the animal (Leviticus 1:4). The forcible laying on of hands symbolically represented the transfer of guilt from the sinner to the perfect animal, the otherwise innocent animal becoming the substitute for the guilty party. Leaning one's weight on the sacrifice suggested something as well of the nature of faith that rests on the object of sacrifice. The result of this transfer and substitution was that "it shall be accepted for him to make atonement for him" (Leviticus 1:4). Peace with God was the goal, and propitiation (atonement) of God's wrath was the means to achieve that goal. This detail proclaimed vividly the gospel truth of vicarious atonement. Typically, it declares that Christ, who knew no sin, was made sin for us "that we might be made the righteousness of God in him" (2 Corinthians 5:21).

(3) The offerer had to kill the animal (Leviticus 1:5). The death of the substitutionary sacrifice symbolically taught the terrible penalty of sin. The demand of God's holy law was absolute and its penalty was severe. God's gracious mercy provided a substitute, but His holy justice could not overlook the broken law. Wages were earned, and wages had to be received (Romans 6:23). That the offerer slew the animal impressed on him the solemn reality that it was his sin that required the penalty; he was personally responsible for the death of the sacrifice. Typically, the slaying points to Christ, "who was delivered for our offenses" and who "died for the ungodly" (Romans 4:25; 5:6). Christ's dying as the perfect sacrifice was the only way that God could be both just and the justifier (Romans 3:26).

(4) The priests sprinkled the blood of the victim on the altar (Leviticus 1:5). This use of the blood shed through death did something positive. Whereas death was the necessary penalty of sin, the blood shed through death was the specific means of

propitiation, satisfying the wrath of God. Sprinkling the blood on the altar, the first piece of Tabernacle furniture, symbolically showed that there is no approach to God apart from blood. Typically, it pictures Christ's presentation of the blood of His atonement (Hebrews 9:12) whereby the believer has access into the holy place (Hebrews 10:19). This is the gospel: approach to God is only through the blood of Jesus Christ.

(5) The priests burned the entire sacrifice on the altar (Leviticus 1:9). Whereas each of the bloody sacrifices parallels the first four steps, the burning of the whole victim is unique to the burnt offering. It is this burning that is a "sweet savor" to the Lord (Leviticus 1:9). This "smell that placates" represents that which is pleasing and acceptable to God; it puts His wrath to rest. Atonement having been accomplished by the death and application of blood, the burning is a sign of reconciliation, satisfaction, and consecration. It is a clear prophecy of Christ, who gave "himself for us an offering and a sacrifice to God for a sweetsmelling savour" (Ephesians 5:2).

Cereal Offering

The *meat offering* was a non-bloody cereal offering that was presented to the Lord in association with one of the bloody sacrifices, usually the burnt offering. This offering of grain could be in the form of whole grains roasted in fire, fine flour, or baked loaves. Oil, incense, and salt were required for every offering, but honey and leaven could never be used. The materials for these offerings were produced by man's labor. By presenting the fruit of his labor, the offerer demonstrated his devotion of life, possessions, and occupation to the Lord. Of all the details specified for the cereal offering (Leviticus 2), the prohibition of honey and leaven and the requirement of salt are the most significant for the symbolic and typical truths about the gospel. Whereas the leaven and honey would cause the offering to spoil, the salt would preserve it. It is specifically called "the salt of the covenant of thy God" (Leviticus 2:13). The association of this preservative with the covenant symbolically declared that God's contract with the people was eternal and inviolable. God would not refuse any who came in faith by way of the sacrifice that He had prescribed. Typically, the cereal offering points to Christ, the surety of the covenant, who was completely devoted and consecrated to God and His divine commission.

Peace Offering

The *peace offering* was the last of the sweet savor offerings, and its restrictions were not as rigid as those of the other offerings (Leviticus 3:1-17; 7:11-34). The animal could be a male or a female of any age. The ritual was like the other sacrifices except that it was offered at the entrance to the outer court. The choice inward parts were burned, and the breast and the shoulder were given to the priest. The priest could share them with his family, something he could not do with the other sacrifices. The rest of the animal was returned to the offerer for a communal meal with his family, his friends, and the Levites. This was a time of fellowship between God and man. The peace offering was an object lesson showing that man was reconciled to God; there was peace between them because of the atonement. Typically, it points to Christ, who reconciled believers to God, having made peace through His blood (Romans 5:1, 10). Christ's blood satisfied all the parties concerned: the offended God, the mediating Christ, and the offending sinner.

Guilt Offerings

The *sin offering* (Leviticus 4-5:13; 6:24-30) and the *trespass offering* (Leviticus 5:14-6:7) were the guilt offerings that pictured both the satisfaction of God's wrath against sin (propitiation) and the removal of sin's guilt (expiation). Both of these sacrifices were for specific sins to teach that every sin was intolerable to God and that confession should be as specific as the sins. Although the initial steps of these sacrifices parallel those of the burnt offering and declare the same general lessons, certain specific emphases are especially apparent. The main objective was to put an end to the separation between God and man caused by sin. Sin pollutes and prevents fellowship with God. In each of these sacrifices blood was shed, a reminder that blood was the only means whereby God would forgive sin. These sacrifices particularly picture expiation, the effect of the atonement manward, made possible because of propitiation, the effect of the atonement Godward. Because divine wrath is satisfied, a sinner can be cleansed from the defilement that offends God. This aspect is a vivid object lesson of 1 John 1:7, 9 and 2:1-2, which state explicitly the importance both of confessing sin and of the relationship of Christ's blood to receiving forgiveness.

Perhaps the most distinctive feature of the guilt offerings was the disposal of the sacrificial victims; they were burned outside the camp. This feature finds ultimate significance in Christ's suffering "without the gate" (Hebrews 13:12), the place of shame and uncleanness. In addition, the trespass offering required compensation to the offended party as an evidence of genuine repentance. This act of compensation points directly to Christ, who positively rendered to God everything that the law required and then paid the penalty of the broken law in behalf of His people. The trespass offering combined both the active and the passive obedience of Christ. Significantly, Isaiah refers to the suffering servant as the trespass offering (Isaiah 53:10), who offered to God everything necessary for the salvation of the promised seed. That Isaiah rightly saw Christ as the reality and the fulfillment of this picture prophecy demonstrates how every Old Testament saint saw the sacrifices.

The bottom line is that the ritual ceremonies told the story of redemption. The message they preached in picture is the

same message that we must preach in plainness of speech. God's
Word is central to worship.

THE EXAMPLE OF ISAIAH

Notwithstanding the safeguards for spiritual worship built
into the Mosaic ceremonies, it was not long before religion
degenerated into empty formalism, a mockery of God's ordinances.
The best of form without heart and spiritual perception is always
only form at best. In Chapter 1, which delineates the dangers of
religion, we have already seen how God raised up prophets to
expose religious hypocrisy and to call idolaters to repentance.
Isaiah's analysis of the dead religion of his generation stands as
a classic example of prophetic insight and reformation fervor.
But not only does Isaiah denounce dead formalism; he records
one of the most vivid scenes of true worship found in Scripture.
His famous vision of the Lord, received during the early days of
his ministry, had a profound, immediate, and durative effect on
his life. Although initially just a spectator of heavenly worship,
Isaiah could not remain passive; even in vision-mode, he
participated and resolved to serve his Lord in response to what
he saw of God's glory. Good worship affects life. Interestingly,
Isaiah's vision has him looking in different directions–up, in,
and out–and each perspective was instructive for him and for us.
Isaiah's vision illustrates how worship puts God, self, and others
in their proper places.

Where Worship puts God

Looking up assured Isaiah that God is preeminent and worthy
of humble adoration by all His creatures. Two truths stand out:
God is absolutely sovereign, and worship is absolutely essential.

Absolute Sovereignty

The timing of the heavenly vision puts the accent on God's absolute sovereignty. Uzziah, for the most part had been a good king, promoting peace and prosperity. But when he overstepped his limited authority by entering the earthly sanctuary, God smote him with life-long leprosy (2 Chronicles 26), and now he was dead. Isaiah lifted his gaze away from the funeral bier to see the glorious King in the heavenly sanctuary. The earthly king was dead, but the heavenly King was not. Earthly kings always come and go, but the King of kings abides and rules forever. Isaiah's description of who and what he saw underscores the reality of divine sovereignty (6:1).

First, he saw *Adonai*. The selection of divine titles is always purposeful and instructive, and this one is ironically significant in the context of the dead human monarch. It identifies God as the unique king, the master and owner of everything who has the right and the power to execute His will. Throughout the Old Testament this particular form of the word always and only refers to God, and this fact has theological significance even beyond this immediate context. John 12:41 forthrightly declares that it was the glory of Jesus Christ that Isaiah saw. In the light of New Testament comment, this reference serves as significant proof of Christ's essential deity and reminds us that whether in pre-incarnate theophanies or visions or incarnate revelations, Christ is ever the only visible manifestation of God. Seeing Christ is seeing God, and failing to see Christ renders any attempt to see God in any other way hopeless. True worship is always in terms of the Son.

Second, he saw the Lord exalted–high and lifted up. His being seated on a throne symbolized His sovereign authority and divine "calmness" in light of what appeared to be uncertain circumstances on earth. Uzziah had his problems, but he was a known factor. His sin and swift punishment were shocking and sobering, but at least Isaiah knew the king's situation and could discern cause-effect sequence. But now the king was dead, and not even the prophet knew the immediate future. There is always something about the unknown that is disconcerting. The "book" on Jotham was not yet in, and things were soon certainly going to turn for the worse with Ahaz. But notwithstanding the earthly crisis, everything was under the control of the heavenly throne. The height of the throne emphasized the infinite majesty, glory, and unique worth of the King who sat upon it. The Lord Himself declared, "The heaven is my throne, and the earth is my footstool" (Isaiah 66:1). None other comes close to His glory. Infinitely exalted above everything, He is absolutely independent–unaffected by anything outside of Himself.

Third, he saw the imperial robe filling the royal palace. The long, loose, flowing, glorious garment of divine royalty claimed all available space. As far as the eye could see, only the evidence of God's glory was visible; there was no room for anything else. God may graciously reveal glory, as He indeed has done, but He will not share His glory with any. That is a principal truth for worship.

Essential Worship

After describing the Lord in His majesty, Isaiah draws attention to the attendants to the heavenly throne and their expressions of worship. These spiritual beings, the seraphim or burning ones, strikingly illustrate essential aspects of spiritual worship. They show us mortals how it should be done. The heavenly worship of sinless creatures suggests three noteworthy aspects of worship.

First, worshippers must be subservient to the Lord. This is suggested both by the seraphim's position and their six-winged appearance: "Above it stood the seraphims: each one had six wings..." (6:2). Identifying the antecedent of "it" is crucial. It refers not to the throne, which would put the creature above the Creator, but to the regal robe spreading over the floor of the throne room. These heavenly worshippers were stationed at the base of throne, humbly below the King–the only proper place where true worship can occur. The most noticeable feature of seraphim is their six-winged configuration. Each pair visually suggests something of their subservience. The pair of wings covering the faces was a sign of reverence: the seraphs were so in awe of the divine glory that they could not look directly at its brightness. The pair covering the feet was a sign of holy humility: these creatures were conscious of their depth below the infinite God. The pair for flying was a sign of sanctified service, always the logical corollary to worship. True worship never breeds passivity, and the seraphim stood ready to do the Lord's bidding. After all, they were servants. If sinless creatures assume such a lowly position before the Lord, how much more must sinful men–notwithstanding their redemption–be cautious not to presume a place of attention that would distract from the sole object of worship!

Second, worshippers must ascribe praise to the Lord. Verse 3 records the content of the heavenly worship service: "And one cried unto another, and said, Holy, holy, holy is the LORD of hosts: the whole earth is full of his glory." In what appears to be antiphonal chorus, the seraphim kept crying out to each other in declaring and acknowledging divine perfections. The threefold repetition of "holy" is a means of expressing the superlative. They ascribed infinite holiness to the One exalted above them. Holiness is that divine perfection that sets God infinitely apart from anything and anyone else. He is wholly holy; He is unique; He is like nothing else. That holiness or separateness extends to His entire being and applies to every other of His glorious perfections. This superlative declaration ascribes to the Lord His intrinsic worth, marking Him as the only legitimate object of worship. Significantly, the seraphim directed this ascription to the LORD of hosts, Jehovah of armies. Jehovah, of course, is the personal name of the one true and living God that is so rich in significance (see my comments about this name in Chapter 3). Its association with the word "armies" addresses His authority over all creation that stands ready at His command to accomplish His will; He is the Commander-in-Chief. In yet another way, He is worthy.

Not only does the threefold "holy" instruct about worship, but it must be included in the theological database of proof texts for the essential deity of Jesus Christ. Remember that the New Testament unequivocally identified Jesus as the One Isaiah saw in this vision and that the Old Testament never uses the name "Jehovah" for any but the one true God. That Jesus is Jehovah, therefore, is irrefutable evidence that He is God. This is the essential theological import of this text rather than its being an argument for the Trinity. Notwithstanding the beauty of the hymn that assigns a separate holy to each of the Persons of the sacred Trinity, each of whom is indeed intrinsically worthy of worship, the text specifically focuses on Christ as the One seen and, therefore, the One to whom this ascription of infinite holiness is specifically directed. A belief in the Trinity is an essential component of orthodoxy, and I have already argued that true worship must be Trinitarian. There are ample ways of establishing the truth from the Scripture; I just don't think that this text is applicable. In commenting on this verse, John Calvin with his typical impeccable exegesis supports my claim.

> The ancients quoted this passage when they wished to prove that there are three persons in one essence of the Godhead. I do not disagree with their opinion; but if I had to contend with heretics, I would rather choose to employ stronger proofs; for they become more obstinate, and assume an air of triumph, when inconclusive arguments are brought against them; and they might easily and readily maintain that, in this passage, as in other parts of Scripture, the number "three" denotes perfection. Although, therefore, I have no doubt that the angels here describe One God in Three Persons, (and, indeed,

it is impossible to praise God without uttering the praises of the Father, of the Son, and of the Spirit,) yet I think that it would be better to employ more conclusive passages, lest, in proving an article of our faith, we should expose ourselves to the scorn of heretics. And, indeed, the repetition points out the unwearied perseverance, as if the Prophet had said, that the angels never cease from their melody of singing the praises of God, as the holiness of God supplies us with inexhaustible reasons for them. (*Commentary on Isaiah*, 205)

Another ascription of praise is the recognition that "the whole earth is full of his glory." Glory refers to all God's manifested assets as well as the excellence of all His perfections and works. The majestic glory that fills the heaven overflows to all the realms of creation, which, like the seraphim, join together their multifaceted parts to enumerate the evidences of God's glory (see Psalm 19). This unification brings God's transcendence to balance with His immanence. He is both far and near–a complexity hard to conceive but motivating of praise. God's incomprehensibility testifies to His intrinsic worth and warrants all the worship we can render to Him. To worship is to stand amazed in His presence.

Third, worshippers must get ready for God's presence. The experience of God's presence occurs whenever and wherever true worship happens: "And the posts of the door moved at the voice of him that cried, and the house was filled with smoke" (6:4). As Isaiah watched and listened to the chorus of angels worshipping the Lord, he witnessed a scene revealing something remarkable: God manifested His presence *because* of worship. Shaking and smoke were common images representing God's presence and its attendant circumstances (see, for instance, Isaiah 4:5; 64:1-3). That the shaking and smoke were caused by the sound of praise is inexplicably amazing, but that's what it says. Would that this image would sink in. We must worship with the anticipation that

God will graciously manifest His acceptance of our worship with unmistakable evidences of His presence. Too often we go through "worship motions" routinely and thoughtlessly without any expectations of consequence. To expect nothing is to get nothing. But God has promised to draw nigh to those who draw nigh to Him. What Isaiah saw was visionary symbolism, so we should not necessarily expect physical quaking or visual theophanies, nevertheless, we have every right to expect God to move within our hearts as with our hearts we give voice to praise.

Where Worship puts Self

Although Isaiah was just a spectator of the heavenly worship, he was profoundly moved by what he saw. No one who really sees the Lord can remain the same. His looking up caused him to look within, and that introspection awakened him to vital individual applications.

Admitting Personal Insignificance

Being impressed by the sight of God and being satisfied with self are mutually exclusive. Isaiah's response to the heavenly vision is sobering and should be representative: "Then said I, Woe is me! for I am undone; because I am a man of unclean lips, and I dwell in the midst of a people of unclean lips: for mine eyes have seen the King, the LORD of hosts" (6:5). He had just seen the unfallen seraphim covering their faces before the holy God, and how much more did he as a fallen man recognize his limitations. His expression of "woe," a sigh of calamity, conviction, and contrition, led to his confession. Whether his admission of "being undone" refers to his being reduced to silence or to his being on the brink of ruin, doomed to die, it is a terrifying and startling self-evaluation. He felt his unworthiness and lamented that his unclean lips disqualified him from joining in the chorus of praise. The light of God's glory exposed his sin to his own conscience, and lips once called to preach could not now render praise. The nearer to God one draws, the more sensitive to sin one becomes. Introspection serves a good purpose, but it always leads to depression. It is a means to a better end; and thus, it must never terminate in self. The better end is its motivation to look away from self to the Lord who is able to qualify the unqualified for worship. Putting self in the proper place is integral to putting God in His.

Recognizing the Greatness of Grace

Isaiah's own heart condemned him, but God is greater than the heart and knows all things (1 John 3:20). He knows well how to remedy man's sin, supplying those unfit for His presence with the requisite clean hands and pure hearts. Isaiah had recognized the need created by his uncleanness, and now he learns that God's grace provides what he needs. Grace always finds a man where he is, but it never leaves him there. The grace in view is not saving but sanctifying grace. Isaiah was already saved, but he needed grace for holiness. Thankfully, there is grace to sanctify as well as to save.

In a symbolic gesture, one of the seraphim, whose ceaseless worship contributed to Isaiah's sense of guilt, used its pair of flying wings to come as a flaming and ministering spirit to serve as God's attending agent in behalf of the prophet (see Hebrews 1:6-7, 14): "Then flew one of the seraphims unto me, having a live coal in his hand, which he had taken with the tongs from off the altar: And he laid it upon my mouth, and said, Lo, this hath touched thy lips; and thine iniquity is taken away, and thy sin purged" (6:6-7). This symbolism points to some salient truths. Isaiah had specifically confessed the sin of his lips, and God specifically touched his lips. God's forgiveness is as specific as man's sin. The scene also points to the connection between the place of sacrifice and its provision for forgiveness. Singeing the lips with a coal from the altar vividly pictures the removal of the obstacles to fellowship and service. The same fire that consumed the victim, appeasing divine displeasure, cleanses the sinful saint from his guilt, assuring him of divine favor and acceptance. When sin is atoned, guilt is gone. What the vision portrays is realized in the cleansing blood of the Lord Jesus Christ. Isaiah's burnt lips illustrate the New Testament's proclamation: "If we confess our sins, he is faithful and just to forgive us our sins, and to cleanse us from all unrighteousness" and "the blood of Jesus Christ his Son cleanseth us from all sin" (1 John 1:9, 7). The bottom line is that without divine cleansing, there can be no participation in worship.

Submitting to Service

Worship breeds service; indeed, true worship and fervent service are inseparable. Isaiah had seen the example of the seraphim's flying wings that poised them for ministry, so now with lips qualified for worship, he expresses his eager willingness to do whatever God wanted done: "Also I heard the voice of the Lord, saying, Whom shall I send, and who will go for us? Then said I, Here am I; send me" (6:8). Willingness to serve should flow from worship-enabling grace; it is the reasonable response to that grace. Significantly, this commitment to service occurred after the removal of guilt and not in order to it. Far too frequently, serving the Lord is suffered as a kind of penance with a view to increasing favor with God. This kind of guilt-motivated service tends to drudgery and leads to burnout. Being conscious of grace and consumed with a sight of the sovereign Christ, however, generates a happy service that may very well lead to physical and even emotional fatigue, but never to spiritual enervation. Throughout his prophetic career, Isaiah never lost sight of the "Holy One" that first moved him to submit to God's call for service. That is a key lesson. A worshipping people will be a serving people.

Where Worship puts Others

Isaiah's outward look put in focus a people who would not be naturally inclined to listen to his message, but whom he felt impelled to minister to. This result of his looking outward is somewhat tangential to our worship theme, but in order to complete my thoughts on the topic of his chapter, I will briefly sum up the lesson. The path of service is seldom smooth. Verses 9-13 reveal something about the mission of the prophet and his message. The mission field was hard and discouraging, but how people respond to our service to the Lord is not the criterion for service. Those to whom Isaiah preached were uninterested, spiritually ignorant, and unresponsive, and people haven't changed any since then. But regardless of how discouraging the mission, power inhered in the message. Sometimes that power was a savor of death. Hearts were made fat, incapable of feeling the operations of grace; ears were made heavy, dulled and stopped up from hearing the word of grace; and eyes were smeared with paste, blinded to the beauty of grace (6:10). But sometimes that power was a savor of life. There would be a remnant according to grace (6:13). The message has the power to transform sinners into a holy seed.

But the key point is that it was Isaiah's vision of Christ and His sovereign glory that motivated his service to a world of sinners. Although not by means of internal vision, we can see what Isaiah saw in the more sure Word of Testimony that we possess. Our response, then, ought to mirror his. Worship puts everything in its proper place; it puts everything in proper perspective. Isaiah's experience is our example. Let's follow it.

The Example of John

The New Testament, as well as the Old, illustrates worship. Nowhere are the examples of worship more clear and numerous than in the Book of the Revelation. Unfortunately, this book is more often viewed as a crystal ball to the future than it is a blueprint for worship. That is too bad. Undeniably, the book addresses "things which must shortly come to pass," but the opening words give hint to the interpretational key: "The Revelation of Jesus Christ, which God gave unto him" (1:1). Let me render this in a way that more explicitly expresses the contextually intended sense: "the Revelation about Jesus Christ, which God gave concerning Him."

Revelation teaches that we are not to be blind or ignorant about the world and where it is headed; predominantly, though, it teaches that we are not to be blind or ignorant about Christ. After all, it is to Him that everything in this world is headed. It is at the name of Jesus that every knee will bow and every tongue will confess "Jesus Christ is Lord, to the glory of God the Father" (Philippians 2:10-11). That sounds like worship, and John records a vision of at least a part of its actualization. He sees an innumerable mass of humanity from all over the globe joining in heavenly worship, "Saying, Amen: Blessing, and glory, and wisdom, and thanksgiving, and honour, and power, and might, be unto our God for ever and ever. Amen" (Revelation 7:12). The language of Revelation 5:13 seems to echo Paul's precisely: "And every creature which is in heaven, and on the earth, and under the earth, and such as are in the sea, and all that are in them, heard I saying, Blessing, and honour, and glory, and power, be unto him that sitteth upon the throne, and unto the Lamb for ever and ever."

So to a church living in troubled times and threatened by hostile enemies (the circumstance of every church in this dispensation), John draws attention to Christ. It is seeing Christ and worshipping Him for His infinite worth that put all of life in proper perspective–the present as well as the future. Worship's affecting life is a consistent biblical focus.

Although expressions of worship are scattered throughout the book, some extended passages in particular provide graphic examples of worship themes that ought to control all worship. For instance, the heavenly scene recorded in Revelation 4 and 5 identifies two principal themes for worship linked to the sight of God's throne. Chapter 4 highlights the throne of government based on God's sovereign rule as the Creator. After describing the mysterious and majestic throne, John records the words of the heavenly worshippers: "Thou art worthy, O Lord, to receive glory and honour and power: for thou hast created all things, and for thy pleasure they are and were created" (4:11). Then in chapter 5, attention falls on the throne of grace and the mediatorial rule of the Redeemer. The words of worship focus on the Lion of the tribe of Judah, the Root of David (5:5)–in other words, the Christ. They center on the credentials of His person, the preeminence of His position, and the power of His passion. With Christ in sight, the angels and the redeemed join together in praise: "Worthy is the Lamb that was slain to receive power, and riches, and wisdom, and strength, and honor, and glory, and blessing" (5:11). The logical link between creation and redemption occurs throughout Scripture and is both a proper theme and a reason for worship.

Although that heavenly scene powerfully exemplifies ideal worship, I want to outline some thoughts from John's opening vision of Christ that charted the course for everything else he saw about Christ in his series of sometimes strange visions. So many of the descriptions of Christ in this opening vision recur throughout the book. John never got over what he saw of the exalted Christ. Resisting the temptation to make a full exposition of this passage, I offer this synopsis that illustrates the necessary centrality of Christ in worship. John's vision of Christ that led to his worshipping Christ is a good example for us.

The Glory of Christ's Presence

Although John was in exile suffering persecution in a dismal place, what he saw of Christ's glorious presence turned the night to day, and a dreary place to heaven on earth. In vision, John sees seven lampstands, which are identified as seven churches representing the church of Christ with all its various needs and problems (1:12, 20). But most remarkably, John saw Christ in the middle of the church (1:13). The following chapters expose a church with problems, failures, and weaknesses, but notwithstanding all those issues, Christ was with His church as Immanuel. This suggests something vital about gathering together as a church of believers. When the church gathers, it should expect the presence of Christ and should conduct itself accordingly. A whole lot of the nonsense that takes place in so many churches would not, if those who gathered would be sensitive and responsive to the special presence of the Savior in the midst. That's not the particular point of John's vision, but it is an important implication for worship.

The Glory of Christ's Person

Being in Christ's presence overwhelms the senses with the glory of His person. Part of worship is just to describe and to reflect on the nature of His person. John sees Christ as the exalted Man and the eternal God. That Christ is described in terms of His likeness to the Son of man and His high-priestly wardrobe (1:13) identifies Him as the ideal and exalted Man who has earned entrance to and a place of honor in heaven. His dominion is eternal yet earned by His perfect work. During the earthly manifestation of His incarnation, He was the meek and lowly Jesus. But now forever in the heavenly reality of His incarnation, He is exalted over all–everything is under His feet (see Psalm 8). But just as John sees Him as absolute Man, so he sees Him as absolute God. His glory is not only earned (as Man), but also inherently His by right (as God). He is infinite (1:8, 11, 17), eternal, and immutable without any limitations. His person has intrinsic and infinite worth; thus, He is the proper object of worship.

The Glory of Christ's Perfections

John could not see the person of Christ without being overwhelmed with perfections of His character. What he saw is difficult to picture, but the truths are in the symbolism and not in some visible reproduction or representation. The point is clear: the glory of the incarnate Christ that was veiled on earth is fully revealed in heaven. Three attributes of Christ shine through. First, He is omniscient (1:14). His white hair represents His wisdom, and His flaming eyes represent His infinite intelligence and penetrating perception. Nothing can hide from His knowledge; all things are open before His eyes. His unfailing discernment between true and false ought to sober every would-be worshipper. He knows the heart. Second, He is omnipotent (1:15). His powerful voice testifies to His irresistible authority, and His brass feet represent His inflexible and irresistible justice. Third, He is sovereign. His absolute authority is evident in His rule over the church–the stars representing the ministers are in His hand (1:20). Ministers own a delegated authority, but Christ is the sole Head and King of the church. His authority is also evident in His righteous justice–the sharp two-edged sword is in His mouth (1:16). His having the keys of death and hell demonstrates His authority over life itself (1:18). His sovereignty is evident in His shining face–His countenance is as bright as the sun (1:16). Ironically, a face that on earth was covered with the vile spittle of man now radiates divine glory.

The image is significant. Just as even a momentary gaze at the brightness of the earth's sun affects the perception of everything else, so being blinded by the Sun of Righteousness will affect everything else that we see. That's the secret for life in general; it's the secret for worship as well.

Christ's glory is inherently His, yet by worship, too, He is glorified. When John saw the Lord's glory, he fell prostrate at His feet (1:17) just as Ezekiel did when he saw the same Christ hundreds of years earlier (see Ezekiel 1:28). True worshippers always assume the low station lest attention be drawn away from the worshipped. So impressed was John with the sight of Christ that he introduced the record of his vision with a doxology directed to One he was about to describe in all His glory: "to him be glory and dominion for ever and ever. Amen" (1:6).

John's worship experience while he was in the spirit on the Lord's Day is just one more example for us to follow. The principles of worship extracted from his, Isaiah's, and Moses's examples are reiterated multiple times and in multiple ways throughout the Bible. The Lord has given clear instructions, imperatives, and reasons to worship Him. He has also given us the opportunity to observe what worshipping Him looks like. Sometimes it just helps to see it done, to see those principles actually put into practice. These persons did it, and so must we—no excuses.

CHAPTER 7

PARADIGMS FOR WORSHIP

Imperatives, instructions, and illustrations concerning worship occur throughout the Scripture. But nowhere are the theme and theology of worship more surface, central, and pervasive than in the Book of Psalms. The Hebrew title for this book that we call "Psalms"–thanks to the Septuagint–is "Praises." That says something and hints at the book's prime purpose. Although written by multiple inspired poets over a span of centuries,[1] its canonical order framed by doxologies sets the collection in five units–according to both Jewish and Christian traditions a miniature Pentateuch.[2] I hesitate, however, to draw forced lines between the five books of Psalms and the five books of Moses since there is no strict correspondence in the order of themes as they appear in the Pentateuch and the Psalms. To me, it is artificial to identify Books 1 to 5 with Genesis to Deuteronomy specifically or respectively since the "books" were not written in that order and since the authority of inspiration rests in the composition not the collection procedure.[3] Nonetheless, I think the Penta-division is an intentional canonical marker to suggest that this worship manual does in fact mirror the Mosaic corpus that reveals the essence and foundation of God's covenant purpose and the inception of God's redemptive program. There is hardly a covenant theme introduced in the Pentateuch that does not find poetic and worshipful expression in the Psalms.[4] "Let the redeemed of the LORD say so" (Psalm 107:2a) could well sum up the function of the Psalter in its totality and in each of its constituent parts.

This book of praises is a divinely inspired handbook of worship–God's "how-to" book of worship. Only the supernatural operation of inspiration can explain the book's remarkable unity in spite of the inevitable diversity caused by its multiple authorship. Since the writers of Scripture did not originate what they said but rather were moved by the Holy Spirit to say what they said (2 Peter 1:20-21), the only legitimately logical conclusion is that the personal and sundry ways that each expressed his feelings, fears, doubts, joys, sorrows, and desires are paradigms illustrating how God expects worshippers to express themselves. The Psalms give patterns for both individual and corporate worship, guiding worshippers in how best to communicate to God in response to His gracious communication. Worship entails meeting with God with ears attentive to His Word, and while the worshipper is to stand more ready to hear than to speak (Ecclesiastes 5:1-2), he is not to stand silent. The Psalms teach us how to give voice to praise and to prayer, the suitable expressions of worship.

I love the Psalms. I love to read them, pray them, teach them, preach them, and sing them. I love the elegant yet simple beauty of the poetry with all of its rich imagery, the essence of which is transferable and retainable in translation–most unusual for poetry. I love their themes and theology. There are so many things about the Psalms that beg for and deserve attention, and what needs to be said even here in developing my proposition has the potential of expanding beyond my intent. So I can only be suggestive, resisting temptation to offer a theological analysis of the book or expositions of specific psalms. I can envision myself writing a commentary on the Psalms someday–just not today.[5] My proposition for now is simply that the Psalms are paradigms for worship and as such mark a path for worshipping the Lord in the beauty of holiness.

FOCUS OF THE PSALMS

The principal focus of the Psalms is God. Given that God is the sole object of true worship, it should not be surprising that He would be the focal point in a worship manual. Remember that one of the preeminent precepts of true and spiritual worship is that it must be theocentric (God-centered) and not anthropocentric (man-centered). The Psalter highlights this precept both by what it says and by what it doesn't say. It says volumes about God, but conspicuous by comparative absence are references to men and their achievements, even those who rendered great and notable service to the Lord. Indeed, references to specific individuals are incidental, and none celebrate what these individuals did for God, but rather what God had done for them. That itself gives a clear directive for worship, and it is a principle we have already underscored: worship is about God and not about man. Far too frequently, modern "worship" directs attention to man's accomplishments, motivating the congregation to imitate some biblical character's traits or behavior, or it attempts to make the people either feel good or sometimes even feel bad (the old guilt motivation) about themselves. God receives only the incidental reference.

The divinely inspired paradigms elevate the Lord to His rightful place, ascribing to Him the infinite worth of His person and the glory of His works (praise) and appealing to Him for His necessary mercies (prayer). Proving this statement requires the kind of thorough theological analysis and multiplication of examples that I cannot offer here. But even a cursory reading of the Psalms–which, by the way, I don't recommend–reveals how consistently the Lord is in view. It is impossible not to notice how frequently the name and various appellations of God occur throughout the collection, directing attention, praise, and prayer to His person. For instance, the covenant name of God that is so wonderfully linked to His gracious redemption and faithfulness, Jehovah (usually LORD in the AV), occurs almost seven hundred times scattered throughout the one hundred fifty Psalms. In addition, the hundreds of other direct references to God in the Psalms via His many other titles, each of which declares some self-revealed truth about God, support the claim that God is central in biblical worship. There is little wonder that David declares, "O LORD our Lord, how excellent is thy name in all the earth!" (Psalm 8:1 and 9).

Praise, however, is to be offered not only because God is who He is, but also because He is like He is and because He does what He does. Therefore, following the inspired paradigm for worship requires giving attention to the divine perfections and works. In regard to His perfections, the bottom line is that there is no God like our God, and a whole of lot of worship can occur just by reflecting on and recounting His infinite, eternal, and unchangeable virtues. The greatness of God and His glory are indisputable facts (see Psalms 135:5 and 138:5 for forthright declarations). Let me suggest a little exercise. Here is the description of God in the *Westminster Larger Catechism*, 7.

> God is a Spirit, in and of himself infinite in being, glory, blessedness, and perfection; all-sufficient, eternal, unchangeable, incomprehensible, every where present, almighty, knowing all things, most wise, most holy, most just, most merciful and gracious, long-suffering, and abundant in goodness and truth.

As you read through the Psalms, mark how the Psalms could provide the biblical support or proof of each of the statements. I dare say that it will be virtually impossible to select any Psalm without finding some reference to or evidence of one or more of God's attributes.[6]

Similarly in regard to God's works, there is plenty to worship about. In one place, David announced his worship agenda in terms of God's acts: "I will praise thee, O LORD, with my whole heart; I will shew forth all thy marvelous works" (9:1). A key exercise of worship is to reflect on what God has done, is doing, and will do; the Psalms address each of these perspectives—particularly in terms of creation, providence, and redemption with all the respective implications and applications for both the righteous and the wicked. The association of creation and redemption is a thoroughly biblical link,[7] and as suggested by the Sabbath mandate, the two together identify necessary themes for worship. Remember how Exodus 20 links the day to creation whereas Deuteronomy 5 links it to redemption. Throughout, the psalmists illustrate how these uniquely divine works are reasons for praise and motives for prayer.

I cannot finish this section concerning the Psalms' focus without reference to Christ. As we have seen over and again, no true worship is possible apart from Jesus Christ, the only way, truth, and life. It should not be surprising, then, that the inspired "how to" book of worship includes so much about Christ. In His post-resurrection, heart-enflaming conversation with the two disciples on the way to Emmaus, the Lord started with Moses and expounded the whole of what the Old Testament Scriptures said about Him (Luke 24:27). And then to the gathered disciples He said specifically, "These are the words which I spake unto you, while I was yet with you, that all things must be fulfilled, which were written in the law of Moses, and in the prophets, and in the psalms, concerning me" (Luke 24:44). Therefore, to miss finding Christ in the Old Testament is to miss the essential message of that book, including the Psalms. Indeed, finding Christ in the Psalms is a sure thing. It follows that if Christ is in the Psalms, and the Psalms are about worship, then worship is in some way about Christ. The Psalms were an effective means of keeping the messianic hope before a worshipping people. Although the Psalms cannot speak of Christ in historical terms since the eternal Son had not yet become man, there is hardly a truth about Christ's person, nature, or work that does not find expression–all of which have implications for worship. His humanity and deity, His death and resurrection, His mediatorial offices (prophet, priest, and king), His first and Second Advents are all part of the Psalms' messianic theology. The Israelites knew what it meant to sing of their Redeemer.

Although I would love at this point to start at the beginning of the Psalter and expound every messianic text, that would–like every other "not-in-the-outline" impulse I have had in this project–take us way beyond our defined scope and purpose. In considering this theme, I refer you to my earlier work *Beginning at Moses: A Guide to Finding Christ in the Old Testament*. What I need to say here, I have already developed in that book. After suggesting and explaining some hermeneutical principles to employ in identifying messianic references,[8] I offer a synopsis of selected messianic Psalms. Here is a synopsis of that synopsis. Psalm 2 reveals Christ as the object of saving faith. Psalm 8 reveals Him as the ideal man. Psalm 16 reveals Him as the resolute Servant whose view of His God, His people, and His mission fueled His determination to endure the suffering for the glory that was certain to follow. Psalm 22, one of the places in Scripture that demand the removal of our shoes because we are on holy ground, reveals Christ as the suffering and successful Savior. Psalm 110, revealing Christ as the King and Priest, is a compendium of theological truths concerning the person and mediatorial operation of Christ, from His place in the Trinity to His Royal Priesthood to His final triumph over every enemy.[9]

A whole set or category of Psalms designated as Royal Psalms spotlights the person of the king and always points in some way to Jesus Christ, the Ideal King. Many more Psalms either in part or in whole, in fact or in type, direct attention to Christ. When you find Christ in the Psalms, remember that you have found Him in the book of worship and song. That is essential. Any biblical paradigm for worship will have Christ as a principal part. The Psalms make it unmistakably clear that kissing the Son–that is, paying homage to Him–is foundational to true religion and to true worship (Psalm 2:12). Acceptance before God is always in reference to Christ.

FORMULA IN THE PSALMS

Not all Psalms are the same. Some are communal; others are individual. Some are joyful; others are doleful. Some confess sin; others claim righteousness. Some exude confidence; others express doubt and even despondency. Some make petitions; others render praise. Some are logically reasoned; others are emotionally random. You get the point–the Psalms are not identical. Any regular reading of the Psalms draws attention to this diversity; it can't be missed. It is not supposed to be missed since every Psalm with its own particulars is the product of divine inspiration and therefore the testimony of divine intent. In one way or another, each Psalm is a part of the divinely defined paradigm to instruct and to guide to proper worship. Not every distinctive model must necessarily be incorporated into every worship occasion, but together the patterns define the substance of worship mechanics.

Opinions differ as to how to catalog the diverse patterns. Some give precedence to content, and others try to discern structural forms that may restrict and consequently identify the kind of content. Avoiding criticism or analysis of the techniques for classifying the Psalms, I want briefly to identify some commonly recognized categories of Psalms that constitute a formula for worship in their identification of appropriate ingredients to be included. This formula details the kind of things that God expects and desires from a worshipping people. The order is arbitrary on my part and reflects only my limitation to address one thing at a time.

Ingredient 1: Praise and Thanksgiving

Since true worship is all about God, praise and thanksgiving for His person and for His works are always integral elements in biblical worship. Although expressions of praise and thanksgiving magnifying God's name and celebrating the manifold evidences of His greatness occur in most Psalms regardless of whatever else may be expressed, some Psalms exclusively eulogize the Lord. A few sample texts will illustrate. They usually include imperatives to praise, reasons for praise (focusing on the Lord Himself or His creative and redemptive works) and resolutions to praise again. These Psalms wholly given to praise/thanksgiving are often designated as hymns. Hymns are sometimes but not always marked by a literary devise called inclusio, which simply means that the beginning and the end are the same or very similar. It's like the bread slices of a sandwich between which is the meat. Here are some hymn examples. Psalm 8 begins and ends with a pronouncement of God's greatness– "O LORD our Lord, how excellent is thy name in all the earth" (vv. 1, 9). In between the two declarations, the psalmist gives evidences of God's glory, grace, and greatness that prove the excellence. Psalm 103 begins and ends with a call to personal worship–"Bless the LORD, O my soul" (vv. 1, 22). Between the imperatives to bless the Lord are reflections on the multiple and varied manifestations of God's mercy and might that motivate the ascription of blessing. Psalm 135 (like Psalms 145-150) starts and finishes with "hallelujah"–"Praise ye the LORD" (vv. 1, 21).

The first "hallelujah" leads to a delineation of God's goodness and greatness with specific descriptions of His grace, uniqueness, sovereignty, eternal immutability, and compassionate care, all of which give justification for praise; the only fitting conclusion is another "hallelujah." Psalm 136 begins and ends, "O give thanks unto the LORD (God of heaven, v. 26)...for his mercy endureth for ever" (vv. 1, 26), and repeats the closing refrain in every verse, "for his mercy endureth for ever." The statement occurs twenty-six times, but not once too often considering the multiple reasons for giving thanks in celebration of who the Lord is (Jehovah, the absolute God and Sovereign), of what He can do (wonders), and of what He has done in terms of creation, redemption, providential care, and timely grace.

Ingredient 2: Confession of Sin

Drawing near to God in worship has restrictions. Psalm 24 poses a question, the answer to which would seem to disqualify most of us from worshipping God at all: "Who shall ascend into the hill of the LORD? or who shall stand in his holy place? He that hath clean hands, and a pure heart..." (24:3-4a). Without those clean hands and pure hearts, worship is impossible. Sin defiles and hinders fellowship with God–something we know both theologically and experientially. But God in His grace and mercy has provided the means for cleansing from sin, thus fitting His worshippers for His presence; He has marked the path leading to forgiveness. "If we confess our sins, he is faithful and just to forgive us our sins, and to cleanse us from all unrighteousness" (1 John 1:9). John sums up the promise; the Psalms implement it. David testified that confessing sin really works: "I acknowledged my sin unto thee, and mine iniquity have I not hid. I said, I will confess my transgressions unto the LORD; and thou forgavest the iniquity of my sin" (Psalm 32:5). The Psalms illustrate what God expects in the kind of confession that not only leads to restoration for fellowship but also constitutes a necessary component in worship.

Expressions of confession and pleas for divine mercy occur throughout the Psalter, but seven Psalms are traditionally classified as penitential (6, 32, 38, 51, 102, 130, 143). Psalm 51 is perhaps the best known of the penitential Psalms, occasioned by David's sin with Bath-Sheba. The logic and progression of his confession provide a good example to follow in both individual and corporate settings. David begins with a plea for forgiveness, making no excuses for his sins and acknowledging that if forgiveness comes, it comes from God's grace, mercy, and compassion (51:1-9). He then pleads for a spiritual renewal and restoration to joy and fellowship in God's presence (51:10-13). Finally, he argues the link between his being forgiven and the worship experience (51:14-16). All of the outward exercises of worship are pleasing to the Lord when accompanied with the sacrifices of a broken spirit and contrite heart (51:17). Confession of sin is part of the necessary humility and submission required of all worshippers in God's presence.

Ingredient 3: Lamentation

Being in God's presence in spiritual worship is a happy relief from the responsibilities and anxieties of life, but it is not a narcotic that dulls the senses to the stuff of life. A great many things in the world seem to threaten God's people and even contradict what is true about God. The Psalms teach that worship includes expressing those concerns and petitioning God for defense and deliverance. These Psalms, whether dealing with individual matters or community concerns, usually include a cry for the Lord to hear the complaint, a summary of the distressing or dangerous circumstance, a confession of trust in the Lord, a petition for divine intervention to reverse the circumstance, and a resolution to praise the Lord. Psalm 13 illustrates the pattern.

David begins by directing a transparent question to the Lord that shows his despair: "How long wilt thou forget me O LORD... how long shall mine enemy be exalted over me?" (13:1-2). He then makes his petition for the Lord to do something before the enemy prevailed: "Consider and hear me, O LORD my God" (13:3). Finally, he confesses his trust and breaks out in song praising the Lord for His intervention: "But I have trusted in thy mercy; my heart shall rejoice in thy salvation. I will sing unto the LORD because he hath dealt bountifully with me" (13:5-6).

A legitimate ingredient of worship is bringing God to bear on issues that without divine attendance would seem to jeopardize His glory or at least to obscure our vision of His glory. The circumstances of life–those in our private little worlds or in the larger world around us–have the potential to create a tension in our hearts between experience and creed, that is, what we believe about God. When experience assumes precedence over creed, we don't feel much like worshipping. Walking by sight is always deleterious to walking by faith. The Psalms direct us to factor God into current situations; true religion is always relevant to life. It is good in worship to dwell on God's faithfulness and the sensibility of trusting Him regardless. Praising God tends to put everything else in proper perspective, even life.

Ingredient 4: Imprecation

Biblical worship includes praying for the vindication of God's glory, His cause, and His people. This vindication often involves His judgment on those who oppose His glory, His cause, and His people. These imprecatory prayers for divine judgment to fall upon the wicked reflect a righteous sense of God's justice, a righteous hatred of sin, and a righteous jealousy for God's glory and kingdom (see, for example, Psalms 35, 69, 109, and 137). Imperative to our understanding of the Imprecatory Psalms is the realization that they never involve personal issues or vindictiveness. The Scripture of both the Old and New Testaments demands love for personal enemies (see Exodus 23:4-5; Leviticus 19:17-18; Matthew 5:38-45); hence, imprecatory prayers are not a biblically sanctioned "voodoo" means of sticking it to personal enemies. That God's people find relief and deliverance when God judges His enemies is a felicitous corollary but never the motive behind the prayers. True prayer always has God's glory as its principal end and driving cause. The imprecatory Psalms, along with the multiple imprecations scattered throughout Scripture,[10] always reflect the highest motive and are just as much a part of the divinely inspired paradigm for worship as the Hallelujah Psalms or any other. Christians have every right and warrant both to declare God's Word in announcing judgment upon the unrighteousness and to pray for God's will to be done. Love for God demands both the declaration and the prayer. Consider how the psalmist identified himself with God and follow his example: "Do not I hate them, O LORD, that hate thee? And am not I grieved with those that rise up against thee? I hate them with perfect hatred: I count them mine enemies" (Psalm 139:21-22).[11] To pray for God to execute His righteous judgment upon the wicked is equivalent to praying for the advancement and extension of His kingdom. I would submit that following this paradigm is a part of what Christ Himself instructed about prayer when He taught us to pray, "Thy kingdom come. Thy will be done in earth, as it is in heaven" (Matthew 6:10). An imprecatory prayer that follows the principles of God's paradigm specifies that general petition. It is a most Christian thing to do, and to do in worship.

Ingredient 5: Ethical Instruction

True and biblical religion pervades life. In contrast to the postmodern propensity for separating different spheres of life into unrelated compartments, biblical religion demands that a saving relationship with God defines and directs every experience and relationship in life. There can be, therefore, no disconnect between worship and life. Remember the requirement of Psalm 24 that restricts worship to those who are ethically and morally pure (clean hands and pure hearts). Recall as well Jeremiah's condemnation of those who committed every conceivable sin yet assumed that God would be pleased with their professed worship (the famous Temple Sermon in Jeremiah 7). Not surprisingly, in the God-given handbook on worship, ethical demands are placed on would-be worshippers. Psalm 15, for instance, demands honesty and prohibits slander; Psalm 82 demands justice, humanitarian and equitable treatment to the defenseless; Psalm 131 requires humility. Some of the Psalms that seem to deal predominantly with issues of piety and ethics are referred to as Wisdom Psalms (for instance, 37, 49, 73, 112, and 127-128). The examples could go on and on, and it is obvious that in this venue I cannot begin to enumerate all the specific instructions in godliness that the Psalms detail. Let the canonical introduction make the salient point. Significantly, standing over the entire Psalter is the contrast between the two ways–the way of the righteous and the way of the ungodly. The godly man must be separate from sinners and must find his delight in God's Word (Psalm 1). Before issuing the first imperative to praise the Lord, the Psalms identify the kind of life expected of those who would worship God. The Psalms consistently link life and worship. Worship does not leave religion or God in the realm of theory.

As I said at the beginning of this section, there is no consensus on how to classify or categorize the Psalms. What I've suggested in terms of the formula of worship illustrated in the Psalms is somewhat artificial, but it summarizes the things that ought to be included in biblical worship. The scope of the Psalms is huge, including petitions addressed directly to God, complaints and confessions of both private and public sins, pleas for deliverance and revival, acknowledgments of confident trust in the Lord, and grateful praise of God through broad as well as specific descriptions of His infinite worth. The Psalms sometimes make their worship point by reflecting on history (78, 105, 106, 135, and 136). Psalm 78:2 forthrightly declares the recital of history to be parabolic: it is like something else. God uses history as a paradigm of His saving acts and purposes for His people. The historical Psalms parallel Paul's assessment of the same history as being recorded for examples and admonitions (1 Corinthians 10:6, 11). Other times the Psalms make their worship point with predictive prophecy; many of the messianic Psalms illustrate this. Whether through history or prophecy, attention is fixed on the unfailing purpose and providence of God that achieves His glory and His people's good through His redemptive acts–all matters of worship.

FUNCTION OF THE PSALMS

There is no question that the Psalms teach us how to worship; the question is how we are to use the Psalms in worship. What should be their function? David's introduction of a psalm as part of the celebration occasioned by the ark's return illustrates the function of psalms in public worship (1 Chronicles 16). Interestingly, the psalm sung first on that day became in the Psalter either in part or in whole what we know as Psalms 96, 105, and 106. It was used more than once. Similarly, some of the superscriptions identify the liturgical use of particular psalms. Psalm 30, for instance, was for the dedication of David's house. Psalms 120-135 were designated as the songs of ascent, traditionally understood to have been part of the celebration of the pilgrimage feasts. Psalm 92 is marked as a song for the Sabbath. Additional instructions recorded in the Septuagint designate other Psalms for specific days of the week (1st day–24; 2nd day–48; 4th day–94; 6th day–93). First Corinthians 14:26,

Ephesians 5:19, Colossians 3:16, and James 5:13 confirm the place of the Psalms in New Testament worship as well.

Evidence is that the early church followed the biblical pattern and incorporated the Psalms into the services of public worship. Certainly, the Reformation with its revival of congregational singing relied heavily on the Psalms, even–some would argue–exclusively.[12] The point to be taken is that there is both biblical and traditional precedent for using the Psalms in worship. It is not my concern here to enter into any of the debates or controversies that have arisen regarding exclusive psalmody or inclusive hymnody.[13] I want simply to recommend four functions that the Psalms ought to have in worship. I'll not comment much because I discussed each of these generally in some detail in Chapter 4, The Liturgy of Worship.

First, *read the Psalms*. Every worship service must include the public reading of the Scripture. Although this public reading should not be restricted to the Psalms, the Psalms by their very nature accomplish much of what is desired in the public reading. With their commands to praise and give thanks, many of the Psalms lend themselves to use at the beginning of the service to call the people to worship. In addition, the Psalms exhibit a theological completeness that will keep the whole course of God's redemptive operation in view if they are read systematically. Johnson offers an interesting array of quotations to this effect.

> In his 1528 "Preface to the Psalter," Luther refers to the Psalter as a "little Bible." He says, "In it is comprehended most beautifully and briefly everything that is in the entire Bible." He calls it a "short Bible," in which is provided an "entire summary" of the whole "comprised in one little book." Before him Athanasius (ca. 296-373) referred to the Psalter as an "epitome of the whole Scriptures." And Basil (ca. 330-70)

called it a "compend of all divinity." All that the Bible teaches
is found in summary form in the Book of Psalms.[14]

Second, *pray the Psalms*. Since so many of the Psalms are
themselves prayers addressed directly to the Lord, following the
paradigm requires praying–the specifics as well as the patterns.
Remember how almost every statement in Jonah's very personal
prayer in the belly of the fish repeated either verbatim or very
close to verbatim some line from the Psalms (Jonah 2). Jonah
prayed with inspired words; that is a good way to pray both
privately and publicly. There is hardly a better way to learn to
pray than to pray through the Psalms, personalizing the inspired
words. There is hardly a better way to insure that public praying
is scripturally sound than to utilize the words of Scripture.
Spontaneous praying does not preclude using the Psalms.

Third, *preach the Psalms*. It is significant to me that the first
sermon preached on the day of Pentecost took a text from the
Psalms. After Peter appealed to Joel's prophecy to explain what
was happening on the eventful day, he began to preach Christ,
taking Psalm 16 as his text, and he didn't finish before commenting
on Psalm 110 as well (Acts 2:25-36). Acts refers to more than
one apostolic sermon that used the Psalms (see, for instance,
Acts 4:25 referring to Psalm 2). In light of the full compendium
of theological truths and life issues addressed in the Psalms, any
preacher ought to find abundant sermon material. Once you learn
something about the structure and style of the poetry, the Psalms
almost outline themselves. They are eminently "preachable."

Fourth, *sing the Psalms*. Among other purposes, the Psalms
were made for singing. That they were sung in their original
settings and continued to be sung in both Jewish and Christian
worship is indisputable. You don't have to be a Presbyterian to
know the rich history of Psalm singing in Reformed worship
traditions, particularly among the Scottish Covenanters. I
personally believe that there is a scripturally warranted place

for God-glorifying and biblical hymnody in worship but not to the exclusion of singing the inspired Psalms. Singing the Psalms will help dispel what has become a common notion even among the most conservative that singing is preparatory for worship. I reiterate what I've already argued–proper singing is not preparatory for worship: it is worship. Singing the Psalms, the divinely inspired hymnbook, is singing what God wants sung.[15] Even the hymns that we sing ought to follow the patterns and themes suggested in the Psalms; that's what paradigms are for. I would suggest that singing the Psalms is a safeguard against singing inappropriate hymns and spiritual songs. Singing the Psalms and using them as a pattern for singing other things will insure the proper kind of words.

Since the tunes have not been preserved, and thus were not inspired, common and sanctified sense must operate. Again I will not venture commentary beyond my competence about music style (see Appendix 4), but I will make a statement reflecting common and sanctified sense. The tunes ought to fit the words and be fit for the One to whom the songs are directed. Remembering that worship singing is not for personal entertainment but for service unto God will automatically exclude what is generally referred to as contemporary Christian music (CCM). The date of composition is not the issue. Something written yesterday might well be appropriate and honoring to God; something written centuries ago might well be spiritually disgusting. Joyous Psalms ought to have joyous tunes; praise Psalms ought to have majestic tunes; penitential Psalms ought to have doleful tunes. Some things just make sense. Sing the Psalms.

The Psalms teach us that we are to meditate on God, His person, His works, and His Christ. The Psalms teach us to declare, to describe, to praise, to give thanks, to pray, to vow, to sing. The Psalms teach us the paradigms for worship; they teach us to worship. God has given us a handbook and hymnbook all in one place. Let's use it to His glory.

CONCLUSION

Contemporary! Traditional! Divisive words–particularly when referring to methods of worship. That's how I started this book, and I have done nothing through it to resolve the tension generated by this worship-war jargon. Although I am aware of the kind of worship styles generally associated with the two words and have my opinions regarding those modes of worship, I don't think they are the best words to identify the core, crucial issues of worship. In my religious environment, "contemporary worship" smacks of compromise and always leads to a "slippery slope." On the other hand, "traditional worship" is a mark of fundamental faithfulness. But contemporary is not always synonymous with wrong, nor does traditional always signify right. To the darkness and deadness of medieval Romanism, Reformation worship was a contemporary perversion of what had become tradition. Sometimes contemporary is good, and traditional is bad.

I don't want to trivialize the matter, but what is contemporary today may become traditional tomorrow. At some point contemporary practices either become obsolete, giving way to the next contemporary practice, or transition to traditional. Much of what we know today as traditional used to be contemporary. I've acknowledged before that I'm not a church historian, but my guess is that what we regard as traditional worship services today don't look much like the worship services of the early church, even that church prior to papal influences and perversions. For instance, the *Didache*, a manual of church instruction dating to about 100 A.D., allowed warm water for baptism only as a last resort and required the one baptizing and the one being baptized to fast for one or two days prior to the baptismal service (see *Didache* 7:2, 4). Somewhere along the way a new tradition was born, and no one today would question the validity of a baptism based on water temperature or the eating schedule of the participants. I was at a conference recently where a colleague from another conservative institution read a paper on worship. He made the insightful observation that much of what passes for traditional worship in many fundamentalist churches today is the consequence of having brought the evangelistic tent-meetings of a hundred fifty years ago inside the church. I think he's right. As a result, the focus of church services shifted from worship to motivational messages invariably concluding with altar calls for immediate decisions. So traditional has this become to some that even to alter the altar call is to be suspected of disobedience to the Great Commission. But that's not the way it used to be.

So the criterion for conducting or evaluating worship cannot be in terms of tradition. I know this is going to sound simplistically pious, but the only legitimate criterion for evaluating and determining worship is the Scripture, our only rule for faith and practice. If being biblical is the standard of worship, then there may even be cherished aspects of "traditional worship" that have to be adjusted or abandoned. Being biblical means having the resolve to either change or not change depending on what the Bible says. That's why *The Beauty of Holiness* is subtitled *A Guide to Biblical Worship*, not necessarily traditional worship.

Having come to the end of my self-imposed outline for this book, I admit that there are many specific issues that I have not addressed. I have intentionally not interacted with proponents of particular points of contention in the worship wars. That needs to be done, but drawing every line of application is beyond the scope of what I wanted to do. I think sometimes in controversy we get so engrossed in the specific issues that we lose sight of the bigger problem of which the specifics are only symptoms. Let me use music as an example here since it seems always to be the front concern. There is a better way to determine what kind of music is appropriate for worship than just to debate about music styles. That has its place in the argument, but I'm saying that even those ignorant about music theory and composition have a means of making proper decisions if they understand from the Bible what worship is all about. I have chosen in this study to focus on the bigger issues that should resolve all the specific matters. I want to think that applying the biblical principles and directives for worship should without my comment answer the questions concerning the legitimacy of drama or dance or CCM or snake handling or sacerdotal enactments or whatever else.

Applying the truths that guide us to biblical worship should solve any arguments about specifics, but that is not always easy or cut-and-dried. The application of truth doesn't always look the same in every age. Whether or not we want to admit it, the application of truth is culturally and temporally elastic. Before you misunderstand me, please read carefully what I said. Truth itself is timeless, universal, and unchangeable; the application of truth is multifaceted. The application of timeless truth may very well look different in diverse times and places. For instance, God's Word commands His people to be separate from the world; that is a timeless requirement. For a while in ancient Israel, that separation entailed not rounding off the corners of the head and not marring the corners of beards (Leviticus 19:27). In the 1960s– when I was a teenager–those grooming habits would have marked societal and parental rebellion. Holiness would have looked different to Moses from what it did to my dad who made sure my hair was constantly trimmed. It seemed as though I was getting a haircut every time I turned around. But that's just a memory, not my point. The point is that there is more than one legitimate way to apply the same truths, even truths about worship.

In this book, I have essentially argued for worshipping according to the regulative principle: that's good Reformed tradition. For those who may be reading the conclusion first, the regulative principle allows in worship only such practices as the Scripture sanctions. But even here, we must grant some latitude. I don't think, for example, that the regulative principle requires that the tunes used by the Psalm-singing Scottish Covenanters would necessarily be the ones used by my Presbyterian brothers in Kenya. To what extent culture can legitimately affect worship is something that needs to be addressed; I acknowledge that and lament that it is a subject too extensive for the focus of this project–just one more thing this book fails to consider.

So while admitting that I have not addressed important issues that beg for answers, I offer what I believe are foundational principles extracted from the Scripture to guide toward biblical worship. This is a *guide* to worship, not a manual. If I have proposed any overarching rule to follow, it is that worship is all about God. Decisions, therefore, about how to worship Him are based not on personal preferences but on God's own Word that prescribes and describes what pleases Him. Worship is not entertainment for spectators; it is sacred service rendered to the Lord. It is true that the Scripture orders us to clap our hands (Psalm 47:1). But whatever our cultural and temporal equivalent of that may be, I guarantee you that it has nothing to do with offering applause to a singer or any other musician for some performance. Worship elevates the Lord; it never spotlights a "worship leader," whatever that means. Interestingly, there is a whole bank of worship words in the Bible, all of which focus on some attitude, posture, or activity, but the Hebrew word in the Old Testament and the Greek word in the New Testament most often translated "worship" both have the essential component of bowing down or showing obeisance. In true worship, all deference and homage are humbly directed to God. Without reverence, a happy gathering may be possible, but biblical worship is not. Acceptable worship always flows from a true knowledge of God that always generates a genuine fear of Him that always follows His revealed will.

Seven chapters mark significant "waypoints" in this guide (that's GPS jargon for marking points of direction). Chapter 1 issues a warning against the potential dangers of worship. True worship is a matter of the heart and must be offered to the Lord not only with reverence but also with wholehearted consecration. Genuine sincerity, according to Jesus, must mark every true worshipper (John 4:24). The danger is that men can turn even biblically ordered practices into idolatry and then convince themselves that God is pleased. Sample exposés of Israel's religion from the Major Prophets underscore the timeless and sobering truth that God is never satisfied with external religion divorced from sincere heart devotion to Him. Worship is an exercise of faith. Appendix 1 considers the same theme from Malachi's autopsy of dead religion. It is not formal liturgy that kills worship; it is a cold heart.

Chapter 2 addresses the bedrock, the object of worship. It seems almost too obvious to state, but God is the only rightful object of worship. Two points stand out: (1) Worship is theocentric, and (2) worship is Trinitarian. Worship is all about God in the Persons of the sacred Trinity. God alone is to be worshipped; God the Father, God the Son, God the Holy Spirit, being equally God, are to be worshipped. I don't think any professing Christian would deny this in creed, but true worship involves more than just a creedal affirmation of God's exclusiveness. Worship expresses itself in total devotion to the One affirmed to be the one true and living God. This chapter explores what it means to obey the greatest of all the commandments, to love the Lord with all the heart, soul, and might. Loving God is worshipping Him for all He is worth.

Chapter 3 is the corollary to identifying God as the sole object of worship; He is the subject of worship as well. If worship is all about the Triune God, then God must be the topic of worship. God's august person, attractive perfections, and awesome works sum up the biblically restricted themes for worship. Worshipping God is worshipping about Him. Faithfully following this waypoint excludes the man-centered focus that characterizes so much of what takes place in both contemporary feel-good-about-yourself services and traditional get-yourself-right services. I'm not opposed to feeling good or doing right, but we're talking about worship.

Chapters 4 and 5 address the mechanics of biblical worship, how it is to be conducted. Chapter 4 sums up the liturgy or components of biblical worship. The Bible does not provide an order of service, but it does reveal the essential elements that constitute a divinely ordered service. The essential elements include the reading of the Scripture, prayer, preaching, and singing. These essential elements are identified both by express commands and explicit examples in the Scripture. None of these are solo acts; speakers imply hearers. Again I emphasize that worship is not a spectator activity; all present must be engaged. That's one reason biblical worship does not include drama or concerts. There is nothing amusing about worship. Chapter 5 continues the how to worship theme by considering the aids that God has given His people to help them worship. God made the Sabbath for our benefit and gave it to us for our spiritual welfare and enjoyment. By resting from sin's curse and thus having undistracted time to remember God's redemption, man could devote himself completely to the Lord in praise and thanksgiving. Unhindered and concentrated worship takes time, and God gave man time to do it. For the church, Christ ordained baptism and the Lord's Supper as visual words of grace and redemption. They are sensible signs to declare gospel truths and, when observed in faith, they make worship easy. It is a terrible tragedy that these aids to worship are so often reduced to perfunctory additions or insertions to whatever else is happening in a service. I would recommend designating special services devoted solely to baptism or celebration of the Lord's Supper. We should take full advantage of the helps the Lord has given.

The final two chapters consider biblical examples and patterns of worship. It always helps to see something done. Not only does the Bible issue imperatives and give instructions regarding worship, but it also shows that worship can occur just as God wants. Chapter 6 surveys and expounds some classic examples: the Tabernacle, the seraphim, and John's experience on Patmos. If we can learn to follow these models, God will be pleased with our worship. Each example we looked at was God-centered and Christ-filled. Chapter 7 considers the divinely inspired handbook of worship, the Psalms. The inspired songs illustrate what praising and praying look like and provide a paradigm of principles that define the content and techniques for worship. If there is such a thing as a worship manual, the Book of Psalms is it. It would be possible to learn just about everything we need to know about worshipping from the Psalms alone.

The bottom line is that the Bible can bring peace to the worship wars if we will think through what it says and go where it leads us. I have sought in this book simply to mark some key considerations concerning where the Bible is leading us in worship. I've taken the title for this book from the closing words of Psalm 29:2: "Give unto the Lord the glory due unto his name: worship the Lord in the beauty of holiness." The two imperatives in this verse encapsulate the whole argument of the book by linking the logic and the manner of worship. Logically, we are to worship the Lord because He deserves it. His infinite worth is the mandate for worship (the glory due His name). Practically, we are to worship by bowing down in the beauty of holiness. To worship in holy beauty requires a behavior and demeanor distinct from worldly behavior and practices. The place and exercise of worship must be uniquely special. Introducing worldly elements into worship in order to attract worshippers defies what worship is all about. May God give us all the courage and resolve to let the Bible be our guide and not to be afraid to obey it, regardless of how out of sync it may put us either with contemporary or with traditional perversions of worship.

It was my prayer at the beginning of this project that the Holy Spirit would help us see how big God is and how small we are and to worship Him accordingly. If God has in any way answered that prayer, I give my humble thanks.

APPENDIX 1

THE MESSAGE OF MALACHI: AN ANALYSIS OF DEAD RELIGION[1]

By proclaiming the glorious prospects of the Messianic Age, Haggai and Zechariah inspired the discouraged returnees from Babylon to be diligent in their service to the Lord and to complete the reconstruction of the fallen temple. Although the nation was still under foreign domination, Jerusalem lay in ruins, and David's throne was empty, the prophetic message of peace and prosperity and the promise of Divine presence was enough to encourage the people for the task at hand. The temple was soon completed. The only thing missing was the experience of the greater glory that Haggai predicted would fill the second temple. But almost a hundred years passed without the realization of the expected promises. The nation remained subject to the same foreign power, and there was no immediate prospect for a king on David's throne. The people were not experiencing the blessings that they assumed God had promised and that they thought they most certainly deserved. Believing that they had done everything God had demanded, they grew increasingly impatient with the divine delays. Because God did not act according to their agenda or schedule, they began to doubt His word and His ability to keep His promise. It is not unusual for God's people to struggle as they seek resolution to the tension between what they believe and what they experience. The Scripture records many examples of this faith/experience conflict as do our personal diaries. But the people to whom Malachi unburdened himself were guilty of more than the normal struggles of faith. These people had developed serious misconceptions of God and of the nature of true, spiritual worship. God was someone who owed them things, and religion was a means of manipulating God for a better life.

God raised up Malachi to put things in the right perspective. In an artful, unrelenting, irrefutable dialectic, Malachi exposed the worthless religion and arrogant self-perspective of these people who thought more of themselves than of God. In his inspired theodicy, the prophet made it unmistakably clear that the blame for any lack of blessing rested on their spiritual deadness and not on God's unfaithfulness. Although written over twenty-four hundred years ago, Malachi's message is tragically relevant for today. Although the mechanics of worship may be different, the same mercantile, self-focused religion lives on. A perfunctory, dead, external, formalistic religion has never satisfied God. Malachi's analysis of the dead religion of his day is a casebook for God's modern-day messengers who must expose the same kind of spiritual death, proclaim the same warning, and prescribe the same remedy.

THE AUTOPSY OF DEAD RELIGION

Malachi's dialectic style of disputation is obvious and requires no comment here except to acknowledge the prophet's skillful use of it to advance the logic of his argument.[2] With a series of six cutting propositions, Malachi penetrated to the core issues that marked Israel's dead worship. His procedure was impeccable. He made the proposition, and then in answer to the predictable denial, he gave irrefutable evidence of the truth of the proposition. Although his procedure betrays the logic of the lawyer, the subject of his analysis (dead religion) hints at the work of a pathologist performing an autopsy. The purpose of an autopsy is to discover the cause of death by examining the corpse for signs of decay and malfunction. Often discovering the cause of death in one person leads to preserving of life in many others. As a theological pathologist, Malachi meticulously examines, exposes, and identifies the causes and signs of dead religion and spiritual decay. So putting this twist on Malachi's disputation, I want to give a synopsis of his autopsy report of dead religion. In keeping with the seminar topic of worship, it is my purpose to avoid technical issues of Hebrew exegesis and to focus on the relevant overall message.

Incision One: Insensitivity to Grace

The first incision revealed insensitivity to grace. Malachi's first pronouncement was a simple, yet profound declaration of divine love: "I have loved you, saith the Lord" (1:2). The first and fundamental evidence of spiritual trouble was the denial of that love: "Wherein hast thou loved us?" (1:2). Like a selfish child that cries "nobody loves me" when he does not get his own way, Israel had interpreted their circumstances as evidence that God did not love them. Because they were not experiencing the material blessing they thought they deserved, they denied the reality of the freely declared love of God. Malachi proved God's love in terms of unmerited election and unfailing preservation (1:2-5). God's loving Jacob and hating Esau were not petty emotional displays earned by the behavior of Jacob and the misbehavior of Esau or their descendants. Rather, loving and hating were issues of deliberate divine choice. God accepted Jacob and rejected

Esau. No reason for the choice of Jacob is given; the choice is explicable only in terms of grace. Whereas Esau received what he deserved, Jacob did not. For Israel to doubt God's love in the light of election and preservation was the height of ingratitude. Sensitivity to grace, on the other hand, always fosters thanksgiving and the realization that God's love is not to be measured by things but by the reality of a personal, intimate relationship with the Lord Himself. Notwithstanding our theological differences on the mechanics of divine election and grace, religion will thrive and live well when and if God's people are overwhelmed with the amazing and wondrous grace of God.

Incision Two: Insincere Worship

The second incision revealed insincere worship. In 1:6-7 Malachi made two general accusations against the priests: that they were despising God's name and that they were polluting the bread on the altar. They, of course, denied the charges, and then Malachi proved the accusation and issued a stern warning. Although Malachi directed the charges against the priests, the application extended to the nation as a whole since priests, by definition, were the representatives of the people. As a rule, the spiritual state of the laity will not be better than that of the clergy (cf. Hosea 4:9). Although the priests were ordained to teach God's law by word and by example (2:6-7), they seemed more concerned with pleasing the people than with pleasing God. They fostered an easy, insincere religion that was full of ritual and empty of spirit and truth. Malachi's twofold accusation suggests two distinctives of insincere worship.

First, insincere worship reveals irreverence toward God. True, spiritual worship is theocentric, evincing a proper knowledge and acknowledgment of God. In verses 6 and 14, the Lord of Hosts identified Himself as a father, a master, and a great King, whose name is worthy of fear. Each of these titles, including the Lord of Hosts, focuses on God's eminent position, authority, honor, and power. Such a God deserves all the reverence, respect, and awe that the creature can give, and all that the creature can possibly give is infinitely insufficient to esteem Him for all His infinite worth. Notwithstanding the Lord's infinite greatness and innate honor, they despised His name. The word despise means to think lightly of or to make light of. It is a significant contrast to the word *honor*, which involves the idea of weight or heaviness. Whereas God deserved to be regarded as heavy, they regarded Him as light. A light regard for God is never conducive to spiritual worship. Significantly, the key words for worship in both the Old and New Testaments suggest the idea of bowing down before the Lord. True worship cannot exist until man sees himself as little and God as big. Malachi's generation was more concerned with self-issues than with God's glory. They regarded their own concerns to be more weighty than the Lord, and that affected their religious behavior. Tragically, many modern church services display the same light regard for God. Worship services have given way to entertainment hours and testimony times drawing attention to man's sacrificial accomplishments for God rather than directing hearts to bow before the holy Person of the Lord.

Second, insincere worship expresses itself in empty ritual: a form of worship without the reality of truly seeking the Lord. Malachi accused the priests of offering polluted bread on the altar (1:7). The word *pollute* designates something that is ceremonially impure; it is unfit for worship. It may be something acceptable in other contexts, but it is inappropriate for the place of worship. They were guilty of regarding the holy place as a common place. Any offering was good enough for God, even if it was blind, sick, lame, or mauled (1:7-13). Carelessly, thoughtlessly, and heartlessly, they went through the motions of worship, assuming God would be satisfied with whatever trinket they threw His way. The whole routine had become a nuisance (1:13). The Lord made it clear

that He was not satisfied and would not accept their offerings
(1:13). He cursed any who would treat Him with such contempt
(1:14). He particularly held the priests responsible, cursing them
for disobedience (2:1-2), rebuking their descendents (2:3), and
bringing them to shame (2:3, 9).

The situation in modern Christianity is no better. On the
one hand, many are bringing unfit and inappropriate things
into the place of worship. "Seeker-sensitive" services are flexibly
designed to eliminate religious shock by infusing cultural norms
with a bit of gospel. Worship as entertainment prevails over
worship as service rendered to God. The whole controversy
about worship style has degenerated into arguments based on
personal preferences rather than on scriptural principles. On
the other hand, many regard worship as mere duty, a necessary
nuisance. With trinkets of church attendance and formalistic
and empty routine, they salve the conscience believing that
God will be satisfied with whatever takes place inside church
walls. Dead religion exists in churches where people sway and
run the aisles as easily as in churches that follow a strict liturgy.
Malachi's message sounds the warning clearly that God will
never be satisfied with thoughtless, heartless, religion regardless
of the form it takes, whether traditional or contemporary.

Incision Three: Instability of Families

The third incision revealed unfaithfulness in human
relationships (2:10-16). Loose worship and loose social morality
always go together; carelessness about God affects everything.
In 2:10-13 the prophet accused the people of corrupting the
covenant with God by intermarrying with the heathen. Men
had broken faith with their first wives, violating their marriage
contracts (2:14). Malachi showed how sinful this behavior was
in three ways. First, he reminded them that when they divorced
their wives, they sinned against God. God had witnessed their

covenant vows, and He expected them to fulfill them. Second, he told them that intermarriage with unbelievers was wrong because God had chosen Israel to be a separated people. They were repudiating God's purpose for them by behaving like the world. Third, he declared that God hated divorce. God had made woman to be the perfect complement for man, pairing them together and uniting them into one flesh. Divorce breaks the bond that God had sealed. It is not without significance that in Malachi's day as in ours the home was a battleground rather than heaven on earth (Deut. 11:21). The breakup of homes is irrefutable evidence of hearts that are not right with the Lord. The home is always the test of how real religion is.

Incision Four: Inaccurate Views of God

The fourth incision revealed misconceptions of God. Dead religion tends to define God based on sight rather than faith, on appearance rather than reality. The apparent prosperity of the wicked contrasted with the apparent adversity of the righteous caused the self-righteous to question the justice of God (2:17). Because they were not enjoying the prosperity they thought they deserved, they concluded that God was not fair and that He was more pleased with sinners than saints. Dead, formal religion breeds a security and carnal confidence that will sooner find fault with God than with self. In a bold anthropopathism, God charged the nation with wearying Him with their words. They had made Him sick and tired by their constant complaining and selfish perspectives. Faith knows that the prosperity of the wicked is only apparent and temporary. It is foolish, therefore, to envy the wicked because they are under God's certain wrath and condemnation. Faith knows that this life, even at its worst, is the best it will ever be for the ungodly and that this life, even at its best, is the worst it will ever be for the godly.

Incision Five: Insufficient Giving

The fifth incision revealed the failure to give to God the required tithes and offerings (3:7-12). This act of robbery was another evidence of dead, heartless religion. The tithe demonstrated recognition of God for His gracious supply of the bounty of life and thanksgiving for His goodness (cf. Lev. 27:30). Significantly, when the people had a heart for God, giving was abundant and natural (cf. Exodus 35:21, 29). But now as one more evidence of their spiritual malady, they withheld offerings from God and forfeited great blessings. Giving to God is not a bargaining device or an investment token to get more from God; it is, rather, an expression of the enjoyment of the Lord Himself. The requirement for tithes and offerings certainly refers to the liberal giving of material possessions, but it extends in principle to giving spiritual things as well. The more believers find satisfaction in the Person of God rather than in possessions, the more freely they will give themselves and all they have to the Lord. Dead religion selfishly hordes; living religion selflessly gives.

Incision Six: Improper Motives for Service

The final incision in Malachi's autopsy of dead religion exposed improper motives. In 3:13 the Lord accused the people of stout words. The word *stout* means hard, severe, or sharp. Their impudent, presumptuous words had expressed violence toward God. In 3:14 the Lord identified precisely what the stout words were: "It is vain to serve God and what profit is it that we have kept his ordinance." This suggests that their motive for serving God was personal gain–religion for profit. Calling service to God vain means that they saw it as useless, insubstantial, without value. That obedience was without profit means that they received no increase. The word *profit* is a weaver's term used of a piece of cloth that has been cut. The imagery is suggestive even if anachronistic. They had served the Lord, and they wanted their cut. When they saw no profit, they saw no reason for serving any more. To serve God for profit is a faithless act, reflecting a materialistic spirit. Ironically, when blessing is defined in terms of material things that in turn become the goal of devotion and service, real blessing and reward from God will never be recognized. How often this same deadness characterizes today's church. Fulltime Christian service is often rejected because it does not pay. Those in such fulltime service often moan over their sacrifice rather than rejoicing in their privilege. Some give to the Lord as if making an investment; they give to get. Wrong motives always kill good religion.

THE ANSWER TO DEAD RELIGION

I can only offer some cursory observations to far-reaching truths. According to Malachi, God's answer to dead religion was the coming Day of the Lord. In 3:2 the prophet asked, "Who may abide the day of his coming?" In 4:1 he described the coming day as a time of burning in which neither root nor branch would survive. Beginning with Obadiah, the first of the writing prophets, until this final Old Testament prophet, the announcement of the Day of the Lord, in part, delineated God's ultimate answer to sin. By simple definition, the Day of the Lord is the period in which God directly interrupts the affairs of time for either the judgment of the wicked or the blessing of the righteous. The Day of the Lord is when eternity breaks into time. Although there have been multiple Days in which God has so intervened, there is yet one final, eschatological day that is certain to come and of which all the preceding days are in some way typical. Judgment, restoration, Messiah, and Millennial blessing are all common themes developed within the context of the Day of the Lord.

Although Malachi touches most of these common themes, at the heart of his message is the Messiah. In typical prophetic fashion, he fuses elements of the first and second advents of Christ. It was not his purpose to supply data for a strict eschatological chronology, but rather to focus on the implications of Christ's coming—whether His first or second. For his argument, the certain *fact* of Messiah's coming was more crucial than the when. Indeed, the undefined *when* aided in the forceful application of the fact.

Part of Malachi's purpose was to correct some tragic misunderstandings about Christ and His kingdom that characterized the thinking of his generation. Many had a Messianic hope, but the Messiah of their anticipation was not the Christ of God; they were in for a surprise. Malachi's corrective echoed that of Amos, who three centuries earlier pronounced a woe on those who desired the Day of the Lord and who declared it to be a day of darkness rather than the light they anticipated (Amos 5:18-20). Practitioners of dead religion tend to assume that God is on their side and that He will destroy their enemies, when in reality they themselves stand in jeopardy of judgment. Similarly, many today have notions of a Jesus, who in fact is another Jesus; they too will be surprised when the real Christ appears. True worship, whether in the old or new dispensations, depends on the proper understanding of Jesus Christ. Christianity has always been the one true religion.

Malachi makes some significant statements in identifying the real Christ of God. First, the coming Christ is God. This is both logically implicit and lexically explicit. Logically, 3:1 is the immediate answer to the final question of 2:17: "Where is the God of justice?" The Lord of Hosts basically declares that the God of justice is coming. The Lord of Hosts says, "I will send my messenger, and he will prepare the way before me." He follows that statement with "The Lord, whom ye seek, shall suddenly come to his temple, even the messenger of the covenant…behold, he shall come." The shift between the first and third person in the declaration of the Lord of Hosts hints at the mystery of the Godhead. On the one hand, the Lord of Hosts says that a messenger will prepare the way before me and then, on the other hand, speaks of the messenger of the covenant, who is the Lord, that he shall come. The coming One is both identified as, yet distinct from, the Lord of Hosts.

Lexically, the One coming to His own temple is the Lord. The articular form "the Lord" occurs only eight times in the Old Testament and refers uniquely to deity. Like the more common form of the word without the article it designates God as the master, owner, and controller of all. He cannot be manipulated or used. What a corrective to Israel's theology this was! With a bit of perspicacious sarcasm, the prophet indicated that the Lord whom they were fervently seeking and delighting in (3:1) was not God's Christ. Whereas they wanted a savior that they could manipulate for personal advantage and who would deliver them from their troubles, the real Christ was the sovereign Lord who rules, but is not ruled. Unless they were truly seeking and hoping for the real Christ, the coming of the Lord would not be their deliverance, but their doom.

Another significant identification of the Messiah is that He is the Messenger of the Covenant. The term *messenger* designates one who is sent on a mission with a particular work and objective to accomplish. Its association with covenant links His business to the whole redemptive plan of God. Whether speaking in general terms of old and new covenants or in specific terms of the covenants with Abraham, Moses, or David, at the heart of each covenant institution is the message of God's salvific purpose in the one person of His Son. Christ is God's promise of grace.

Given the misconceptions of the Messiah in Malachi's day, the prophet focuses on the consequences of the wrong notions about Christ. The Messenger that is going to come suddenly and unexpectedly to His temple comes on a mission of cleansing and judgment. Interestingly, the word translated "suddenly" occurs about twenty-five times, usually in a context of disaster or judgment–another hint that the Messiah of their anticipation was not the real Christ. The images of fire and soap illustrate an aspect of the Messiah's work of judgment. As fire separates dross from the metal and as soap separates dirt from clothes, so the Messiah will do a cleansing and purifying work. In part this is the gracious solution to the questions of 3:2. Only those with clean hands and pure hearts can abide the day of His coming and stand when He appears. The beauty and grace of the gospel is that Christ provides the necessary cleansing. But there is a judgment work that will be executed on the dirt and dross. 3:5 makes it clear that judgment is well earned and deserved. The prophet lists seven sins that are clear violations of God's law, the standard of judgment. The closing accusation in the verse is that they do not fear the Lord. That the Scripture so often links fearing God with knowing God suggests the ultimate, judgment-deserving sin is ignorance of God. Judgment on such sinners is the execution of justice. In their self-righteousness, they asked, "Where is the God of justice?" Woe to those who desire justice without Christ.

Another important part of Malachi's answer to dead religion is the attention given to Messiah's antecedent: a forerunner with an Elijah-type ministry (3:1; 4:5-6). This has significance in terms of both advents of Christ. Although Malachi does not specifically identify this special messenger, the Gospels affirm that John the Baptist fulfilled this preparatory ministry for Christ's first advent. Similarly, Revelation 11 reveals two yet unidentifiable witnesses who during the Tribulation will in the spirit and power of Elijah and Moses preach the gospel of repentance before Christ's glorious second coming. Such ministry is always a necessary prerequisite for preparing people to be ready for the coming of the Lord.

The immutability of the Lord is the guarantee that every aspect of the covenant will be fulfilled (3:6). God had a purpose for the sons of Jacob that the sins of Jacob's sons in the fifth century BC could not frustrate. Psalm 89, the great commentary on the Davidic covenant, echoes the same theme of divine pledge (verses 28-29, 34). In verse 34, the Lord declares that He will not alter the thing that is gone out of His lips. The word *alter* is the same word used in Malachi 3:6 to declare that God will not change. Both texts anticipate the New Testament affirmation: "For all the promises of God in him are yea, and Amen" (2 Corinthians 1:20). There is but one unchangeable answer to dead religion: the Lord Jesus Christ.

ANTITHESIS TO DEAD RELIGION

Again, I can only be suggestive, but simply stated, the antithesis to dead religion is living religion. Although most of Malachi's message exposes deadness, he does feature aspects of living religion that stand in marked contrast to the prevalent spirit of his day. His description of living religion concerns both how true worshippers see the Lord and how the Lord sees them. This contrast is a fitting conclusion and suggests the necessary corrective to all guilty of dead religion.

First, true worshippers fear the Lord (3:16). Fearing God is knowing God and living with constant awareness of Him. It includes awe, worship, respect, and the dread of displeasing the Lord. Those who truly fear the Lord recognize Him as an essential factor of life, and they live with reference to Him. Fearing God is the foundation for true worship and the motivating directive for ethics. Second, meditation characterizes living religion. Those who feared the Lord thought upon His name (3:16). The word for think means to meditate, to regard, to take inventory. This is more than a casual, routine, thoughtless devotion time; it is a conscious reckoning that God and all He is (i.e. the name) is the great asset and real wealth of life. True worship–whether private or public–is thinking time. Thinking time is never wasted time. Finally, God's discerning between those who serve Him and those who do not (3:18) identifies living religion as an active religion. Serving is the reverse side of meditation. To meditate without service is religious daydreaming; to serve without meditation is heartless busywork. Meditation gives motive to service; service gives expression to meditation. Living religion invades all the routines of life.

The Lord always knows those who belong to Him, and He is the rewarder of all who truly seek Him. Three special truths stand out that reveal God's genuine concern for His people. First, He carefully attends to them. The prophet declared that "the Lord hearkened, and heard it, and a book of remembrance was written before him" (3:16). God has a keen interest in His own, and He is not unmindful of those who are mindful of Him. He will always be found of those who seek Him (cf. 1 Chronicles 28:9). Second, He claims His people as prized possessions (3:17). The word jewels designates a special, royal treasure. It highlights the protected and privileged position of believers before the Lord. Finally, He treats His people as family (3:17). As members of God's family, true worshippers enjoy all the benefits of protection and provision that flow from the Heavenly Father.

The difference between dead religion and living religion is literally a matter of life and death. Not only are the contrasts evident now, but the consequences are eternal. "All that do wickedly shall be stubble...but unto you that fear my name shall the Sun of righteousness arise with healing in his wings" (4:1-2). May Malachi's analysis of dead religion direct all who read it to a vital relationship with the Lord. May it, indeed, generate a genuine seeking and delight in the Messenger of the Covenant, who came once and who is coming again.

SOME THOUGHTS ON WOMEN IN THE CHURCH

Two specific texts (1 Corinthians 14:34 and 1 Timothy 2:11-12) seemingly deny women any right to public participation in the church, thus restricting them to passive spectators. Two important hermeneutical principles must operate when interpreting these texts. (1) God never contradicts Himself–His Word is always consistent. Therefore, specific, restrictive texts must be interpreted not only in their immediate context but also in light of the larger context of the whole of Scripture. (2) God reveals and establishes His truth both by precept and examples. Applying these principles identifies both what is permitted and what is prohibited for women in the place of public worship.

WHAT IS PERMITTED

It is clear that women played an active and important role in the New Testament church. Paul includes several women in his greetings to the church in Rome and comments on their important service (Romans 16:1, 3, 6, 7, 13, 15). In Philippians 4:3, the apostle mentions women who labored with him in the gospel, apparently in the same capacity as Clement.

First Corinthians 11 is a key passage that regulates the woman's role in the place of public worship particularly. It is important to note that a role Paul regulates in one text he would not prohibit in another–that would constitute a contradiction which would be incongruous with the very nature of Scripture. In this text, Paul defines the head-covering requirement that gives women the right to pray and to prophesy. Although praying can be either private or public, prophesying serves no private function–it is always a public operation. This would suggest the reference would be to public praying as well. The word "prophesy" is a general term, having a wide and elastic range of usage. Since general words are capable of referring to any or all of the elements in their semantic range, individual contexts determine how restrictive or inclusive the word is to be understood. The New Testament sense of this word "prophesy" includes the declarative act of preaching as well as praising and giving of thanks by declaring or testifying concerning what God has done. In this passage, Paul does not restrict the sense of the word, and it would be arbitrary to limit the sense of the word only to musical praise when applied to women. So, whatever disagreement may exist concerning the nature and relevance of the head-covering restriction, the passage is clear that women who submit to the head-covering restriction can, indeed, participate in public praying and prophesying.

The Scripture provides significant examples of women engaged in prophetic activity. Miriam was a prophetess who led the women in joining the worship of the entire congregation in celebration of the Exodus (Exodus 15:20-21). Deborah was a prophetess who gave the Lord's word to direct deliverance from the Canaanites and composed an inspired song of praise declaring the Lord's work (Judges 4-5). Although her ministry is not detailed, Isaiah's wife is called a prophetess (Isaiah 8:3). Huldah was a prophetess who played a major role in declaring the Lord's word to Josiah (2 Chronicles 34:21-28). While it may be argued that God used Deborah only because there were no qualified men, that would hardly be the case for the others who ministered at times when God-called men were also active (Moses, Isaiah, Zephaniah, Jeremiah).

If in the Old Testament dispensation, women had a function in public ministry, it follows that the New Testament dispensation would see an increase rather than a squelching of that female participation. This is, in fact, part of Joel's Pentecost prophecy (Joel 2:28-29). Joel predicted the day in which there would be a massive effusion of spiritual power that would come on all flesh, enabling both genders and all ages to prophesy. Acts 2 records the amazing fulfillment of the prophecy when the Holy Spirit empowered and gave utterance to all who had gathered in the upper room. Acts 21:9 specifically notes the prophetic activity of Philip's four daughters. Sandwiched between a reference to Philip's evangelistic efforts and Agabus' prophetic word to Paul, it is not likely that this prophetic ministry was limited to providing special music at their father's evangelistic campaigns. Therefore, it seems clear that both by precept and significant example the Scripture permits women a right and role in public worship and ministry.

WHAT IS PROHIBITED

Suffice it to say that the New Testament limits the leadership of the organized church to men. God has ordained men to be elders who have the responsibility to govern and to teach the church and has given men to be deacons to aid the elders in the church's operation. So for women to assume the occupation of pastor or any official church office would go beyond their right.

It remains to consider the two restrictive texts. First Corinthians 14:34-35 is in the immediate context in which Paul demands orderly conduct in public worship (vv. 29-40). It would appear that the injunction for women to keep silence addresses a particular violation of order in the Corinthian assembly in which women were disturbing the meeting by asking questions or disputing over what had been preached. Rather than asserting themselves publicly, they were to ask their husbands privately about the content of the prophecies, discernment, etc. In public worship, women are not to be forward but to give evidence of their submissiveness that is part of the divine order.

The kind of silence Paul has in mind is specifically defined by the statement, "they are commanded to be under obedience, as also saith the law." Paul's use of "law" in this context invites consideration of the whole Old Testament revelation (see 14:21 where he refers to Isaiah as law). Nowhere does the Old Testament command women to be silent but rather–as illustrated above–gives witness to those most vocal in service to God. Genesis, however, does record that by ordinance of creation God ordained a hierarchical relationship between man and woman. Man was first created, and then woman as his necessary complement and opposite. The roles and functions of both man and woman were set from the beginning. The whole history of humanity flows from Adam's headship over both Eve and the race that followed. It is important to emphasize that this divinely established subordination of woman to man existed from the original creation, was not the consequence of the curse, and was not, therefore, reversed by redemption. Tragically, sin corrupted and perverted the relationship as previewed in Genesis 3:16. The gospel can heal the hurts of those perversions, but it does not eradicate a relationship established for pre-fallen humanity. This "creation" law is precisely what Paul argues in 1 Corinthians 11 where he defines the proper guidelines and decorum for women's participation in public worship. So what Paul prohibits in this context of 1 Corinthians 14 corresponds to what God has already made clear: it is women's submissiveness and not their absolute silence that is according to law. The problem was not that the Corinthian women were talking in public worship, but they were doing something in what they were saying that violated the command for submissiveness. The rule against speaking cannot be absolute given what the Scripture teaches and illustrates elsewhere in both the Old and New Testaments, but it does prohibit an assertive participation that would either disrupt the service or violate the functional subordination that God has ordered for women. That is the law.

In 1 Timothy 2:8 Paul instructs men when praying to do so without wrath and doubting and then in verse 9 continues the praying instructions to women by adding that they should do so in modesty, humility, and self-control. He then gives instructions not on how they are to pray but on how they are to learn and teach. That she is to learn in silence in subjection parallels precisely the caveat in 1 Corinthians 14. The silence pertains to maintaining quiet and peaceful order in the assembly and does not forbid an active participation in her scripturally legitimate praying or prophesying. Properly understanding Paul's prohibition against a woman teaching requires attention to the tense of the infinitive "to teach." It is a present tense, which suggests that Paul forbids women assuming the occupation of teacher, which ministry is reserved for the pastor/elder. This is substantiated by the next infinitive, which prohibits her exercising dominion over men. By law of Greek grammar, the second infinitive defines, explains, or restricts the significance of the first. In other words, Paul says that what he means by a woman not teaching is that she must not have a position that exercises dominion over men. There is a kind of teaching in the church that is based on a God-given authority for leadership, and therefore, would exclude participation by women. God-called and God-equipped teachers who have official authority in doctrinal interpretation and instruction are gifts to the church (1 Corinthians 12:28-29 and Ephesians 4:11) and are limited to men. Consequently, the New Testament does not sanction women pastors or elders. Since the Scripture excludes women from having an official teaching office, the session of the church would not have the authority to permit or to ask women to fulfill the office or teaching ministry of an elder. So a woman's keeping silence is equivalent to being in subjection to the God-ordained leadership, not being mute in regard to permissible praying or prophesying.

There is indeed a divinely ordered hierarchy between men and women that must be maintained and evidenced within the church. The Scripture specifically defines the respective roles and regulates the behavior of both male and female in the place of public worship. A woman's submission to the authority placed over her and her obedience to the biblical prescription for evidencing that submission frees her to open her mouth in prayer and in testimony to the word and work of the Lord–particularly when she is so instructed to do by those in authority in the church.

APPENDIX 3

THOUGHTS ON HEAD COVERING FOR PUBLIC WORSHIP: AN EXPOSITION OF 1 CORINTHIANS 11:2-16

The Word of God is the only rule for faith and practice. Christian conduct must be the reflection of biblical standards rather than expedient conformity to changing style or habit. This principle is applicable to every area of Christian life, not the least of which is worship. *The Westminster Confession of Faith* makes a significant statement regarding religious worship: "The acceptable way of worshipping the true God is instituted by himself, and so limited by his own revealed will, that he may not be worshipped according to the imaginations and devices of men" (21.1). First Corinthians 11 establishes some of the divinely revealed guidelines of acceptable worship. In this chapter, the apostle Paul deals with two essential aspects of public worship: head covering for women and proper observance of the Lord's Supper. Unfortunately, the regulations concerning head covering have either been misinterpreted or through expediency relegated to the sphere of local Corinthian custom which has no applicability to modern, American Christianity. It is my position that the shifting customs of society do not influence or abrogate the imperatives of Scripture. Therefore, the mandate of 1 Corinthians 11 that women must worship with covered heads is as binding today as it was in the first-century church.

THE AUTHORITY OF THE REGULATION (vv. 2, 16)

Paul begins by praising the Corinthian Christians for keeping the ordinances that he had delivered to them. Although the word "ordinance" may have the idea of tradition, it does not suggest that the requirements were of human origin or imagination. Indeed, these traditions delivered by the apostle constituted the revealed Word of God. The word designates that which was given to the apostle, who had the duty and authority to convey the received message to the people. Consequently, the word identifies the following context as being divinely revealed truth. To assign the passage to an ancient local custom with no present application is suspicious exegesis. Paul's closing remark in verse 16 confirms the authority of the regulation. Paul is dogmatic; he will not tolerate contentiousness in regard to the matter of head covering. The apostle claims that the churches of God have no such custom. Although some expositors identify the "custom" as the contentiousness, it is more appropriate to associate the "custom" with the practice of head covering. The churches of God have no custom that permits Christian women to participate in public worship with uncovered heads; therefore, there is no room for contention or debate in the matter. It is significant that the apostle refers to the churches of God. The plurality of churches removes this from the sphere of localized custom.

To identify as custom what the Scripture explicitly says is not custom is untenable and dangerous. To ignore the authoritative imperative of God's Word is disobedience.

The Existence of an Hierarchy (v. 3)

There is an hierarchy in God's order. This hierarchy is the basis for Paul's instructions concerning the proper manner of worship. The imagery of the "head" represents the threefold hierarchy of man to Christ, woman to man, and Christ to God. The head is the governing organ; it is that to which all else is subordinate. The Headship of Christ is a frequent theme in the New Testament. In His anointed office Christ is the Mediator and Sovereign over all things (cf. Ephesians 1:22). While Christ is the head of every man, God is the head of Christ. Because Christ is the "very and eternal God, of one substance and equal with the Father" (*Westminster Confession of Faith*, 8.2), this is a subordination of function. The use of the title Christ is appropriate for as the Messiah, Christ was chosen and anointed to perform His unique function (cf. Isaiah 42:1). The subordination of function rather than of essence that exists between the Father and the Son aids in understanding man's headship over women. Similarly, although no essential inequality between man and woman exists, a subordination of role and of function does. In God's order, man has a position of authority over the woman. This is true not only in the marriage relationship but in the relationship everywhere. There is no doubt that the Gospel of Christ has done much to give the woman a position of honor. There is honor for both man and woman in their respective yet different roles. God expects this created difference to remain valid and obvious in the church.

THE IMPLICATIONS FOR WORSHIP (VV. 4-6)

The difference between man and woman must be reflected in public worship. The terms "praying" and "prophesying" are important in this context as one of public worship. The word for "pray" is perhaps the most general term for prayer and is appropriate for public prayer. Although prayer is not essentially public, prophesying serves no purpose apart from the public context. In Paul's contrast of prophecy and tongues, it is clear that prophesying serves both to edify the church (1 Corinthians 14:4) and evangelize the lost (1 Corinthians 14:24). Prophesying is more than predicting the future or preaching the Word in a ministerial capacity although these are important aspects of the word. If these ministerial operations were the only aspects of the word, women would have no legitimate right to participate, for they are to learn in silence and have no authority to teach men (1 Timothy 2:11, 12). In this context, however, the praying and prophesying are acceptable activities for women whose heads are covered. Part of public worship is the "singing of psalms with grace in the heart" (*Westminster Confession of Faith*, 21.5; Colossians 3:16; Ephesians 5:19). It is significant that this form of praise—that is part of public worship—is designated as prophesying (1 Chronicles 25:2, 3). Legitimate prophesying by women may not be restricted to praise (see Appendix 2), but it certainly includes this important element of worship.

If men exercise their right to worship with any covering upon their heads, they disgrace their head, Christ. Conversely, if women exercise their right to worship without a covering upon their heads, they disgrace their head, man. Any violation of God's established order is ultimately an affront against God Himself. Although the requirements for man and woman are stated with equal clarity and authority, they have not received equal obedience. Whereas few men would be so irreverent as to wear a hat during worship, many women demonstrate equal irreverence by worshipping with uncovered heads.

Head covering for women is distinctively Christian. In the Jewish community men were to pray with their heads covered. In the pagan Greek community, both men and women worshipped with uncovered heads. The new Christian practice established by the apostle was contrary to the customs of the first-century world. Conformity to custom was not an option that the apostle allowed for either the ancient or modern church. The uncovered head for men and the covered head for women became a symbol of the divinely established order in Christ. Symbols are designed to represent spiritual reality. Although the reality exists independently of the symbol, a willful rejection of the symbol represents rebellion against the reality.

Indeed, failure to comply with the requirement not only constitutes apparent rebellion against God's order, but it degrades the woman herself. If the woman participates in worship with uncovered head, she is one and the same with one who has been shaven. Paul uses two synonyms to describe what ought to be done to the one who dishonors her head. The word translated "shorn" implies the cutting short of hair with shears whereas the word "shaven" implies the use of a razor. There are two possible implications connected with this extreme cutting of the hair, both of which involve great shame for the woman. It may be the mark of prostitution. It has been suggested that shorn hair was the "scarlet letter" to identify publicly those who had been guilty of sexual impurity. That would be shame for the woman who professed faith in Christ. If this is the imagery, it was a shame no more severe than worshipping with the head uncovered. On the other hand, it may represent the extreme behavior that is the logical extension of the act of improper worship. If the woman sets aside the head covering in worship and thus erases the symbol of her subordination to man, she might as well be consistent with her expressed attitude and shave herself, thus, completely removing what Paul identifies as her glory (v. 15). For woman to abandon her God-given role and usurp the authority and function of man is to leave a position of honor and to bring shame upon herself. To avoid the shameful implications the woman ought to have her head covered.

ARGUMENTS FOR OBEDIENCE (VV. 7-15)

In order to substantiate his claim of woman's subordination and his demand for the appropriate symbol in public worship, the apostle argues from two facts–creation and nature. The difference between man and woman is by virtue of creation. Man has the duty or obligation not to cover his head (a symbol of subjection) because he is the image and glory of God. Genesis 1:27 indicates that the woman also is in the image of God, but Paul adds that man is the glory of God and woman is the glory of man. This glory refers not to divine majesty but to that which brings honor. Man was the climax, the crown of God's creative work. He enjoyed a position of honor before God that woman did not share because there was no woman. The creation of woman was different and constituted woman as the glory or honor of man. It is a position that belongs exclusively to woman. Verses 8 and 9 give the reasons for the thesis of verse 7. Woman is the glory of man because her origin was from him and man's origin was independent of her. The purpose of woman's creation was directly connected to man (Genesis 1:18-22), but the purpose of his creation was independent of hers. That Paul concentrates on creation rather than marriage places the same responsibility on both single and married women.

Because of the woman's place dictated by creation, she ought to have power on her head (v. 10). The word translated "ought" both here and in verse 7 is a term expressing obligation or duty; consequently, there is no option or choice in the matter. The expression "power on her head" requires explanation. The word "power" has the idea of right or authority. It is the same word that describes the teaching of Christ in contrast to the scribes (Mark 1:22) and designates the right or privilege given to believers in Christ to become the children of God (John 1:12). By a figure of speech called metonymy, the word "authority" designates the symbol of that authority–the head covering. It is the head covering–the symbolic recognition of subordination–that gives to woman the right, authority, and privilege to approach God and participate in public worship. Recognition of proper place and function in God's order is essential to acceptable worship. Head covering is a symbol of that recognition.

The final statement of verse 10, "because of the angels," adds a sobering thought to the obligation. Because the word "angels" can have the simple idea of messenger, some have identified the angels here as the ministers of the church (cf. Revelation 2, 3). This adds little to the verse, and it is best to interpret the word in its usual sense as the supernatural created beings. On other occasions, Paul suggests that these angelic creatures are witnesses to man's activity (1 Corinthians 4:9; Ephesians 3:10; 1 Timothy 5:21). Job 38:7 indicates that the angels (sons of God) were witnesses of creation. This fits nicely with the context. Women are to worship with covered heads, not only for public testimony before men, but also as testimony to the angels who witnessed their creation and know their ordained position.

Verses 11 and 12 are a warning against drawing the wrong conclusion about woman's position of subordination. Galatians 3:28 teaches that in the sphere of faith all share the same benefits of salvation whether male or female. Although in the created order woman's position is subordinate, it is not an inferior or less dignified position. The relationship between man and woman is complementary. The word translated "without" in verse 11 means separate, apart, or by itself. It suggests the interdependency between male and female which is best served when men and women move within their proper spheres.

Both creation and natural generation support the thesis of interdependency. Both woman and man owe their existence to the other. The preposition "of" in verse 12 expresses the idea of source or origin. At creation woman came from man. The preposition "by" expresses the idea of mediation or agency. In natural generation man comes through the woman. Paul concludes that all this has its source in God.

Having established woman's subordinate role, Paul commands his readers to determine for themselves the appropriate application (v. 13). He asks whether it is a suitable or proper act for a woman to pray without the symbolic head covering. The word for praying is the same as in verses 4 and 5; therefore, the context is still dealing with public prayer. Although Paul does not explicitly answer the question with a yes or no, the answer is implicitly clear. It is not proper behavior for a woman to participate in public worship without the head covered.

Paul's final argument is from nature (vv. 14, 15). Nature itself teaches that there is an essential difference in appearance between man and woman. The word "nature" can have various senses in the New Testament: natural endowment, natural disposition, natural order, or species. The idea of natural disposition or characteristic is the appropriate sense here. Paul is essentially appealing to the general consciousness which recognizes that, according to the natural disposition of things, a man should not have "long hair." For a man to have this kind of hair is a shame to him. The word "shame" literally has the idea of "without honor." The position that rightly belongs to man is sacrificed if he has "long hair." A proper understanding of "long hair" is essential to the context. There are two words for hair: *thriks* which is hair as hair and *kome* which is fixed hair. *Kome* is the word used in this context. There is nothing in the word that dictates length. Rather, it represents that hair which is ornate, a hairdo. It is that coiffure belonging exclusively to the woman. It is contrary to nature for a man to have a distinctively feminine hairstyle. Whereas this *kome* is dishonorable for man, it is the glory of the woman. Even apart from the matter of precise length, there must be a clear difference between masculine and feminine hairstyle. To erase this distinction within the natural sphere is rebellion against God's ordinance established at creation. Just as the hairstyle in every day life identifies male and female, so in public worship the use of head covering symbolizes their respective positions before God. If the distinction is part of the natural sphere, it is fitting for the Christian woman, who acknowledges and enjoys her God-given position, to wear the divinely ordained symbol of that position in public worship.

The final statement of verse 15 has been the source of a common misinterpretation of the whole passage. Some interpreters claim that the only head covering intended is the hair. Therefore, if a woman worships with hair on her head, she is in perfect compliance with Paul's instruction. The context is clear that there must be a distinction between men and women in public worship in regard to their head. In verse 6 Paul explicitly says that women ought to be covered whereas in verse 7 he says "a man indeed ought not to cover his head." If it is proper for women to worship with hair on their heads, it is improper for men to worship with hair. It is preposterous to interpret the passage as saying that women must have hair, but men must be bald while worshipping. Although preposterous, it is the only logical conclusion if the head covering is simply the hair. God does not require the absurd. Rather than stating an absurdity, the final statement provides an additional reason for God's demand for head covering. This statement is part of Paul's illustration from nature and must be understood in that context. In every day life–apart from public worship–the *kome* has been given for a veil. The normal significance of the preposition "for" is substitution. Consequently, the *kome* has been given in the place of a covering. Proper understanding of this statement depends on the meaning of the word translated "covering." The word is *peribolaion,* a compound word whose component parts mean to put around. Although the word occurs only here with reference to the head, its transparent meaning of "wrap around" together with its usage elsewhere suggests the idea of a veil that would enclose the entire head. For instance, in Hebrews 1:12 the word refers to a vesture or mantle that would be wrapped around the body. Similar references to clothing occur in the Septuagint, the Greek translation of the Old Testament (cf. Ezekiel 16:13; 27:7). This veil, which would hide the face, would be a mark of degradation and humiliation. Even in the sphere of nature this mark of second-class citizenship has been replaced by the *kome,* the mark of glory. It is not this sign of degradation that Paul requires in worship. It is significant that this word does not occur in the specific instructions of verses 5 and 6 regarding the head covering for women. There the apostle does not specify a particular kind of covering. He demands simply that something be on the head during the period of public worship. That temporary covering, rather than being a mark of degradation, is the symbol of authority that entitles the woman the place of worship.

In simple terms the message is clear. If the hair is woman's glory, then the Christian woman ought to cover her glory in the place of public worship where attention is to be directed to God and away from self. No flesh should glory in His presence (1 Corinthians 1:29).

APPENDIX 4

SOME THOUGHTS ON THE MEANING OF MUSIC FROM A CHRISTIAN WORLD VIEW

By Paul Overly (D. Mus.)[*]

Music has meaning! Music wouldn't be my vocation if I didn't believe in its profound ability to communicate. A debate persists concerning whether music has the ability to communicate moral meaning universally—whether meaning is inherent in the music or comes from an outside reference point. While we know about this debate in the context of church music issues, it also occurs in other academic venues. Some researchers, already predisposed to reject absolutes, reject universal musical communication theoretically (although some will admit an inexplicable

---

[*] Dr. Overly is a friend on the music faculty of Bob Jones University. He has used some of my thoughts on worship in a class he teaches, so I thought it would be a good idea to use some of his here. He has offered this informal essay for which I'm grateful. His competency in music certainly exceeds mine.

consistency in the way music communicates without advocating absolutes). Other formalists dismiss cultural or other influences and look for meaning solely within the music itself. We do not and cannot know all of the details of musical communication. However, a biblically informed world view demands that music, while it may well be affected by outside influences, must have an ability inherent within itself to communicate across culture and class, and as Christians we must be careful to utilize it a way that glorifies God.

All music emanates from one source, our Creator God. The most basic elements of music are present in creation. Pitch and its organization into the harmonic series are naturally occurring acoustical phenomena. Time—and hence our concepts of rhythm—began with creation. The regular motion of the ocean waves and perhaps more importantly the beating of the human heart point to rhythm's natural existence. The singing of the birds, the roll of thunder, and the sound of the wind rustling through the treetops reveal to us divinely created tone colors and differing dynamic levels. It is then no wonder that when Job speaks of God's presence in creation, he tells us that the morning stars sang together.

Not only is music present in creation, but Scripture further reveals that God and not man is the author of music. The prophet Zephaniah informs us that our Lord joys over His people with singing—a thought too wonderful to comprehend. But it demands our recognition that music is not a human invention. The writer of Hebrews presents Christ singing the praises of the Father in the midst of His church. Although music is not a human invention, only humanity, created in God's image, is capable of creating music in this world. Birds sing, but only the song God gave them. Waves crash, but only when God allows them. But only man, with eternity set in his heart, can take the elements of music, compose, and thus communicate to fellow man.

How does this communication occur? Music is the most abstract of our art forms, and it contains a process of communication that we can never completely understand on this side of glory. Music's foundation in God necessitates the conclusion that it must communicate to all humanity created in His image. Scripture reveals clues as to how this musical communication across cultural boundaries occurs.

Scripture frequently reveals music as an expression of emotion. A cursory examination of the Psalter makes this clear, but many other passages reveal it as well. Laban claimed that he wanted to give Jacob a proper send-off filled with music and mirth. When the Lord provided water in the wilderness for the Israelites, they sang with joy, "Spring up, O well." Upon hearing of the death of Saul and Jonathan, David composed a lament. After thorough investigation, John Makujina in Measuring the Music postulates that music universally communicates our general emotions—we are unlikely to mistake a happy song for a sad song no matter the culture. Certainly the human response to rhythm and especially tempo seems universal. The beating of our heart provides a constant rhythm to our lives, and it quickens and slows as our emotions (or the level of excitement produced by those emotions) change.

Another clue to musical universality lies in the place music has assumed through thousands of years of human civilization. In genealogies at the beginning of Genesis, Moses, by mention of Jubal, reveals music as a vocation in the earliest of recorded civilization. Scripture reveals its use as a part of daily work (i.e. the vintage shouting of the treaders in Isaiah), as part of civic celebration (i.e. the Song of Miriam), as part of war (note the response of Joshua in Exodus 32 or Gideon's use of trumpets), and most importantly as part of religious worship. Secular historians, sociologists, and ethnomusicologists would point to those same uses (this list is not exhaustive) in pagan culture as well. One of my colleagues at Bob Jones University had the unique experience of hearing an unsaved, atheistic musicology professor lecture that every culture has a music specifically set apart for worship. If we all experience the same emotions in a basic societal structure, our music no matter the culture will have some level of universal communication.

A question then follows—why does music sound so different in different countries. There can be no doubt that the development of civilizations in relative isolation to each other (an isolation that had its genesis at Babel) led to distinctive organizations of the musical elements. The individual musical styles that developed communicated directly and in some cases almost exclusively to the populace for which they were intended. Hence we have today a diverse cornucopia of music representing many different cultures, and yet as I've already noted, music has some ability to communicate in a universal sense. One's culture certainly has a great effect on how one perceives music. In some ways it seems virtually impossible to separate music's formal meaning from the cultural filter through which it flows. For the Christian however, the filter of culture, while not superfluous, must remain secondary. Scripture alone must be our rule for faith and practice.

As the reader has probably by now figured out, one purpose of these musings is to give a brief commentary on the musical choices of Christians and evangelical Christian churches today. The prevailing wisdom of today proposes that we must take our society's popular, commercial music and wed it with lyrics that present a Christian worldview. The argument usually runs something like this. Music cannot communicate universally; it is amoral and has no inherent meaning. Therefore, we can utilize our culture's popular music and reassign its meaning and use for our own purportedly well-intended purposes. After all if lots of people like it (and we wouldn't call it popular if they didn't) then lots of people will come to our churches, be exposed to the gospel and be saved.

We've already seen that there are compelling biblical reasons to believe that music can communicate in some universal sense, and it certainly seems ludicrous to call something amoral that God must have created and called good. Therefore a brief assessment of our society's (or any society's) popular music is in order. Certainly anything that God created, man in his sinful nature can corrupt. Civilizations since the beginning of recorded history have developed within their cultures music that manifestly communicates sinfulness. This is clear both from Scripture and from even a cursory study of music history. Our modern culture is no different. It has created a popular music that communicates meaning totally antithetical to Christianity. If ever there was a universal cultural understanding of what this music means, it exists in the meaning of our pop culture's music. Read any popular magazine, read an article from a scholarly journal, notice how people react in Japan or Russia or the British Isles, or New York City or Pickens, South Carolina to "the music of this world." The performers, songwriters, producers, and consumers revel in the meaning of their music. Its meaning as assigned by our culture could not be clearer.

The meaning of this music, however, cannot be solely derived from culture. The formal elements themselves within the music of our popular culture define the music as well. The elements of pop music as noted by any reputable music text—its typically loud dynamic levels, distorted timbres (vocally and instrumentally), the overriding rhythmic elements—point to the fact that our culture's assessment of the music and the formal elements within the music are in close conformity the one with the other.

The question that now must be asked is whether a popular music's meaning can reasonably be reassigned by a segment of the culture for its own purpose. The CCM community labors mightily and shamelessly in this regard. They compare their artists to secular counterparts and their music to secular genres. In their thinking the music has no meaning that the text does not give it. This reasoning borders on absurd. Here in South Carolina the Confederate battle flag has become a racial flash point. The popular notions about the flag–even if those notions are historically unwarranted– would render it unlikely that by mere declaration the flag would become a symbol of racial unity.

The perception of current society will identify it as an emblem of oppression regardless of claims to the contrary. Musical meaning is much more powerful than a symbolic flag that lacks intrinsic meaning. Music that our worldly culture has already embraced as its own (and whose inherent elements unreservedly support the worldliness) cannot be biblically legitimized by a Christian subset claiming "it doesn't really mean all that." In the eyes of the world and most of the church, this "rock and roll Christianity" is an unqualified success. It can claim nearly a billion dollar industry, now largely owned by secular companies. Very large churches and smaller assemblies desperately seeking to attract people have centered their worship upon it, and it seems to work in building crowds. But what seems to work is not always what is right. We must look at success through a different paradigm. If this use of music cannot be validated by Scripture, then this movement is an unqualified spiritual disaster, one that must rejected by a people whose lives are guided by God's word.

In the final analysis, why does this discussion matter? The practice of contemporary worship has become so common in so many churches that it is hardly questioned. But there is reason not only for question but also for alarm. Although there is arguably room for disagreement on the particulars of musical communication, there are biblical principles that should factor into all Christian use of music. When I reflect on music's origin in creation and in our Creator, I must marvel at the gift with which I have been entrusted. I must endeavor to learn it thoroughly, to teach it carefully, and to perform it joyfully. If God joys over me with singing then my music must echo back His praise.

> So my song must swell the chorus
> While the angels' praises ring.
> I, a sinner saved and pardoned,
> Have more cause than they to sing.

- From *My Song*, a poem by Bob Jones, Jr.

CONTEMPORARY WORSHIP AND THE NEXT GENERATION OF FUNDAMENTALIST LEADERS

By Dr. David L. Burggraff[*]

INTRODUCTION

Worship is once again becoming a focus of discussion. Throughout Christian history, public worship has attracted attention, stimulated discussion, and even provoked contention.[1] The wrestling match today between college-age students and seminarians and their pastors is over contemporary worship styles

---

[*] Dr. Burggraff is former president of Calvary Theological Seminary in Lansdale, Pennsylvania, and now serves as vice president for spiritual formation and ministry development of Clearwater Christian College in Clearwater, Florida. I heard Dr. Burggraff read this paper at a conference and was greatly impressed with his insight, and he graciously granted permission to include it here. I include it here because it expresses the same concerns about worship from a Fundamental Baptist perspective. I think you will find it most instructive.

and music. But before we get into "how much contemporary is contemporary?" we would do well to heed Harold Best's advice on "contemporary":

> It does not take long in this culture of ours for something to become antique. Just go to a flea market, a swap meet, or even an antique shop and you will find things for sale labeled as collectible, desirable, or even nostalgic that, yes have issued from as nearby a time as the seventies or eighties. The nineties are surely next, and given the speed with which the techno-commercial side of culture assures quick obsolescence, oldies may not have to become gold to be sold. Contemporary worship is certainly here to stay and has fast become one of the forms of traditional worship and, in the sense just cited, an oldie. . . . In one sense, therefore, the question to the prospective churchgoer is "What brand of out-of-styleness do you prefer?" In another, it is "To what extent are you willing to change when leadership thinks it's time to change?" . . . The one remaining question then would be "Who decides on change, the leadership or the followership?"[2]

Why do we worship the way we do? Why is there such variety of worship styles among Christians? Who is correct? How has worship changed since New Testament times? What is Biblical and what is traditional? And, the focus of this session, how is contemporary worship impacting the next generation of fundamentalist leaders? This session is an attempt to discuss those questions, particularly the last question.

1.   MAJOR CATEGORICAL EXPRESSIONS OF WORSHIP

	FREEDOM	FRONTIER	FORMAL
Focus:	Spirit-centered	Bible-centered	God-centered (mystical)
	Feeling-oriented	Audio-oriented	Visual-oriented
Examples:	Charismatics, Pentecostals	Bible churches, Baptists Reformed, Methodists	Episcopalians, Lutherans, Catholics

Spontaneity (laxity)   Structure (liturgy)

←——————————————————————————→

2.   THERE IS A GROWING EMPHASIS ON THE RENEWAL OF WORSHIP

In the Believers' Church tradition (us, and those similar to us), proclamation from the Scriptures is the focal point of worship. However, the monotony and emptiness of the worship service in a great many churches today has contributed to discussions dealing with changing how worship should be done.

But some of the changes may actually be leading to the denigration of worship. First, there is a revival of interest in the Anglican and Catholic liturgy. Sometimes this has been expressed in a desire to make the Eucharist or "Lord's Supper" the focal point of worship. The question which is disturbing some today is whether the effort to reach back into a liturgical heritage in order to strengthen our worship may bring with it the medieval theology which was expressed in that liturgy. Second, for the modern worshipper, worship is often defined exclusively in terms of the individual's experience. Worship, then, is not about adoring God but about being nourished with religious feelings, so much so that the worshiper has become the object of worship.[3] Third, there's the dumbing-down effect seen in public education and culture in general, along with 150 years of revivalism that– armed with songs geared to working up the masses–approaches church solely as an evangelistic crusade, and the drive to compete with MTV and be "relevant," thereby pleasing the tastes of the congregation.[4] All of this together erects almost insurmountable barriers we must overcome if we are to truly worship the Lord.

3.   TRADITIONAL NORTH AMERICAN EXPRESSIONS OF WORSHIP

During the first sixty years of the twentieth century, traditional Protestant worship settled into eight major traditions:[5]

Liturgical tradition — emphasis on beauty

Reformed tradition — emphasis on the centrality of the Word

Anabaptist tradition — concern for community and discipleship during worship

Restorationist tradition — commitment to weekly Communion

Revivalist tradition (Baptist, Methodist, evangelicals) - concern to move toward the invitation and call sinners to repentance

Quaker tradition — call to silence and waiting for God to speak

Holiness tradition — emphasis on the need to break through and achieve sanctification in worship

African-American tradition — emphasis on soul worship

Robert Webber opines that three things characterize these traditions.

> First, for the most part they are tied into a print form of communication. . . . Each tradition has a prayer book, a hymnbook, or bulletins; is primarily verbal; and is given to one-way communication. Second, traditional worship is predictable. For example, a Baptist living on the East Coast in the fifties will experience the same form and style of worship on a West Coast visit because the same can be said for every denomination and fellowship. . . . Third, traditionalists are also worship isolationists. They seldom worship outside of their own tradition because they are denominational loyalists. When taking a vacation, these traditionalists look in the Yellow Pages for a church of their own denomination. The result? Worship never changed. It looked and felt the same everywhere and at all times before 1960. It was a comfortable, never-to-be-questioned security.[6]

Then came the change(s). Webber goes on to describe these phenomena.

> Then came the liturgical renewal in the sixties and the seventies. . . . Subsequently, every major denomination produced new books and resources in worship renewal. There were at least movements emerging in different degrees among traditional churches that included the following new interests: (1) concern to restore the theology of worship, (2) new attention to the historic fourfold pattern of worship, (3) a rethinking of the Eucharist, (4) a restoration of the Christian year, (5) new questions about the role of music and the arts in worship, and (6) concerns about how to intensify the participation of the congregation.[7]

Webber goes on to comment that the emphasis on renewal the past two decades has not been without its problems. "Something was missing in both the traditional and contemporary worship renewal. What was missing in one was the strength of the other. The traditional church was missing the sense of a real and vital experience with God. The contemporary movement was missing substance."[8]

4. CURRENT NORTH AMERICAN EXPRESSIONS OF WORSHIP

Currently, Christians in North America are expressing their worship to God through six major approaches:

Formal-Liturgical Worship

Traditional Hymn-based Worship

Contemporary Music-driven Worship

Charismatic Worship

Blended Worship

Emerging Worship

How Has Worship Changed through the Centuries? – Survey of Christian Worship

I. The Ancient Church (first five centuries of church history)

    A. Second Century worship shows strong influence of the synagogue.[9]

        1. Christian worship, like that of the synagogue, holds to the centrality of Scripture. It was the Jewish custom to read and comment on the Scriptures. Portions from the Pentateuch and the prophets were read.

        2. The church, like the synagogue emphasized prayer. There is a correspondence in the time of prayer. The first Christians observed the daily hours of prayer practiced in the synagogue: the third hour (Acts 2:15), the sixth hour (Acts 10:9), and the ninth hour (Acts 3:1).

        3. The second century expression of worship is seen in a letter, The First Apology, by Justin Martyr (he is explaining to an unsaved Emperor how Christians worship).

        "On the day called Sunday there is a meeting in one place of those who live in cities or the country, and the memoirs of the apostles or the writings of the prophets are read as long as time permits. When the reader has finished, the president in a discourse urges and invites [us] to the imitation of these noble things. Then we all stand up together and offer prayers. And, as said before, when we have finished the prayer, bread is brought, and wine and water, and the president similarly sends up prayers and thanksgivings to the best of his ability, and the congregation assents, saying the Amen; the distribution, and reception of the consecrated [elements] by each one, takes place and they are sent to the absent by the deacons."

B. Third Century

1. Prayers were said while people stood with their arms stretched heavenward or folded on the breast as in ancient Jewish worship. The Scriptures were read from a rostrum. It was the custom to stand during the reading of the Gospels to accentuate the fact that these books are the most precious of the New Testament because they speak directly of the Savior. It is generally recognized that while certain parts of the service were fixed, there was nevertheless a great deal of freedom. The prayers were not yet fixed, and the liturgy was not so completely structured that free worship could not be contained within the generally accepted order.

2. The chief officiant of worship was either the bishop or the minister or ministers, depending on the size of the congregation. The deacons were also highly involved in worship. They directed the people, read the Scriptures, led in prayer, guarded the doors, maintained order, presented the elements, and helped to distribute them. The people were also involved. They assisted in the readings and played their part in

the drama with responses, prayers, and alms.

C. Fourth and Fifth Centuries – dramatic change in
understanding: God is present, heaven has come to
earth; therefore, display it.

   1. Influence of the culture: The Eastern world-view was
informed by the Hellenistic (Greek culture) love for
the aesthetic. Hellenistic propensity toward beauty
gave shape to the rich colors of the fresco painted
walls, the simple beauty of the icons, and the colorful
vestments of the clergy. The concern of Eastern
worship was to bring heaven down to earth and
transport earth to heaven. It is born of the conviction
that we earthlings join in that heavenly assembly.

   2. Church leaders taught that since earthly worship joins
heavenly worship, God is present – display it. For this
reason developed the mystical presence of God in the
ceremony and the liturgy. This sense of the mystical
is communicated especially in the development of the
sanctuary screen.

II. The Medieval Church (500-1500 A.D.) – the Mass
develops, ceremonial worship

A. More and more worship became a ceremonial action
in itself, performed for the sanctification of those
participating. This is most noticeable in the gradually
increasing separation of the clergy.

B. During the early centuries, the organized church
converted many pagan festivals and customs and invested
them with Christian meaning. This strategy had its
definite advantages in Christianizing the Empire but also
suffered the disadvantage of an unhealthy influence from

the mystery cults. Furthermore, the church distanced
itself from the people even more as it increasingly
viewed itself as a hierarchical institution rather
than a body. The church dispensed salvation. The
liturgy, especially the Eucharist, became the means of
receiving this salvation. The Eucharist (i.e., Catholic's
transubstantiation) was elevated above the Word.[10]

C. A major result of the mystical view of worship is that
the Mass became an epiphany (manifestation) of God.
**The Mass assumed the character of a sacred drama
that was played out by the clergy while the people
watched.**

III. The Reformation church (1500 A.D.)

A. People expected all sorts of benefits and advantages from
hearing Mass. The priest saying the Mass took the place
of worship by the people and became a legalistic means
of buying salvation. This view struck at the heart of the
Christian message and perverted the essential nature
of the Christian faith. The overthrow of the Mass as a
sacrifice was necessary.

B. The Reformers insisted on the restoration of the Word to
its ancient and proper place in worship.

1 The Reformation was fueled by a commitment to
reform the church's worship and message of salvation.
With regard to her worship, the Regulative Principle
was put forth, stating that "Nothing should be
introduced or performed in the churches of Christ for
which no probable reason can be given from the Word
of God." (Bucer)

2 "This is the sum of the matter: that everything shall be done so that the Word prevails. . . . We can spare everything except the Word. We profit by nothing so much as by the Word. For the whole Scripture shows that the Word should have free course among Christians." (Luther, quoted in Thompson, Liturgy, West, Ch, p. 98)

C. Zwingli went even farther than Luther in insisting that the people were to give ear to the Word of God alone. Consequently, he did away with the Mass. In addition, he abolished organs as well as other music, vestments, pictures, and anything else that would detract from the centrality of the Word. Quarterly communion, rather than weekly communion, became standard in the churches. Influence extended through the English Puritans to the Baptists, Presbyterians, Congregationalists, and Independents and spread through them to most of American Protestant Christianity.

D. The Anabaptists

The Anabaptists not only rejected ceremonies in worship but also the necessity of formal public worship. It was their conviction that the true church was an obedient and suffering people whose daily walk with God was of utmost importance. This walk climaxed in the gathering of Christians together for prayer, Bible reading, admonition, and the Lord's Supper in the informal atmosphere of the home. They thus refused to attend the worship of the state church and met in secret at various times in an unscheduled and impromptu manner.

IV. The Modern Church (16th Century-present). Many of the
    following features became part of our worship.

A. Emphasis on non-liturgical worship

The anti-liturgical movement among mainline
Christians originated with the Puritans in England.
The emphasis shifted away from the use of a prayer
book to spiritual worship and spontaneous prayers. The
Congregationalists rejected the use of written prayers,
insisting that prayer should be from the heart, directed by
the Spirit of God.

B. Emphasis on understanding

1 Congregationalists developed a commentary approach
   to the reading of Scripture that opposed what they
   called "dumb reading." The reader, usually the
   minister or one trained in the Scripture, always made
   comments on the meaning and interpretation of the
   text as it was being read (i.e. exposition).

2 Presbyterians also practiced "lecturing." This lecturing,
   or sermon, was to consist of three parts: the doctrinal
   content of the text, a development of the argument,
   and the application of the text to the hearer. For
   this reason ministers were to be highly trained in
   the use of the original languages and theology. They
   were cautioned, however, against using the original
   languages in the pulpit.

3 From the earliest records of the **Baptist** churches of the
   17th century we learn that the major portion of the
   worship time was spent in preaching (or prophesying,
   as it was frequently called) from Holy Scripture. In
   Article 19 of the 1611 Confession of Faith of the
   Gainsborough Church, the main elements of worship
   are delineated. The church was "to assemble together

to pray, prophesy (expound the Scriptures), praise God, and break bread." This congregation was observing the Lord's Supper each Sunday, and a few Baptist congregations continued that practice for a short time. However, in the Baptist churches the general practice quickly reduced the frequency to a monthly observance of the Supper for at least two reasons: They were afraid of the repetition which might lead them back toward a sacramental emphasis like the Catholic Mass, and they did not want to threaten the centrality of biblical preaching in their worship.

C. Emphasis on experience – Pietists: 17th Century

Pietism was a movement against dead orthodoxy. It began in Lutheranism in the seventeenth century. The key to Pietist worship is found in the stress on conversion. In conversion, worship centered on the personal experience of the worshiper in worship and was followed by a rigorous ethical walk in personal life. In this way the corporate worship of the congregation and systematic order of congregational action were gradually replaced by the stress on individual experience in worship and a personal walk with the Lord.

D. Emphasis on revival – Revivalists: 18th and 19th Centuries

The mark of Revivalism was the introduction of field preaching and camp meetings. The services developed a style of praying, singing, and preaching of their own. The main concern was evangelism – communicating the gospel of Christ to the unconverted. Consequently, the services were designed as an appeal to the unconverted to become converted. It was never the intention of the leaders that these revival services replace the worship in the church. However, the revival approach was gradually assimilated by the church and here and there replaced Sunday morning worship.

E. Charismatic emphasis, spontaneity – Charismatics: early-to late-20th Century

It is difficult to describe contemporary charismatic worship. In the main, however, it is the full and active participation of every member as the key to charismatic worship. This emphasis is expressed in five concerns: body, ministry, spontaneity, praise and joy, and community and love.

F. Emphasis on Change – Modern evangelicals: late 20th Century.

1 Don Hustad offers the following insights:[11] During the last several years, many churches have become convinced that the worship order they had always followed, and especially the music they used, was suddenly out of date! Almost overnight, often without careful study and discussion, both order and materials were changed radically, or a "contemporary" service was added to the schedule to accommodate the stile moderno, the nuovo musicae. Just as quickly, the church organized itself into opposing camps.[12]

2 To the present day, many evangelicals have exulted so much in their "free," non-liturgical identity, that few of their scholars have paid attention to the theology and practice of corporate worship. In their more mundane, year-round worship life, Sunday services have resembled evangelistic crusades or Bible study gatherings.

3 The early 1960s saw the advent of both the "worship celebration movement" and the charismatic renewal movement, signaling the beginning of the end for the serious movements of worship thought and action. They developed and propagated a philosophy of worship based on their theology and expressed in simple "praise-and-worship" songs and performance-oriented contemporary Christian music.

4 Finally, in the 1980s the church growth movement recommended "consumerist" choices in worship in order to reach the Baby Boomers. . . . Evangelicals took their advice seriously because of the centrality of evangelism in their consciousness—and because they weren't able to identify the theological and liturgical issues at stake. Thus, a logical, almost inescapable progression of historical events set the stage for the current worship revolution, which has been the source of some creative growth and much bruising conflict in today's church. (Hustad, p. 20; italics mine.)

5 Millard Erickson has similarly observed of this phenomenon: Anyone alert to what is going on in evangelical American churches is aware of the shift toward a more informal, experience-centered style of religion. Celebration is replacing meditation, praise choruses are supplanting hymns, worship teams have succeeded robed choirs, organs are sitting unused in favor of guitars, hymns are replaced by words projected on a screen or inserted in the worship folder, casual attire is worn instead of Sunday-go-to-meeting clothes. One church leader, observing that a change-oriented congregation had just installed an organ costing over one million dollars in the new sanctuary, commented, "think how many guitars that would have bought." This youth-oriented trend is gaining momentum.[13]

The Newest Phenomena: The Emerging Generation and the Emergent Church Why is it Becoming the New Model?

Counselor and writer Chuck De Groat, in "A Growing Hunger for Honesty and Authenticity," describes what is happening in Christian homes on a regular basis today.[14] He writes about the reaction many parents are living through when their college-age son (or daughter) returns home after being at school at the "big university."

> He returns home for his first break, and you begin to notice some strange and disturbing patterns. As you ask him about his faith, he's elusive. At church on Sunday, he seems uncomfortable and irritable. You begin wondering if this is it – the moment every Christian parent dreads. Has your son abandoned the faith?

> At Sunday dinner, you muster the courage to ask. And his response floors you. *Dad and Mom, I've got something to share with you. I'm frustrated with church. It doesn't tackle the deep issues I wrestle with.* Here it comes. This is it. You grab each other's hand. And then he says it.

> *Dad and Mom, what ever happened to the old hymns? My campus director plays guitar, and he's got all these old hymns that I never hear in church anymore, and they are so relevant to my struggles. And what ever happened to the Lord's Supper? Man, that's the good stuff . . . that's where I can lay it on the line with Jesus and bring Him my fears and dreams. And what ever happened to the Bible? When I was young, I loved hearing the stories and struggles of faith. They reached me. I wish our pastor told fewer jokes and focused on some of the real life stories in the Bible and the church.*

You don't know whether to cry or laugh.

De Groat then adds that today, "parents are telling more and more stories like this one. A strange convergence of ancient ways of faith and radically new forms of expression is happening. And it's happening in ways that might surprise you." What he describes is the emerging generation's faith, and the resultant expression of that faith in the emerging church.

Is The Emergent Church Another Reformation?

In *The Younger Evangelicals*, theologian, pastor, and author Robert Webber describes "a new evangelical awakening" happening primarily among young men and women.[15] It is influenced and guided by the "young in spirit" who sense the need for an evangelical revival. The leaders of the "young in spirit" include the likes of Sally Morgenthaler, Brian McClaren, Stanley Grenz, and others who offer a vision of the church bathed in the "historic substances of the faith" lost in the past 25 years of ministry and reset in the "new cultural condition of the twenty-first century."[16]

As advocates of a modern Reformation, these elders of a movement sometimes called "the emergent church" see the hope of evangelical Christianity resting in a deconstruction of modern, Enlightenment methods that they see both radical liberalism and fundamentalism. Traditional evangelicals (1950-1975), they say, embraced the modern worldview with its affinity towards evidentialism, foundationalism, and rationalism. Meanwhile "pragmatic evangelicals" who followed (1975-2000) overreacted by abandoning much of the historic substance of faith for an ahistorical, consumer-friendly, market-driven and therapeutic form. Led by mega-church pastors, popular authors, and a band of well-intentioned Christian brothers seeking to re-invent Christianity in a new, relevant form the result was a de-historicized Christianity lacking substance, appealing to its consumers by imitating culture rather than creating it.[17]

The new, emerging church (2000-) led by the younger evangelicals involves a re-commitment to the depth and substance of historic Christianity, without the fundamentalism or liberalism that characterized much of the church of the twentieth century. Within these churches one is apt to see a focus on the Trinity and God's transcendence ("it's not about me"), a fondness of mystery ("don't pretend you have all the answers"), a desire for honesty ("don't make church a show"), space for lament ("I need to know God hears my cries"), the language of story ("don't give me more principles . . . show me how I fit into God's story"), and a craving for community ("size isn't proof of God's presence; love is").

The Emergent Church – Fad or the Future?

We are living in a day of great interest in "spiritual" matters (i.e., as seen in recent years by the popularity of Dan Brown's books, The Da Vinci Code and his Angels and Demons). Yet a change is occurring. Leading emergent church proponent, Pastor Dan Kimball writes:

> In the 1970s and 1980s, God raised leaders to give
> new life and vision to dying churches. God used
> and still uses churches that employ seeker-sensitive
> methodology to draw hundreds of thousands of people
> across North America back to Jesus and His church.
> The values of these churches were birthed specifically
> out of the leaders' desire to identify with the people

they were hoping to reach. Even if a church did not fully embrace a seeker-sensitive strategy, many churches at least adopted many of its contemporary approaches to ministry. The emphasis on creating a place for seekers to come meant emphasizing the weekend service as the entry point to the church. Contemporary architecture was developed for worship buildings along with new approaches to preaching and communication. Dramas, videos, and production staff were added to larger churches to help make the weekend services more professional. Evan Garth Brooks-like headset microphones were used to show that we really are keeping up with the times and are hip to current culture.

Based on my observations and conversations, however, I think that many of these very things are contrary to what emerging generations value and are seeking in their spiritual experience.

We are very likely to see the pattern of past generations repeated. As churches lost touch with the culture and didn't connect with younger generations, the seeker-sensitive movement was born. This time, however, it is the seeker-sensitive movement that loses touch as it grows more and more disconnected with the heart of emerging generations.[18]

The back cover of Kimball's book explains that the seeker-sensitive movement revolutionized the way evangelicals did church and introduced countless baby boomers to Christ. "Yet trends show that today's post-Christian generations are not responding like the generations before them. As we enter a new cultural era, what do worship services look like that are connecting with the hearts of emerging generations? A few excerpts from Dan Kimball's book are insightful.

Currently in our culture, when someone refers to a seeker-sensitive worship service or approach, they many times are referring to a methodology or style of ministry—a strategy of designing ministry to attract those who feel the church is irrelevant or dull. This often involves removing what could be considered religious stumbling blocks and displays of the spiritual (such as extended worship, religious symbols, extensive prayer times, liturgy, etc.) so that seekers can relate to the environment and be transformed by the message of Jesus. Generally, seeker-sensitive services function as entry points into the church, and the church offers deeper teaching and worship in another meeting or setting. (p. 24)

He explains how the change is taking place, the differences in today's post-seeker-sensitive era.

A post-seeker-sensitive worship promotes, rather than hides, full displays of spirituality (extended worship, religious symbols, liturgy, extensive prayer times, extensive use of Scripture and readings, etc.) so that people can experience and be transformed by the message of Jesus. This approach is done, however, with renewed life and is still "sensitive" as clear instruction and regular explanation are given to help seekers understand theological terms and spiritual exercises. . .

Many of the very things that we removed from our churches because they were stumbling blocks to seekers in previous generations are now the very things that are attractive to emerging generations. . .

But our culture is changing. Previous generations grew up experiencing church as dull and meaningless, and so the seeker-sensitive model strove to reintroduce church as relevant, contemporary, and personal. But emerging generations are being raised without any experience of church, good or bad. . . .

In recent times, the wave of change came to the church with the seeker-sensitive movement. Another wave of change is now breaking on our shores. This should not surprise us. Time passes, new generations are born, cultures change, so the church must change. We see this in ancient church history, . . . Many call the change we are now experiencing as moving from the modern to the postmodern era. Some call it moving from a Christian a post-Christian culture. . .

The type of change I am talking about is not just about what happens in the church service, with the music, or with the small group strategy. These are only surface issues. It is really a revolutionary change that affects almost everything we do— even what comes to mind when we say the word church. . . .

It is a reality, and emerging church leaders must be students of world and church history so we can gain perspective on all of this. . . As the emerging church returns to a rawer and more vintage form of Christianity, we may see explosive growth much like the early church did. (Pp 25-29; See "Emergent Mystique," *Christianity Today*, Nov 2004.)

Comparisons: Traditional/Pragmatic/Emergent

	TRADITIONAL	PRAGMATIC	EMERGENT
Cultural Situation	Modern Worldview Industrial society Post WWII	Transitional paradigm, Technological society, Vietnam War	Postmodern Worldview, Internet society, War on terrorism
Communication Style	Print/Verbal	Broadcast/ Presentational	Internet/ Interactive
Attitude towards History	Distinctives of 20th century fundamentalism	Fresh start, Historical forms not "relevant" today	Need wisdom from past. Road to future runs through past
Generation	Booster/Traditional	Boomer/Innovative	20-somethings/ Xers
Theological Commitment	Christianity as Rational Worldview	Christianity as therapeutic/ Answering Needs/ Jesus as Friend	Christianity as community of faith/ Ancient-Reformation
Apologetics Style	Evidential/ Foundationalism	Bridge between evidential and personal, pragmatic	Embrace metanarrative/ Embodied faith
Ecclesial Paradigm	Civil religion/ Christ of culture	Culturally-sensitive and market-driven/ Christ above culture	Missional, counter-cultural/ Christ transforms culture
Church Style	Neighborhood churches, rural	Mega-churches, suburban, market-driven (targeted)	Small churches, cities, inter-cultural
Leadership Style	Pastor-centered	Manager-CEO led	Team ministry, priesthood of all
Youth Ministry	Church-centered programs	Outreach, fun programs	Prayer, Bible study, worship, social action

Education	Sunday school, Information-centered	Generationally targeted, need-based	Inter-generational, Not information but formation
Spirituality	Keep the rules	Prosperity & success	Authentic embodiment
Worship	Traditional	Contemporary	Convergence
Art	Restrained/Suspicious	Art as Illustration	Incarnational
Evangelism	Mass Evangelism	Seeker services	Process-relational
Social Action	Small program in church	Need-driven (AA, abortion, etc.)	Transforming culture

Shift in Approach to Worship Services[19]

MODERN CHURCH (Seeker-Sensitive)	EMERGING CHURCH (Post-Seeker-Sensitive)
Worship "services" in which preaching, music, programs, etc. are served to the attender	Worship "gatherings," which include preaching, music, etc.
Services designed to reach those who have had bad or boring experiences in a church	Gatherings designed to include and translate to those who have no previous church experience
Services designed to be user-friendly and contemporary	Gatherings designed to be experiential and spiritual-mystical
A need to break the stereotype of what church is	A need to break the stereotype of who Christians are
Stained glass taken out and replaced with video screens	Stained glass brought back in on video screens
Crosses and other symbols removed from meeting place to avoid looking too "religious"	Crosses and other symbols brought back into meeting place to promote a sense of spiritual reverence

Room arranged so individuals are able to see the stage from comfortable theater seating while worshiping	Room arranged to focus on community, striving to feel more like a living room or coffeehouse while worshiping
Lit up and cheery sanctuary valued	Darkness valued as it displays a sense of spirituality
Focal point of the service is the sermon	Focal point of the gathering is the holistic experience
Preacher and worship leader lead the service	Preacher and worship leader lead by participating in the gathering
Uses modern technology to communicate with contemporary flare	Gathering seen as a place to experience the ancient, even mystical (and uses technology to do so)
Services designed to grow or accommodate the many people of the church	Gatherings designed to grow to accommodate many people but seen as a time when the church which meets in smaller groups gathers together

On worship, Dan Kimball writes:

> A major criticism of the church today is that it is a modern, Americanized, organized religion that has lost its ancient roots and sense of mystery. But what do emerging generations value? The ancient – the mystery of religious faiths of old. But what do they see when they come to our churches?
> In the emerging church we need to bring back the ancient symbols and talk about the Jewish roots of our faith. For example, our church once asked a Jewish believer to talk to us about Passover and to walk us through a messianic Seder dinner. Another time, he presented a Jewish perspective on the Messiah and his return.
> We also have what we call Hymn Times. We place a large velvet chair on the stage, and before we sing each hymn, someone sits in the chair to read about that hymn, explaining why, when, and by whom it was

written. Good hymns go over really well in a post-Christian culture because they are fresh, unknown, and reek of history. They teach deep theological truth and focus on God and his attributes. As long as people can relate to the musical accompaniment we use, we could easily incorporate numerous hymns into our services. Younger generations seem to love hymns, and we sing many of them. Even a couple in their seventies attend our worship gathering because we do more hymns than the service they had been attending.[20]

For further reading and information on the Emergent Church:

Carson, D. A. *Becoming Conversant with the Emerging Church*. Grand Rapids: Zondervan, 2005.
> An excellent critique on the entire Emergent phenomena and its shortcomings.

Jones, Tony. *Postmodern Youth Ministry*. Grand Rapids: Zondervan, 2001. This book details much about the postmodern phenomenon and its impact on young people.

Kimball, Dan. *The Emerging Church: Vintage Christianity for New Generations*. Grand Rapids: Zondervan, 2003. The best over-all book on this latest movement.

Penning, James M. and Corwin E. Schmidt. *Evangelicalism: The Next Generation*. Grand Rapids: Baker, 2002.

Webber, Robert. *The Younger Evangelicals: Facing the Challenges of the New World*. Grand Rapids: Baker, 2002. The best book on the current views of younger evangelicals.

www.vintagefaith.com. and also, www.emergentvillage.org.

Significant Features That Have Developed As Part Of Our Worship – or – Contemporary Issues: Where Do We Go From Here?

The elements (traditions) discussed below have become commonplaces in our worship services. As the survey of worship shows, it is a history of development and change. Today, the question is being asked: Have the changes been for the better or worse? The following traditions are continual matters of discussion today.[21]

I. Centrality of the Word of God over ordinances in the worship service.

   A. Should the Eucharist ("Lord's Supper") or the Word of God be the focal point of worship?

   "If the church would focus its worship upon God revealed in Christ, it must hear His Word. . . . This hearing of the Word of God, hearing what the Lord of the Church wants to say to His church in its actual situation, is the primary task of the church, the basic human action in worship." (Saucy, The Church in God's Program, p.179)

   B. Placement of the pulpit – central feature among Baptist churches, emphasizes the Word.

   From the Reformation Period on the use of space (location of the pulpit, choir, etc.) became very important. The use of space in Protestants' (as well as Anabaptists and independent groups) buildings was especially marked by the centrality of the pulpit. The symbolic location of the pulpit communicated the renewal of the Word and emphasis on preaching. This became the single most powerful symbolic use of space in the evangelical church. A second feature was to place the communion table under the pulpit or in a less central place. Symbolically, this makes communion less important that preaching.

II. Congregational participation, spontaneity, and change.

The mistake of the medieval period was that the congregation watched worship. In the modern Protestant church the mistake is that the congregation tends to listen to worship. How can we best return to worship that involves full congregational participation?

Furthermore, it is not always easy to find the delicate balance between spontaneity and order. Today much of what passes for spontaneity is irreverent showmanship spawned by a desire to be "unique" and "relevant" rather than obedient and biblical. On the other hand, we must also be concerned not to mistake antiquity and orderliness for authentic New Testament worship in the twenty-first century. After all, cemeteries are both ancient and orderly.

III. Time of worship – importance of Sunday, issue of Sunday PM Service.

"In Christianized countries the civil Sunday with its partial cessation of regular activities has become filled with other activities (special games, opportunities to shop, etc.). Believers, too, are caught up in these secular uses of the Lord's Day. Churches also abandon opportunities to use available hours on Sunday for their activities. The result may soon be that Sunday will be like every other day of the week, requiring normal work hours as well, and believers will be back in the first century trying to find early morning or late evening hours for worship." (Ryrie, Bas. Theo., p. 432). The issue being raised today is over two Sunday services (i.e. the PM service).

IV. Music

Modern worship practices of Baptists singing hymns would have been unthinkable to early Baptists. Early Baptists rejected group singing of "manmade" hymns. A singing congregation might include some non-Christians, and their participation would pollute the worship. The questions today are whether the music is too simplistic, repetitive, etc., for worshiping God. Does our music match Eph. 5:19 and Col. 3:16?

V. Use of the public invitation, revivalism, and conversion experiences as part of worship.

17th Century Pietism emphasis on individual experience and personal walk replaced systematic corporate worship. 18th and 19th Century revival and frontier services became the format for Sunday worship services among Evangelicals and Fundamentalists in the 20th Century. Charles Finney's development and use of the public invitation in 1830-33 revivals in Rochester, NY lead to the use of public invitations whereby the unconverted and sinners were encouraged to come to the "anxious bench" (come to the altar, come forward) at the end of the service.[22] This was quickly adopted by other revival preachers (Moody, Finney, etc.) and into churches (C. H. Spurgeon) and has carried over into the 20th Century.

As we have already noted, many well-meaning, serious-minded, pastors have turned the Sunday service into a revival or, worse, a political rally. What they do not realize is that by changing their priorities from worship to solely evangelism and political action, they are actually weakening their effectiveness in these endeavors. If people do not focus on Christ, worship Christ, feed on Christ, all of life suffers due to a depletion of spiritual empowerment.

CONCLUSION

If you can't go to church and at least for a moment be given transcendence, if you can't pass briefly from this life into the next, then I can't see why anyone should go. Just a brief moment of transcendence causes you to come out of church a changed person. (Garrison Keillor, Cited by Kimball, p.143)

The style and form of worship have been in a state of constant change since the first century. Change in worship will continue. Some of what happens today will pass away as fad. Other things will become the sacred traditions against what future generations will rebel. The music will change. The instrumentation will change. The style of preaching will change. The arrangement of sanctuaries will change. The old songs we love may be forgotten. Old churches will die. New churches will repeat mistakes made by their forbears. Intergenerational conflict will continue. But the gospel of Jesus Christ will go forward.

ENDNOTES

CHAPTER 2

[1] John Calvin, Institutes of the Christian Religion, ed. John T. McNeill; trans. Ford Lewis Battles, (Louisville: Westminster John Knox Press), Book 1, Chapter 11, Paragraph 8.

[2] I am indebted to my friend Dr. Kevin Bauder, the President of Central Baptist Seminary, for suggesting this line of thinking. On one occasion we were together in Florida, and I heard him lecture on the fundamental truth of religion with Deuteronomy 6:4-5 as his text. It generated much thought and spawned a couple of sermons–good lectures or sermons always do that. In fact, I was so engrossed in thought about the issue that while returning home I missed an exit and went about forty miles out of the way. At least, that's the excuse I use for having missed that exit.

[3] "Man's chief end is to glorify God and enjoy him for ever" (*Westminster Shorter Catechism*, 1). For supporting Scripture, see 1 Corinthians 10:31; Romans 11:36; Psalm 73:25-28.

[4] Second Kings 17:24-33 records a classic illustration of this kind of "instrumental worship." Expatriates from various locations began to inhabit Samaria because of Assyria's deportation policy. Because these people did not fear or worship the Lord, He sent lions among them to slay them. They figured that if they learned how to worship the Lord, their lion problem would be solved. Worshipping the Lord was a means to an end, and they kept serving their own gods as well just in case they could get something

from them. Unhappily, this "Samaritan theology" thrives even apart from the threat of lions.

[5] In his analysis of formal religion in the post-exilic community, Malachi exposed the attitude of those who had obviously assigned instrumental value to God and were obviously disappointed when God did not serve what they perceived to be His purpose. "It is vain to serve God: and what profit is that we have kept his ordinance, and that we have walked mournfully before the LORD of hosts?" (Malachi 3:14). For my analysis of Malachi's critique of Israel's religion, see Appendix 1, "The Message of Malachi: An Analysis of Dead Religion."

[6] J. Ligon Duncan III concurs with this assessment of the moral law. "The ten words themselves are a disclosure of God's own nature and not merely a revelation of temporary, social, religious, and moral norms. The first commandment shows us a Lord who alone is God....Because these commandments teach us first and foremost about what God is like, they also provide for permanent direction on how we are to think of God, how we are to worship God, and that God cares greatly about how we think of and worship him." "Does God Care How We Worship," in *Give Praise to God: A Vision for Reforming Worship*, eds. Philip Graham Ryken, Derek W. H. Thomas, and J. Ligon Duncan III (Phillipsburg, N.J., P&R Publishing, 2003), 30.

[7] Duncan again speaks to the point. "For instance, the whole exodus account... stresses that God's people are redeemed in order that they might worship him. Moses' very call emphasizes that God sends Moses to Egypt to deliver his people that they might worship him. Listen to the reiterated emphases of these passages: 'When you have brought the people out of Egypt, you shall worship'(Ex. 3:12); 'let us go a three day's journey into the wilderness, that we may sacrifice to the LORD our God' (3:18); 'let My son go that he may serve [or worship] Me' (4:23); 'let My people go that they may celebrate a feast to Me in the wilderness' (5:1); 'let us go a three day's journey into the wilderness that we may sacrifice to the LORD our God' (5:3). Do not underestimate this repeated language. This is not merely a ruse to get Pharaoh to temporarily release the children of Israel. It is the primary reason why God sets his people free: to worship him. The primacy of worship in a believer's life is, thus, set forth" (29).

[8] Alan Cairns, *Chariots of God: God's Law in Relation to the Cross and the Christian* (Greenville: Ambassador-Emerald International, 2000), 152,154. Cairns goes on to say in his development of the first commandment that the concept of worship "includes every duty that we owe to the Lord" (155). Alan Cairns has been my minister for some twenty-five years, and I listened with

interest and conviction to the series of sermons that gave rise to this book. I would recommend Chariots of God as a thorough and practical exposition of the law with its attendant implications and applications.

[9] For a thorough and convicting delineation of the duties required and the sins forbidden by the first commandment, see Questions 104 and 105 in the *Westminster Larger Catechism.*

[10] My concern at this point is the singular uniqueness of God, but the Shema's statement of God's unity is an essential component of divine uniqueness and leads to our later consideration of Trinitarian worship. That God is one and that He is three are not mutually exclusive truths; indeed it is the very essence of who God really is. Christianity is the only religion that recognizes and affirms this essential dogma. Although the Shema does not specifically identify God the Father, Son, and Holy Spirit, it does speak to the unity of the Godhead. Although no analogy can explain the mystery of the Trinity, the use of the number "one" in the Old Testament at least illustrates the possibility of a single entity consisting of multiple parts. For instance, Ezekiel took two sticks, and he put them together to become one stick, a process which symbolized a single kingdom consisting of two divisions (Ezekiel 37:17-22).

[11] The observation of William G. Shedd, the great 19th century Presbyterian theologian, is significant here. "A believer in the Trinity, in using the first petition of the Lord's prayer, may have the first person particularly in his mind, and may address him; but this does not make his prayer antitrinitarian. He addresses that person as the representative of the Trinity. And the same is true whenever he particularly addresses the Son, or the Spirit. If he addresses God the Son, God the Son implies God the Father. Each Divine person supposes and suggests the others. Each represents the others. Consequently, to pray to any one of the Divine Three is by implication and virtually to pray to all Three." *Dogmatic Theology* (Grand Rapids: Zondervan Publishing House, reprint, 1971), I, 308.

[12] Any good systematic theology text or theological dictionary should provide ample and helpful discussion on these important issues. If you want a clearly concise synopsis of the evidence, see Alan Cairns, "Trinity," in *Dictionary of Theological Terms* (Greenville: Ambassador-Emerald International, expanded 3rd edition, 2002), 494-496.

[13] William G. Shedd, *Dogmatic Theology* (Grand Rapids: Zondervan Publishing House, reprint, 1971), I, 331.

CHAPTER 3

[1] *The Westminster Confession of Faith* also remarks on nature's contribution to the issue of worship. "The light of nature sheweth that there is a God, who hath lordship and sovereignty over all, is good, and doth good unto all, and is, therefore, to be feared, loved, praised, called upon, trusted in, and served, with all the heart, and with all the soul, and with all the might" (21.1).

[2] Psalm 49:16-17 illustrates this rather concrete sense of glory. "Be not thou afraid when one is made rich, when the glory of his house is increased. For when he dieth he shall carry nothing away: his glory shall not descend after him." Put very simply, the rich man cannot take his glory, that is, his money or possessions, with him when he dies.

[3] David's choice of grammar in Psalm 19:1 highlights creation's constant activity in its mission to glorify God. Two aspects of the word "declare" make the point. First, it is a participle, a form used to mark habitual activity. Second, it is a piel form, which sometimes has an iterative idea. Interestingly, what the grammar suggests in verse 1 is stated vividly in verse 2: "Day unto day uttereth speech, and night unto night sheweth knowledge." Every day and every night participate in this unceasing communication.

[4] Paul, similarly, links the idea of riches with glory (see, for instance, Ephesians 3:16 and Colossians 1:27). The expression the "riches of glory" could well be understood as an appositive: "the riches, which are glory."

[5] This is a key point that Stephen Charnock makes in his classic 17th century work, *The Existence and Attributes of God* (Grand Rapids: Baker Books, reprint, 1963). "The first ground of the worship we render to God, is the infinite excellency of his nature...for God, as God, is the object of worship" (I, 206). Again he says, "Worship is so due to him as God, as that he that denies it disowns his deity....It is a debt of justice we owe to God, to worship him; and it is as much a debt of justice to worship him according to his nature. Worship is nothing else but a rendering to God the honor that is due to him..." (I. 212).

[6] I actually had someone question my credibility once because I used this spelling of the divine name in my other books, so let me say a word about why I am using the designation Jehovah to refer to the divine name instead of Yahweh. I would be adamant that the issue is not one of orthodoxy, nor is it a matter of conservatism compromising with or surrendering to liberalism,

as some would argue. I am comfortable using either pronunciation. Without getting overly technical, I will explain briefly the problem.

This name is often referred to as the Tetragrammaton (four letters) because in the ancient script of the Hebrew Bible only the four letters YHWH would have occurred. The Hebrew alphabet consists only of consonants, and consequently, vowel sounds were not part of the writing system. This obviously does not mean that vowels were not part of the language since vowel sounds are essential for any vocalization. There was no problem with reading and understanding the text until classical Hebrew became a dead language (i.e., no longer spoken). Beginning about A.D. 600, a group of Jewish scholars, called Massoretes, devised a system to incorporate vowel signs into the consonantal text in order to preserve and insure the traditional pronunciation of the biblical text. Although the work of these post-Christian Jewish scholars is trustworthy in the majority of instances, occasionally it reflects some peculiar interpretations that originated in humanly generated tradition. It is a common opinion that the disputation over the pronunciation of the divine name results from a rabbinical superstition based on an erroneous interpretation of Leviticus 24:16 that makes blaspheming the name of the Lord a capital offense. According to the superstition, the best way to avoid blaspheming the name was to avoid pronouncing the name. So when YHWH occurred in the biblical text, the Massoretes supposedly inserted the vowels that belonged with the word Adonai, the title usually translated as "Lord" in the Authorized Version. That was to be a clue to all who read the Scriptures that when they came to the word YHWH they were to say Adonai instead. The theory is, then, that when the vowels belonging to the word Adonai are pronounced with the consonants YHWH, Yehovah or Jehovah is the resulting pronunciation. On the other hand, those who prefer the pronunciation Yahweh recognize that God never intended His name to be avoided and that we have every right to voice it. The phonation Yahweh results from linking the name to an old Hebrew form of the verb "to be," which according to Exodus 3:14 seems to be the root source of the word.

So, which is it? The abbreviated form "Ya" (for instance, in the expression "hallelujah") supports the voicing Yahweh. See Robert Reymond's *A New Systematic Theology of the Christian Faith* (Nashville: Thomas Nelson Publishers, 1998), 157 for more evidence for this pronunciation. Some proper names, however, that are compounded with the divine name support Jehovah (for instance, Jehoshua, i.e., Joshua, meaning Jehovah saves or Jehoshaphat, meaning Jehovah judges). I cannot dogmatically conclude and repeat that I do not regard either pronunciation as evidence of conservatism or liberalism. In this venue I am using the vocalization "Jehovah" simply because it is more commonly recognizable to a general audience. After all, a great many fine, well-known hymns use the name Jehovah, and I don't want to change the music. It just wouldn't be the same singing "Guide me, O thou great Yahweh."

[7] That God revealed Himself as Jehovah to His people from the beginning is not a contradiction of Exodus 6:3: "And I appeared unto Abraham, unto Isaac,

and unto Jacob, by the name of God Almighty, but by my name JEHOVAH was I not known to them." I tell my students frequently that the first law of biblical hermeneutics is that the Bible can't mean what it can't mean, and the second is like unto it: the Bible never contradicts itself. There is express biblical data that God had revealed Himself as Jehovah and that the name was in common use long before Moses. For instance, men began to call on the name of Jehovah from the days of Seth (Genesis 4:26), and Adam and Eve knew the name long before that (see for instance, Genesis 4:1). Genesis 15:6 says expressly that Abraham believed Jehovah. It is impossible to believe what is unknown. So whatever Exodus 6:3 means, it cannot mean that Abraham was unaware of the name Jehovah. Rather, the verse is saying that whereas the patriarchs primarily experienced that aspect of God's character indicated by El Shaddai, this generation, whose varied and multiple needs were in the unknown future, could have the assurance that the LORD in the infinite fullness of His Person would be their experience. John Howard Raven (a Reformed and conservative scholar of the late 19th and early 20th centuries) commented thus on the text: "When we examine the usage of the expression to know God and to know the name of God, it is evident that this verse does not mean that the patriarchs never heard the name Jehovah. It means that though they used the name, they had no such deep appreciation of its meaning as God was about to reveal to Moses. To know the name of God means to appreciate by experience the ideas connected with the name, to receive the revelation of God suggested by it, to accept God as he is revealed in it." *The History of the Religion of Israel: An Old Testament Theology* (Grand Rapids: Baker Book House, 1979, reprint from 1933 edition), 49.

[8] I make this statement contrary to some respected notions. Raven's statement is typical: "The thought is not of the Independent, Self-existent One, The Absolute who exists without dependence upon any other" (48). I am, however, in good company. Geerhardus Vos concludes in *Biblical Theology* (Grand Rapids: Wm. B. Eerdmans Publishing Co., 1948, 11th printing, 1980) that the name "gives expression to the self-determination, the independence of God....the name...signifies primarily that in all that God does for His people, He is from-within-determined, not moved by outside influences" (118-119). Similarly, Robert Reymond says that "God in his Yahwistic character is the self-existent, self-determining, faithful God of the covenant" (158).

[9] J. Barton Payne, for instance, says, "'Yahweh' ("faithful presence") is God's testamental nature, or name," in *The Theology of the Older Testament* (Grand Rapids: Zondervan Publishing House, 1972), 148. Similarly, Raven claims that Jehovah is "preeminently the covenant name of God." He continues, "The God who reveals himself to each succeeding generation as each generation has need and as each generation is able to receive the revelation, is the God who can never fail to keep every promise he has made" (48).

[10] Walter Kaiser comments on the debate. "On the etymology and meaning of the name Yahweh, there is almost no agreement. The bibliography in the last century alone would fill a whole book, and there seems to be no end in sight." "Exodus" in *The Expositor's Bible Commentary*, ed. Frank E. Gæbelein (Grand Rapids, Zondervan Publishing House, 1990), II, 323. He goes on to give a brief synopsis of some of the common suggestions. I personally believe that there is root connection even though the proposition "I AM" uses the common form of the verb hyh and "Jehovah" reflects a less common form hwh. At least it is the less used form in biblical Hebrew, although it is the standard form of the root in Aramaic. The question is whether they are really one or two roots. But for now, this involves linguistic arguments not directly germane to our discussion. So notwithstanding how interesting it is, I'm going to let it go.

[11] The transition from this first person declaration "I AM" to the static name Jehovah involves a change of subject, which in Hebrew would be accomplished by changing the first letter of the verb. (Aleph which designates first person becomes yod which designates third person.) "He is" would be the translation of YHWH. Although the name Jehovah would literally translate as "He is," it was the proper form of the name that even the Lord used when referring to Himself. For instance, Exodus 6:6 says, "I am the LORD."

[12] Interestingly, the Septuagint–the Greek version of the Old Testament– translates this important statement in a way that agrees with my analysis. The Greek translation does not preserve the parts of speech of the original Hebrew statement, but it does nicely preserve the sense: "I am the One who is." It translates the first Hebrew verb with a first person personal pronoun as the subject of the finite verb "to be" and the second Hebrew verb (the one I suggest is the subject complement) with the substantive participle of the verb "to be." The same participle construction–"the One who is"– is repeated as the name that sent Moses.

[13] Raven offered the translation, "I Shall Become that which I Shall Become" and then suggested the paraphrase, "I shall show myself to be that which I shall show myself to be" (47-48).

[14] I, 213. Consider also this thought from Charnock, I, 207. "When we see, therefore, the frame of the world to be the work of his power, the order of the world to be the fruit of his wisdom, and the usefulness of the world to be the product of his goodness, we find the motives and reasons of worship; and weighing that his power, wisdom, goodness, infinitely transcend any corporeal nature, we find a rule of worship, that it ought to be offered by us in a manner suitable to such a nature as is infinitely above any bodily being. His being a Spirit declares what he is; his other perfections declare what kind

of Spirit he is....How cold and frozen will our devotions be, if we consider not his omniscience, whereby he discerns our hearts! How carnal will our services be, if we consider him not as pure Spirit!"

[15] *Institutes of the Christian Religion*, ed. John T. McNeill; trans. Ford Lewis Battles, (Louisville: Westminster John Knox Press), Book 2, Chapter 6, Paragraph 1. He also said, "Meanwhile let us not be ashamed to take pious delight in the works of God open and manifest in this most beautiful theater… to be mindful that wherever we cast our eyes, all things they meet are the works of God, and at the same time to ponder with pious meditation to what end God created them" (Book 1, Chapter 14, Paragraph 20). Furthermore, he concluded that "the contemplation of God's goodness in his creation will lead us to thankfulness and trust" (Book 1, Chapter 14, Paragraph 22).

[16] It is interesting just to look at the subject index of any good hymnal and note how many great hymns of praise include references to creation: "All Creatures of Our God and King," "I Sing the Mighty Power of God," "Praise Ye the Lord, the Almighty, the King of Creation," "The Spacious Firmament on High," "Give to Our God Immortal Praise," "Sing Praise to God who Reigns Above," "This is My Father's World," and "How Great Thou Art," just to name a few.

[17] See the *Westminster Confession of Faith* 21.3 and 5 to find praying, preaching, and singing as ingredients of worship.

[18] (Greenville, SC, Ambassador Emerald International, 2003). Based on the message of the book of Daniel, *God's Unfailing Purpose* focuses on the heavenly throne from which God rules according to His perfect and unchangeable will. God is in absolute control of all things–the big issues of the world and the seemingly bigger issues confronting individuals. Daniel's view of history and prophecy shows that God's kingdom is coming and that God's will is being done on earth as certainly as it is in heaven. Daniel's message concerning God's providence is simple: "Not to worry–everything is under control."

CHAPTER 4

[1] Interestingly, the word "liturgy" is essentially a transliteration of a Greek word that refers to the ministration of service. In both secular and sacred Greek literature, the focus of the word is on service or duty, whether voluntary

or imposed and regardless of the sphere in which that service is rendered. However, in the Septuagint it refers principally to religious service rendered by the priests in their sanctuary duties. This special religious sense, set by the LXX, carries over into the New Testament. Paul regarded his ministry as a "liturgy of the gospel" (Romans 15:16) and indeed designated the Christian's consecrated life as reasonable "liturgy" (Romans 12:1). Especially significant are the references in the book of Hebrews that elevate the priestly duties of the old dispensation to the perfect service rendered by Christ (see, for instance, Hebrews 8:2). If anything is clear about the priestly duties, it is that they had to be performed precisely according to divine formula. Any deviation was potentially fatal (consider the Nadab and Abihu incident recorded in Leviticus 10). Deviations from the divinely revealed patterns may not be immediately fatal in this dispensation, but they are serious matters nonetheless.

[2] Though not all-inclusive, Acts 2:42 isolates some of the cardinal components of worship that marked the church from its formal inception, thus indicating that certain procedures and elements were regular: "And they continued stedfastly in the apostle's doctrine and fellowship, and in breaking of bread, and in prayers." The sum of this is preaching, joint participation in worship experience and activity, the Lord's Supper, and formal prayers. Let me make a few comments to justify this summation. First, I interpret the reference to the apostles' doctrine to involve oral communication since this historic reference predates any apostolic writing. The means of communicating apostolic doctrine in public worship today entails both the reading of the inspired Scripture and its exposition. Second, the word "fellowship" refers to what is held in common. In this context, I believe it underscores the importance of collective participation in public worship. Regardless of the individual's role or function in the liturgy, worshippers are participants, not spectators. Colossians 3:16 would indicate that part of that fellowship involves "teaching and admonishing one another in psalms and hymns and spiritual songs, singing with grace in your hearts to the Lord." As translated, this would indicate that psalms, hymns, and spiritual songs were the means of the mutual teaching and admonition. Although singing is an integral part of worship, I would prefer translating the verse with different punctuation, which would more naturally link "with psalms and hymns and spiritual songs" to singing rather than teaching. Here's the whole verse: "Let the word of Christ dwell in you richly, in all wisdom teaching and admonishing one another, with psalms and hymns and spiritual songs singing with grace in your heart to the Lord." Regardless of where the commas are, the verse addresses the fact of collective participation in the worship experience. It also factors in singing as an integral part of service to the Lord. Third, the Greek text literally reads, "the breaking of the bread." It seems to designate particular bread that is identified and set apart. I would suggest, therefore,

that the reference is not just to group dinners, which did occur in the early church (see, for instance, Acts 2:46) but to the celebration of the Communion sacrament. Fourth, the Greek text literally reads, "the prayers." This does not suggest a set of standard or official prayers , but it does suggest formal categories of prayers such as thanksgiving, praise, confession, intercession, supplication, etc.

[3] The lack of detail regarding the formal process of worship in the New Testament does not mean that the first-generation organized church abandoned formal worship. On the contrary, the Old Testament's instruction and emphasis on ordered liturgy established a given in Christian thinking and practice. Something that was clearly developed by the Old Testament would not need to be reiterated with equal detail by the New. It is a novelty of more recent theological thinking that requires New Testament repetition for confirmation of Old Testament truth. Although progressive revelation is a legitimate concept, the fact remains that some truths are more fully developed in the Old Testament than in the New Testament (e.g., the holiness of God, details of creation, etc.). Given the highly structured worship practices detailed in the Old Testament, it would require express prohibitions to the contrary in the New Testament for the early Christians to worship the Lord casually. In the absence of such prohibition, the continuing association with the Temple (see, for example, Acts 2:46; 3:1; 21:26) and synagogues (see, for example, Acts 18:4) would indicate at least in part that structure and form were elements in Christian worship.

[4] The Confession isolates prayer in a separate paragraph: "Prayer, with thanksgiving, being one special part of religious worship, is by God required of all men: and, that it may be accepted, it is to be made in the name of the Son, by the help of His Spirit, according to His will, with understanding, reverence, humility, fervency, faith, love, and perseverance; and if vocal, in a known tongue" (21.3). It continues as follows: "The reading of the Scriptures, with godly fear, the sound preaching and conscionable hearing of the Word, in obedience unto God, with understanding, faith, and reverence, singing of psalms with grace in the heart; as also, the due administration and worthy receiving of the sacraments instituted by Christ, are all parts of the ordinary religious worship of God…" (21.5).

[5] William M. Taylor, a Scottish-born Presbyterian minister of the 19th century, in his book based on his "Lyman Beecher Lectures" to the theological students of Yale in 1876 highlights this truth: "But still it is right that the book should be publicly read, not only that all may see that preacher and hearer make it the ultimate standard of appeal, but also that the minds and hearts of the worshippers may be rightly affected as they draw near to God." *The Ministry of the Word* (London: T. Nelson and Sons, 1876), 214.

[6] Most married couples can experientially explain the difference. Some time ago, my wife gave me a coffee mug with an inscription expressing this distinction: "I know you're talking, but I'm not listening." Too often in personal relationships we hear without listening. More tragically, in our spiritual relationship with the Lord, we more often hear than listen. We just don't pay attention. How often have we read our daily portion of God's Word only to be totally blank about what we read as soon as we have finished? How often have we stood for the public reading of the Bible with our minds wandering to other concerns? Listening is work, whether at home or in church.

[7] Paul's choice of words confirms that his instruction concerned the public reading of Scripture. It is the same word the Septuagint used to designate the contextually explicit public reading of the law by Ezra (Nehemiah 8:8). The Septuagint text of the 1 Esdras, an apocryphal book dating to about 150 B.C., also uses word when describing what appears to be the same event as Nehemiah 8: "...the Levites taught the law of the Lord and read the law of the Lord to the crowd, giving interpretation to the reading" (9:48; my translation).

[8] "Beside publick reading of the holy scriptures, every person that can read, is to be exhorted to read the scriptures privately, (and all others that cannot read, if not disabled by age, or otherwise, are likewise to be exhorted to learn to read,) and to have a Bible." Cited from *The Directory for the Publick Worship of God of 1645*. This directory can be found in most editions of the Westminster Standards.

[9] I would highly recommend Terry L. Johnson's and J. Ligon Duncan's summary comments on this section of *The Directory for the Publick Worship of God* in "Reading and Praying the Bible in Corporate Worship" in *Give Praise to God: A Vision for Reforming Worship* (P&R Publishing, 2003), 143-148. They outline "eleven pieces of exceedingly wise biblical and pastoral counsel" (143) from the 17th century document that remain relevant for 21st century worship.

[10] William Taylor's comments are noteworthy: "We ought not, therefore, to regard this part of the service as of subordinate importance, or to engage in it in a perfunctory manner. Let us feel that we are dealing with the Word of God, and that will produce within us such reverence and docility of spirit, that as we read, the people will be hushed into attentiveness, and will listen, not as unto us, but as unto God." *The Ministry of the Word*, 214.

[11] Again Taylor aptly admonished the would-be preachers, "Remember that it is God's word you are dealing with, and that greater results may be expected from that than from any preaching of yours." *The Ministry of the Word*, 220.

[12] Significantly, giving serious attention to the Word leads to a commitment to obey. For instance, when Moses "took the book of the covenant, and read in the audience of the people," they rightly declared, "All that the LORD hath said will we do, and be obedient" (Exodus 24:7; cf. 19:7-8). Although Israel's pledge to obey was tragically short-lived, it was nonetheless the appropriate response. It is foolish, indeed, to hear the word and not do it (see James 1:22-25).

[13] Significantly, Paul's argument against praying in an unknown tongue was that those who would hear him praying would neither understand nor be edified. "What is it then? I will pray with the spirit, and I will pray with the understanding also: I will sing with the spirit, and I will sing with the understanding also. Else when thou shalt bless with the spirit, how shall he that occupieth the room of the unlearned say Amen at thy giving of thanks, seeing he understandeth not what thou sayest? For thou verily givest thanks well, but the other is not edified. I thank my God, I speak with tongues more than ye all: Yet in the church I had rather speak five words with my understanding, that by my voice I might teach others also, than ten thousand words in an unknown tongue" (1 Corinthians 14:15-19).

[14] Terry L. Johnson and J. Ligon Duncan, "Reading and Praying the Bible in Corporate Worship" in *Give Praise to God: A Vision for Reforming Worship* (P&R Publishing, 2003), 148-149. This article offers a sobering contrast between the past and the present in regard to the place and practice of the pastoral prayer in worship; it then provides a helpful section on recommendations for public praying. The conclusion of the authors is noteworthy. "Even as it makes sense to have the minister preach and administer the sacraments, it makes sense to have him pray. The prayers that we envision are those offered by a man called by God, who saturates his mind with the word of God and spends hours each week on his knees before God. Even as the church has deemed it wise to apply the New Testament admonitions to 'guard the gospel' by entrusting its proclamation through word and sacrament only to those ordained to do so, so also it is both pastorally and theologically wise to leave leadership in prayer in the hands of the minister" (169).

[15] "To speak for God to men is a sacred and responsible task. To speak for men to God is not less responsible, and is more solemn. The public prayers of the pastor are apt to be the models of the devotions of his people; when he leads them in prayer he is really teaching them to pray." Robert L. Dabney,

Lectures on Sacred Rhetoric (1870; reprint, Edinburgh: The Banner of Truth Trust, 1979), 347.

[16] *Lectures on Sacred Rhetoric*, 346. Shedd's comments are likewise significant. "A prayer should have a plan as much as a sermon. In the recoil from the formalism of written and read prayers, Protestants have not paid sufficient attention to an orderly and symmetrical structure in public supplications. Extemporaneous prayer, like extemporaneous preaching, is too often the product of the single instant, instead of devout reflection and premeditation. It might, at first glance, seem that premeditation and supplication are incongruous conceptions; that prayer must be a gush of feeling, without distinct reflection. This is an error. No man, no creature, can pray well without knowing what he is praying for, and whom he is praying to. Everything in prayer, and especially in public prayer, ought to be well considered and well weighed." William G. T. Shedd, *Homiletics and Pastoral Theology* (Edinburgh: William Oliphant and Co., 2nd edition, 1874), 271.

[17] I do offer a brief exposition of Daniel's classic prayer that you may find helpful in *God's Unfailing Purpose: The Message of Daniel* (Greenville: Ambassador Emerald International, 2003), 119-124. You will see there how biblical prayer (1) flows from the Word of God, (2) involves confession, (3) invokes great things from God, and (4) appeals to the supreme motive, which is God's glory. You can find further lessons about biblical praying in my article "Hezekiah's Letter," in *Biblical Viewpoint* (November, 1983) XVII, 37-43.

[18] Although not a paragon of ministerial compassion or concern, Jonah's prayer from the belly of the great fish is a casebook example of what it is to saturate prayer with scriptural language (Jonah 2). Almost every line of his prayer is either a direct quotation from or very close allusion to some line from the Psalter (just look at the cross references in your Bible). Though he repeated the words of Scripture, he adapted and applied the truths to his own unique need and circumstance. Think what we will of Jonah, his knowledge of Scripture that surfaced in this most distressing and disgusting environment depicts a man who knew how to pray. His prayer was in a very private setting, but its pattern and example is appropriate for public praying as well. A key point to remember is this: Jonah did not simply recite scriptural language; he really prayed using scriptural terms.

[19] *Lectures on Sacred Rhetoric*, 345. He further said that "during the 'Dark Ages,' the disgraceful incompetency of the clergy resulted, first, in the introduction of forms of prayer, and, second, in the customary disuse of the divinely-appointed ordinance of preaching. The Reformation reversed all

this. It has become the characteristic of the Popish religion that it makes the liturgical service nearly the whole of public worship, and the Reformed that it makes the sermon the prominent part" (345).

[20] The New Testament uses over thirty words to designate this verbal communication of God's Word, and particularly the gospel. The most common word for preaching in the New Testament (kerussein, 61 times) has the idea of a herald announcing the arrival of a king or proclaiming the king's message. That is precisely what a preacher must do: the message is not his but the King's. The second most common word, from which we get the word "evangelize" (*euaggelizein*, 54 times), means "to announce good news." The noun form of this word is the New Testament word for "gospel." Indeed, there is no better news for people to hear than that Jesus Christ died for their sins and was raised again the third day, all according to the Scripture (1 Corinthians 15:3-4).

[21] R. Albert Mohler, Jr., "Expository Preaching: Center of Christian Worship" in *Give Praise to God: A Vision for Reforming Worship*, 109.

[22] *The Directory for the Publick Worship of God* in the section "Of the Preaching of the Word" sets down some sobering guidelines for how "the servant of Christ, whatever his method be, is to perform his whole ministry." I think these recommendations are worth repeating verbatim.
a. Painfully, not doing the work of the Lord negligently.
b. Plainly, that the meanest may understand; delivering the truth not in the enticing words of man's wisdom, but in demonstration of the Spirit and of power, lest the cross of Christ should be made of none effect; abstaining also from an unprofitable use of unknown tongues, strange phrases, and cadences of sounds and words; sparingly citing sentences of ecclesiastical or other human writers, ancient or modern, be they ever so elegant.
c. Faithfully, looking at the honour of Christ, the conversion, edification, and salvation of the people, not at his own gain or glory; keeping nothing back which may promote those holy ends, giving to every one his own portion, and bearing indifferent respect unto all, without neglecting the meanest, or sparing the greatest in their sins.
d. Wisely, framing all his doctrines, exhortations, and especially his reproofs, in such a manner as may be most likely to prevail; shewing all due respect to each man's person and place, and not mixing his own passion or bitterness.
e. Gravely, as becometh the word of God; shunning all such gesture, voice, and expressions, as may occasion the corruptions of men to despise him and his ministry.
f. With loving affection, that the people may see all coming from his godly zeal, and hearty desire to do them good. And,
g. As taught of God, and persuaded in his own heart, that all he teacheth is

the truth of Christ; and walking before his flock, as an example to them in it; earnestly, both in private and publick, recommending his labours to the blessing of God, and watchfully looking to himself, and the flock whereof the Lord hath made him overseer: So shall the doctrine of truth be preserved uncorrupt, many souls converted and built up, and himself receive manifold comforts of his labours even in this life, and afterward the crown of glory laid up for him in the world to come.

[23] I would recommend the following articles that deal with some of the important issues regarding worship singing: Paul S. Jones, "Hymnody in a Post-Hymnody World" and Terry L. Johnson, "Restoring Psalm Singing to Our Worship." Both of these are in *Give Praise to God: A Vision for Reforming Worship*. See also, W. Robert Godfrey, "The Psalms and Contemporary Worship," Brian Schwertley, "The Biblical Case for Exclusive Psalmody," and Benjamin Shaw, "A Defense of Biblical Hymnody in *The Worship of God: Reformed Concepts of Biblical Worship* (Taylors, S. C.: Christian Focus Publications, 2005).

[24] In deference to my many musical friends who are most expert in music and godly in character, my musical incompetence does not disqualify me from these opinions. Many advocates of what I would regard as biblically aberrant musical practices are accomplished musicians. I agree with the sentiment expressed by Terry L. Johnson in "Restoring Psalm Singing to Our Worship" in *Give Praise to God*, 271. He says, "Singing must have its own inherent properties that God values.... This is a subject concerning which evangelical Christians have paid little attention. The components of song, word and tunes, are both almost universally assumed to be secondary issues, matters of taste or personal preference. Many ministers, who typically have the highest level of theological and pastoral training in a given congregation, turn music matters over to music directors and worship teams.... This indifference flies in the face of the common consent of humanity....The church...is to have its own distinctive music that is, unlike that of the world, characterized by 'weight and majesty.'"

[25] I would say that many of the arguments that I have heard over the years against CCM fail to evaluate and criticize on significant biblical and theological grounds and have done little to dissuade its advocates. For an atypical but extremely helpful biblical and philosophical analysis of the issue, I would recommend John Makujina's *Measuring the Music: Another Look at the Contemporary Christian Music Debate* (Willow Street, PA: Old Path Publications, 2002).

[26] I remind you of the change in punctuation for this verse that I suggested in

note 2 above. The verse would read like this: "Let the word of Christ dwell in you richly, in all wisdom teaching and admonishing one another, with psalms and hymns and spiritual songs singing with grace in your heart to the Lord." I'm not opposed in principle to using psalms, hymns, and spiritual songs as a means of teaching and admonishing one another; I just don't think that's what the verse is saying.

CHAPTER 5

[1] The *Westminster Confession of Faith* 21.6 and 7 expressly state the historic Protestant understanding of the Sabbath:

As it is the law of nature, that, in general, a due proportion of time be set apart for the worship of God; so, in His Word, by a positive, moral, and perpetual commandment binding all men in all ages, He hath particularly appointed one day in seven, for a Sabbath, to be kept holy unto him; which, from the beginning of the world to the resurrection of Christ, was the last day of the week; and, from the resurrection of Christ, was changed unto the first day of the week, which, in Scripture, is called the Lord's Day, and is to be continued to the end of the world, as the Christian Sabbath.

This Sabbath is then kept holy unto the Lord, when men, after a due preparing of their hearts, and ordering of their common affairs before-hand, do not only observe and holy rest, all the day, from their own works, words, and thoughts about their worldly employments and recreations, but also are taken up, the whole time, in the public and private exercises of worship, and in the duties of necessity and mercy.

[2] For a more thorough discussion of some of these matters, such as the shift of Sabbath day from the seventh to the first, I highly recommend the exposition and analysis of the fourth commandment by my ministerial colleague Alan Cairns in *Chariots of God* (Greenville: Ambassador-Emerald International, 2000), 193-209. Also helpful is the work by Joseph Pipa, *The Lord's Day* (Ross-shire, Great Britain: Christian Focus Publications, 1997).

[3] See my analysis of this issue in *Beginning at Moses: A Guide to Finding Christ in the Old Testament* (Greenville: Ambassador-Emerald International, 2nd edition, 2001), 261-268.

[4] That the sabbath principle is a creation ordinance is strong evidence against

identifying it as a Jewish occasion. There was a sabbath long before there was ever an Israel. Geerhardus Vos, a well-known Princeton theologian of the early 20th century, noted the connection between the Sabbath's institution at creation and its universal application: "The duty is based in Exodus…not on something done to Israel in particular, but on something done in the creation of the world. This is important, because with it stands or falls the general validity of the commandment for all mankind." *Biblical Theology* (Grand Rapids: Wm. B. Eerdmans Publishing Company, 1948), 139.

[5] Paul, as well as Jesus, has been misunderstood and has become a point of reference for those appealing to the New Testament as warranting the Sabbath's irrelevance in this dispensation. Three texts in particular supposedly nullify the Sabbath principle, notwithstanding the fact that in their respective contexts none addresses the weekly Sabbath at all: Romans 14:5-6, Galatians 4:10-11, and Colossians 2:16-17. Cairns comments that many Christians wrongly appeal to these passages to support their dismissal of the Sabbath. He says, "Usually, the bare recitation of these texts is considered sufficiently persuasive to dismiss all argument for the permanence of sabbath observance. It is confidently held that at the very least, sabbath observance is not mandatory for Christians, while at its worst sabbath-keeping may become legalism. Never was confidence more misplaced. The texts cited do not teach that sabbath observance has been discontinued or made optional. One vital fact must be noted: None of the texts cited makes any reference to the weekly sabbath. In Judaism there were many ceremonial sabbaths. Being purely ceremonial, they passed away with the coming of the gospel substance of which they were foreshadowings. But the Lord has never spoken a single word about abrogating the weekly sabbath." *Chariots of God*, 199.

[6] Many of the Jewish customs and institutions that were operating when Christ came originated in the historically and religiously crucial period between the Testaments. Broadly speaking, three Jewish groups emerged during the Seleucid regime: the Maccabbeans (military resisters), the Hellenists (political compromisers), and the Hasidim (religious separatists). These groups sum up Daniel's prophecy: "And such as do wickedly against the covenant shall he corrupt by flatteries: but the people that do know their God shall be strong, and do exploits" (Daniel 11:32). The Hellenists and the offspring of the Hasidim remained into New Testament times. Of all the movements developing from this period, the Hasidim (pious ones) were primarily responsible for preserving the religious system necessary for the coming of Christ. Unhappily, the movement that was so faithful in preparing the way for Christ became one of the greatest instruments of opposition when He came. In all likelihood, the Hasidim were the predecessors of the Pharisees (separated ones), the religious order that was most vehemently aggressive in its opposition to Jesus Christ.

There is a terrible irony in that opposition that stands as a sobering warning. In their protest of the pagan encroachments of Antiochus, the Hasidim maintained strict adherence to the law of God and devised safeguards for its protection. In their effort to preserve the sanctity of the law, they specified applications of obedience designed to address the particular pressures of the day. Their motives were good and pure, and I believe that many of them were true believers, waiting and looking "for redemption in Jerusalem" (Luke 2:38). They were the fundamentalists of the day. Tragically, it wasn't long before the traditions of their applications gained equal status and identification with the law itself. What they sought to protect became redefined and perverted in the process. They erected a fence around the law that eventually became the law itself in their thinking. So convinced were they of their religious correctness that they accused the perfectly righteous Son of God of breaking the law. It is true enough that Christ often violated the Pharisaical traditions and transgressed their fence, but the truth of the matter is that in order to keep perfectly the law of God, He had to break the laws of the Pharisees. In their legalistic pride and hypocrisy, it never crossed their minds that they could be wrong.

[7] For instance, the Day of Atonement was a sabbath of solemn rest (Leviticus 23:32). Since the date of the Day of Atonement was fixed at the tenth day of the seventh month (Leviticus 23:27), the actual day of the week on which it occurred would float from year to year, just as birthdays and Christmas do. Every so often the Day of Atonement would fall on Saturday, but every year the Day was a sabbath.

[8] Vos makes this point as well: "The principle underlying the sabbath is formulated in the Decalogue itself. It consists in this, that man must copy God in his course of life" (*Biblical Theology*, 139). Similarly, Gustav Oehler in his famous 19th-century *Theology of the Old Testament* (Minneapolis: Klock & Klock Christian Publishers, reprint 1978), 332 notes, "Man, like God, is to work and to rest; thus human life is to be a copy of Divine life."

[9] Walter Kaiser remarks on this rest theology as it relates to Israel's possession of the Promised Land and then makes a significant link to the Sabbath concept. "Yet there was more to this 'rest' than geography. Rest was where the presence of God stopped (in the wilderness wanderings–Num. 10:33) or where He dwelt (1 Chron. 28:2: Ps. 132: 8, 14; Isa. 66:1)." He concludes by saying that every rest in the Old Testament "was only an 'earnest,' down payment, on the final Sabbath rest yet to come in the second advent." *Toward an Old Testament Theology* (Grand Rapids: Zondervan Publishing House, 1978), 128, 130.

[10] *Theology of the Old Testament*, 334.

[11] Pipa recognizes the importance of this passage for a proper understanding of the Lord's Day and offers a helpful exposition in a chapter entitled "The Great Purpose" in his work The Lord's Day (11-24).

[12] In his book *Puritan Reformed Spirituality* (Grand Rapids: Reformation Heritage Books, 2004), Joel Beeke offers a helpful and insightful discussion of the Sabbath and its place in Christian worship (111-118). His conclusion is noteworthy. "We conclude therefore that to omit or neglect the sanctification of the Christian Sabbath is to disobey God, break faith with the Lord Jesus, and rob ourselves of great blessing. Likewise, to keep the Sabbath as it ought to be kept, according to the teaching and example of our Lord, is a large part of living to the glory of God, and is nothing less than 'to begin in this life the eternal sabbath' (Heidelberg Catechism, Question 103)." (117-118).

[13] *Westminster Confession of Faith*, 21.3, 5. Terry L. Johnson, in his article "The Regulative Principle" in *The Worship of God: Reformed Concepts of Biblical Worship* (Taylors, S.C., Christian Focus Publications, 2005), 24-26, succinctly outlines the principal elements of worship as reading, preaching, singing, praying and seeing the Bible. His reference to seeing the Bible plays off Augustine's reference to the sacraments as the "visible word."

[14] Calvin links the use of the written Word with the sacraments in his attack on papal superstition that "thought it enough if the priest mumbled the formula of consecration while the people looked on bewildered and without comprehension." He went to say, "You see how the sacrament requires preaching to beget faith. And we need not labor to prove this when it is perfectly clear what Christ did, what he commanded us to do, what the apostles followed, and what the purer church observed. Indeed, it was known even from the beginning of the world that whenever God gave a sign to the holy patriarchs it was inseparably linked to doctrine, without which our senses would have been stunned in looking at the bare sign. Accordingly, when we hear the sacramental word mentioned, let us understand the promise, proclaimed in a clear voice by the minister, to lead the people by the hand wherever the sign tends and directs us" (*Institutes of the Christian Religion*, 4. 14. 4). Likewise, the *Westminster Larger Catechism* says, "Christ hath appointed the ministers of His Word, in the administration of this sacrament of the Lord's Supper, to set apart the bread and wine from common use, by the word of institution, thanksgiving, and prayer..."(169). Johnson concurs: "The sacraments are accompanied by extensive Bible reading (e.g., the words of institution and warning) and theological explanation (e.g., the covenant and nature of the sacraments). They are themselves visual symbols of gospel

truths. In Reformed worship the word and sacrament are never separated. Why? Because faith comes by hearing the word of God (Rom. 10: 17)" (*The Worship of God*, 26).

[15] "The grace which is exhibited in or by the sacraments rightly used, is not conferred by any power in them; neither doth the efficacy of a sacrament depend on the piety or intention of him that doth administer it: but upon the work of the Spirit, and the word of institution, which contains, together with a precept authorizing the use thereof, a promise of benefit to worthy receivers" (*Westminster Confession of Faith*, 27.3).

[16] And I would stress this point as well, that they are intended for public and not private worship. They are ordinances of the church and have no place in private celebration.

[17] For more thorough discussions, see D. Marion Clark, "Baptism: Joyful Sign of the Gospel" and Richard D. Phillips, "The Lord's Supper: An Overview" in *Give Praise to God*.

CHAPTER 7

[1] Although many Psalms are anonymous, the superscriptions specify the names of David (73 times), Asaph (12 times), the sons of Korah (11 times), Jeduthun (4 times), Solomon (2 times), Moses (1 time), Heman (1 time), and Ethan (1 time) as being either authors or dedicatees of particular Psalms. Interestingly, the same preposition governing the names can indicate either "by" or "for," so we are not always certain how to understand the status of the person named. For instance, the superscription of Psalm 72 could be translated either "by Solomon" or "for Solomon." At any rate, the inclusion of Moses in the list shows the composition of the Psalms started long before David, and Psalms 126 and 137 with their exilic or post-exilic themes indicate that inspired Psalms were being composed long after David as well.

[2] A frequently quoted Jewish midrash or commentary on Psalm 1:1 says, "Moses gave the Israelites the five books of the Law, and to correspond to these David gave them the Book of Psalms containing five books." This dates around the 10th century A.D. but reflects what seems to be an earlier tradition. Similar statements from Ambrose, Hippolytus, and Jerome reveal that the same tradition existed in the early church. Here are the divisions with

the doxologies that mark them:

Book 1 (Psalms 1-41)–"Blessed be the LORD God of Israel from everlasting, and to everlasting. Amen, and Amen" (41:13).

Book 2 (Psalms 42-72)–"Blessed be the LORD God, the God of Israel, who only doeth wondrous things. And blessed be his glorious name for ever: and let the whole earth be filled with his glory; Amen, and Amen" (72:18-19).

Book 3 (Psalms 73-89)–"Blessed be the LORD for evermore. Amen, and Amen" (89:52).

Book 4 (Psalms 90-106)–"Blessed be the LORD God of Israel from everlasting to everlasting: and let all the people say, Amen. Praise ye the LORD" (106:48).

Book 5 (Psalms 107-50)–a series of doxologies beginning with Psalm 146 and ending with 150 that is a climactic finale not only to the section but to the entire Psalter.

[3] There is evidence that at least two collections–one associated with David and one with Asaph–were in place during the days of Hezekiah (2 Chronicles 29:30). Since some of the inspired Psalms were not yet written, and since the canonical order does not place all of David's Psalms together, it is obvious that Hezekiah's collection neither substantially nor sequentially would have matched our current collection. My guess is that the canonical form took shape in the post-exilic period, most likely under the direction of Ezra.

[4] Bruce Waltke concurs with this basic link between the Pentateuch and the Psalms: "Moses instituted Israel's liturgical elements: its sacred objects, festivals, objects, personnel, and activities. David, Israel's Mozart, transformed the Mosaic liturgy into opera by putting it on the stage of the temple and by accompanying it with the music and the libretto of his psalms." "Theology of Psalms" in *New International Dictionary of Old Testament Theology and Exegesis*, Vol. 4 (Grand Rapids: Zondervan Publishing House, 1997), 1110. Geoffrey Grogan suggests something similar in his explanation of the fivefold division of the Psalter: "Perhaps the reason for the fivefold structure is simply that the story of God's creative and redemptive acts for his people, the wise laws and gift of worship institutions, all recorded in the Pentateuch, should be taken up unto the people's worship as well as being subjects of affirmation and injunction" in *Prayer, Praise & Prophecy: A Theology of the Psalms* (Great Britain: Christian Focus Publications, 2001), 179.

[5] In the meantime, take a look at Grogan's *Prayer, Praise & Prophecy*. I think you will find it to be a helpful development of the theology of the Psalms.

[6] In his comments on the Psalms' emphasis on God's perfections, W. A. VanGemeren draws an interesting line from Moses to the Psalms. Just after

the transgression of the golden calf, God answered Moses's prayer to see His glory with the promise that He would cause His goodness and glory to pass before him (Exodus 33:19, 22). Then on Sinai, the Lord showed Himself to Moses and made a remarkable declaration about Himself: "The LORD, The LORD God, merciful and gracious, longsuffering, and abundant in goodness and truth, Keeping mercy for thousands, forgiving iniquity, and that will by no means clear the guilty..." (Exodus 34:6-7). VanGemeren remarks: "The perfections of Yahweh are those qualities revealed to Israel through Moses...by which the Lord maintains a blessed and meaningful relation with his people. The laments and praises of the Psalms express confidence in the Lord, as he remains the same, even when the circumstances of God's people are continually in flux. The ground for hope lies in the perfections of Yahweh, for he is good, upright, full of integrity, righteous, just, gracious, faithful, loving, compassionate, and forgiving." Van Gemeren then isolates specific perfections, providing examples throughout the Psalms and showing the implications of those perfections for worship. "Psalms" in *The Expositor's Bible Commentary*, Vol. 5 (Grand Rapids: Zondervan Publishing House, 1991), 233-237.

[7] Check these passages for illustrations of this theological connection: Isaiah 42:5-9; 43:1-7; 45:12-17; John 1:1-18; 2 Corinthians 4:6; Colossians 1:13-20. C. Hassell Bullock observes, "What a marvel that the Creator of the world should have intertwined His creative and redemptive designs like warp and woof....Creation is more than the presupposition of redemption. It is God's commitment to redemption." *An Introduction to the Old Testament Poetic Books* (Chicago: Moody Press, 1988), 134.

[8] The key hermeneutical rules include the analogy of Scripture, the uniqueness principle, the type-antitype connection, and the authority of New Testament confirmations. *Beginning at Moses*, 297-298.

[9] See *Beginning at Moses*, 300-320.

[10] In light of a common notion that the Imprecatory Psalms reflect a primitive or sub-Christian spirit, it is particularly significant to note their occurrences outside the Psalms. Interestingly, some of the severest of imprecations come from Jeremiah, the weeping prophet (15:15; 17:18; 18:21-23) and from the apostle Paul himself (Galatians 1:8-9; 5:12; 2 Timothy 4:14). That martyred souls in heaven pray for God's vengeance to be let loose against their executioners dramatically proves the appropriateness of such prayers (Revelation 6:10).

[11] In discussing the Imprecatory Psalms, J. Barton Payne offers five explanations "for the justification of these divinely approved words." Here is a summary of his explanation. (1) They often contain poetic statements that must be interpreted figuratively. (2) They reflect an abhorrence of sin. (3) They consign vengeance into God's hands. (4) They express goals beyond private vindication, namely, God's glory. (5) They reveal God's attitude about sin and therefore stand as warnings to sinners. *The Theology of the Older Testament* (Grand Rapids: Zondervan Publishing House, 1972), 202-203. To this list should be added the fact that some of the imprecations are prophetic of the ministry of Christ (see Psalms 69:25 and 109:8 with Acts 1:20; Psalm 69:4 with John 15:25; Psalm 69:9 with John 2:17 and Romans 15:3).

Waltke offers a helpful explanation of the Imprecatory Psalms in his article on Psalm theology in *New International Dictionary of Old Testament Theology and Exegesis*, IV, 1106. He counts thirty-five psalms that petition God to punish enemies and claims that "they teach sound doctrine" and "are most holy." He sums them up in this way. (1) "These petitions are by saints...who have suffered gross injustices." (2) "They are righteous and just; they ask for strict retribution." (3) "These petitions are full of faith....in them the psalmists trust God, not themselves, to avenge the gross injustices against them." (4) "These prayers are ethical, asking God to distinguish between right and wrong." (5) "They are theocratic, looking for the establishment of a righteous kingdom by the Moral Administrator of the Universe." (6) "They are theocentric, aiming to see God praised for manifesting his righteousness and justice in the eyes of all." (7) "They are evangelistic, aiming for the conversion of the earth by letting all people see that the Lord is Most High over all the earth." (8) "They are covenantal; a wrong against a saint is seen as a wrong against God." (9) "The prayers are oriental, full of figures, especially hyperbole." (10) "They are political." By this he means that the wicked would be exposed for what they were, and the righteous would then side with the offended.

I cite Waltke's explanation because I think it is a good one, but I do so reluctantly because his conclusion tragically misses the point. He says, "Though theologically sound, however, these petitions for retribution are inappropriate for the church...." All I can say is, "O well!"

[12] I'm not a church historian, so researching all the annals and councils for appropriate citations is outside my competence. However, for a readable summary of the Psalms' use throughout church history, I would recommend the article by Terry L. Johnson, "Restoring Psalm Singing to Our Worship" in *Give Praise to God: A Vision for Reforming Worship* (Phillipsburg, New Jersey: P&R Publishing, 2003), 257-286.

[13] Concerning this debate, I have already recommended the counterpoint articles by Brian Schwertley and Benjamin Shaw, which argue for exclusive

psalmody and biblical hymnody respectively in *The Worship of God: Reformed Concepts of Biblical Worship* (Taylors, South Carolina: Christian Focus Publications, 2005).

[14] Johnson, 262.

[15] In his preface to the Psalter, Calvin comments on both the words and the tunes to be sung in worship. "Moreover, that which St. Augustine has said is true, that no one is able to sing things worthy of God except that which he has received from him. Therefore, when we have looked thoroughly, and searched here and there, we shall not find better songs nor more fitting for the purpose, than the Psalms of David, which the Holy Spirit spoke and made through him. And moreover, when we sing them, we are certain that God puts in our mouths these, as if he himself were singing in us to exalt his glory." And then with reference to tunes, he says: "Care must always be taken that the song be neither light nor frivolous; but that it have weight and majesty (as St. Augustine says), and also, there is a great difference between music which one makes to entertain men at table and their houses, and the Psalms which are sung in the Church in the presence of God and his angels." Quoted in Johnson, 272-273.

APPENDIX 1

[1] This is a paper I read at the Bible Faculty Leadership Summit in August, 2002. It is an adaptation of an article I wrote for the *Biblical Viewpoint*, Vol. 32, 1998.

[2] For a concise synopsis of the form and style see Douglas Stuart's analysis of Malachi in Volume 3 of *The Minor Prophets: An Exegetical and Expository Commentary* (Grand Rapids: Baker Books, 1998). Integrating the obvious forms to the message, Stuart effectively illustrates Malachi's use of disputation and chiasm throughout the commentary. By the way, the whole three-volume set edited by Thomas McComiskey is one of the best on the Minor Prophets. In *The Literary Structure of the Old Testament* (Grand Rapids: Baker Book House, 1999), David Dorsey, not suprisingly if you have read Dorsey, recognizes chiasm both in the whole of the book and in the specific units. E. Ray Clendenen argues for three chiastic movements in terms of "the hortatory structures" of problem, command, and motivation in "The Structure of Malachi: A Textlinguistic Study," *Criswell Theological Reviews*, 2.1 (1987).

APPENDIX 5

[1] Paul Basden, "Introduction," in *Exploring the Worship Spectrum: Six Views*, ed. Paul Basden (Grand Rapids: Zondervan, 2004), p. 11. Basden illustrates: "Christ-followers have debated controversial issues—when and whom to baptize, how to observe Holy Communion, how often and how long to preach—only to watch those debates degenerate into rancorous fights and full-blown schisms. For example, Eastern and Western churchmen fought over the role of icons in worship, eventually dividing Christendom; Calvinists killed Anabaptists over the baptism question; Luther split with Zwingli over the meaning of the Lord's Supper; Puritans separated from Anglicans over the priority of the preached Word," p. 11.

[2] Harold Best, "A Traditional Worship Response," in *Exploring the Worship Spectrum: Six Views*, ed. Paul Basden (Grand Rapids: Zondervan, 2004), p. 119.

[3] Alexander Schmemann, *Introduction to Liturgical Theology* (New York: St. Vladimir's Seminary Press, 1986), p. 30.

[4] Monte E. Wilson, "Church-o-Rama or Corporate Worship" in *The Compromised Church: The Present Evangelical Crisis*, ed. John H. Armstrong (Wheaton: Crossway Books, 1998), p. 68.

[5] Robert Webber, "Blended Worship," in *Exploring the Worship Spectrum: Six Views*, ed. Paul Basden (Grand Rapids: Zondervan, 2004), p. 176-7.

[6] Webber, "Blended Worship," 176-7.

[7] Webber, "Blended Worship," 176-7.

[8] Ibid., 178.

[9] The post-apostolic church studied apostolic doctrine and examples, as well as Old Testament doctrines and practices, and developed a full-blown pattern of worship. Cf. Wilson, "Corporate Worship," p. 72.

[10] Harry L. Poe writes: "Worship held a particularly powerful evangelistic sway over the Celtic peoples of western Europe. Druidism, that often romanticized religion of the Celts, included human sacrifice and cannibalism. Believing

that gods inhabited the trees, the Celts sacrificed their victims on trees. They thought that the god entered the body of the sacrifice to receive it. The Celts then drank the blood and ate the flesh of the sacrifice to receive the power of the god. Though the Romans began suppressing this practice in Gaul as early as the time of Julius Caesar, it persisted in the Celtic regions that never came under the jurisdiction of the Empire, notably Ireland, Scotland and Germany. Martin of Tours and generations of monks after him challenged the druids and set up places of Christian worship at the pagan holy sites of druidism. There they offered the sacrifice of the flesh and blood of Jesus. They obtained immortality by drinking Jesus' blood and eating his flesh. It is not surprising that the Catholic doctrine of transubstantiation emerged from the Celtic church in northern Europe, not the Latin church" (Harry L. Poe, "Worship & Ministry" in *New Dimensions in Evangelical Thought*, David S. Dockery, editor [Downers Grove, IL: InterVarsity Press, 1998], p. 437).

[11] Much of this section is taken from Don Hustad's *True Worship: Reclaiming the Wonder & Majesty* (Wheaton: Hope Publishing Co., 1998), pp. 16-20.

[12] In the Foreword of Hustad's *True Worship*, Paul Westermeyer writes: "Twenty years ago Erik Routley noted 'the shocking spectacle of churches feeling obligated to run two services on a Sunday morning, one popular or modern, the other traditional, thus effectively dividing their congregations into two parties which find it convenient not to meet.' Some Roman Catholics who began this procedure after Vatican II have more recently called it into question, while Protestants who were slower to begin it have now vigorously imitated their sisters and brothers without learning from their mistakes" (p. 8).

[13] Millard J. Erickson, *Where Is Theology Going?* (Grand Rapids: Baker, 1994), p. 41.

[14] Chuck De Groat, "A Growing Hunger for Honesty and Authenticity," in the recent issue of *By Faith* magazine (http://www.byfaithonline.com).

[15] Robert Webber, *The Younger Evangelicals: Facing the Challenges of the New World* (Grand Rapids: Baker Books, 2002).

[16] Webber is one of these leaders. A professor of Theology Emeritus at Wheaton College, Webber and a cast of "young in spirit" leaders (see *The Younger Evangelicals*, pp. 14-19) including Sally Morgenthaler, Brian McClaren, Stanley Grenz, and others offer a vision of church bathed in the "historic substance of the faith" lost in the last 25 years of ministry and reset in the "new cultural condition of the twenty-first century."

[17] Webber, *The Younger Evangelicals*, 23-42.

[18] Dan Kimball, *The Emerging Church: Vintage Christianity for New Generations*. (Grand Rapids: Zondervan, 2003), p. 103. ISBN 0-310-24564-8

[19] Adapted from Dan Kimball, *The Emerging Church,* p. 105.

[20] Dan Kimball, *The Emerging Church,* p. 149.

[21] The word *tradition* is repeatedly bashed these days by the marketing gurus. (See the superb critique of Philip Kenneson and James Street called *Selling Out the Church: The Dangers of Church Marketing* [Nashville: Abingdon Press, 1997]). Why is our culture so hostile to tradition? Much of the antipathy arises from a confusion between "tradition" and "traditionalism." Historian Jaroslav Pelikan's brilliant distinction is forever apt that *traditionalism* is the dead faith of the living, whereas *tradition* is the living faith of the dead. In our churches' struggles over such issues as worship forms and styles, traditionalism usually becomes an idolatry of "the way it's always been done." In contrast, to value the Church's tradition is to recognize that our forebears in the faith had many insights into what worship means, that their hymns carried the faith well, and that therefore those tools and forms are vital to immersing us into the presence of God. Moreover, to value tradition does not mean one is closed to new expressions of faith.

[22] Mark A. Noll, *A History of Christianity In The United States And Canada* (Grand Rapids: Eerdmans, 1992), pp. 174-78.

SCRIPTURE INDEX

Genesis

1:18-22	210
1:27	210
3:16	202
3:24	137
4:1	255
4:26	255
15:6	255
16:12	44
18:16-33	86

Exodus

3:5	63
3:12	251
3:14	254
3:14-15	63
3:18	251
4:23	251
5:1	251
5:3	251
6:3	254, 255
6:6	256
15	98
15:1-18	87
15:11	45, 66
15:20-21	200
16:33-34	137
19:7-8	261
19:9-25	82
20	108, 163
20:2	43
20:3	33, 35, 40
20:4	35
20:7	35
20:8-11	108
20:24	126
20:24-25	133
23:4-5	170
24:7	261
25:8	126
25:9, 40	128
25:22	130
25-30	130
25-31	128

29:42	130
29:42-43	36
30:6	130
32	128, 217
32:11-32	87
33:19, 22	271
34:6-7	271
35:21, 29	192
35-40	128
38:8	133
39:42	128
40	128
40:34-38	129

Leviticus

1:3, 10	139
1:4	140
1:5	140
1:9	141
1:11	35
2	141
2:13	142
3:1-17	142
4-5:13	142
5:14-6:7	142
6:24-30	142
7:11	34
7:11-34	142
10	125, 258
17:11	34
19:17-18	170
19:27	179
20:7-8	22
23:27	267
23:32	267
24:8	134
24:16	254
26:11-12	126
27:30	192

Numbers

10:33	267
16	125
17:10	137

Deuteronomy
4:10 82
5 108, 163
5:12-15 108
6:1, 13, 24 48
6:4 45
6:4-5 40, 250
6:5 46
6:6, 17, 25 48
6:12 49
6:12, 6-9 49
6:15 45, 46
6:25 49
6:7-9 80
6:13 48
6:15 53
8:3 80
9:18-20 87
11:21 191
12 126
26:18-19 15
31:9-12 79
31:19-32:44 98

Joshua
24:14 46, 47
24:15 47

Judges
4-5 200
5 98

1 Samuel
1:8-12 87
4 28
4:21-22 34
15:22 10

2 Samuel
2:1-10 87
6 4
7:22 45

1 Kings
4:32 98
8 67
8:22-61 87

8:23 45

2 Kings
17:24-33 250
18-19 25
19:14-18 87
21 30
21:3-7 33
23:6 33

1 Chronicles
13 4
15:15 5
16 172
25:2, 3 208
28:2 137, 198, 267

2 Chronicles
26 145
29:30 270
34:21-28 201

Ezra
9:5-15 87
9:9 73

Nehemiah
1:4-11 87
8 260
8:1-8 79
8:3 82
8:5 82
8:6 82
8:8 91, 260
9 67, 73
9:3 82
9:6 71, 73
9:48 260

Job
8:13-14 23
38:1-40:5 70
38:7 211

Psalms
1 171
1:1 269

1:2	80	51:17	29, 168
1-41	270	65:3-4	34
2	164, 184	69	169
2:6	56	69:4	272
2:12	165	69:9	272
6	168	69:25	272
8	164, 166	69:35	25
8:1, 9	162, 166	72	269
9:1	163	72:18-19	270
11:7	137	73	171
11:4	27	73:25-28	250
13	168	73-89	270
13:1-2	169	74:2	25
13:3	168	76:2	25
13:5-6	169	78	172
15	171	78:2	172
16	164, 174	78:68	25
16:11	36	82	171
19	149	86:5	22
19:1	59, 253	89:28-29, 34	197
19:5	60	89:52	270
19:14	61	90-106	270
21:12	44	92	172
22	164	92:1-2	66
24	167, 171, 172	93	172
24:3-4a	167	94	172
24:3-4	20, 22, 26, 31,	95:6	69
	131, 137	96	172
29:2	5, 183	97:12	67
29:10	72	98	97
30	172	99:1-5	137
32	168	99:3	67
32:5	167	100	70
35	169	100:2-3	69
36:9	135	102	70, 168
37	171	102:25	70
37:4	42	103	166
38	168	103:1, 22	166
40:5	68	104	70, 72
42-72	270	104:24	71
47:1	180	105	172
48	172	105:1-2	61
49	171	106	172
49:16-17	253	106:48	270
51	168	107	72
51:1-9	168	107:2a	160
51:10-13	168	107:2	73
51:14-16	168	107:8, 15, 21, 31	73

107-150	270	1:5	17
109	169	1:5b-6	16
109:8	272	1:5-9	16
110	164, 174	1:7-8	16
112	171	1:10-15	18
119:18	96	1:11	18, 19, 20
120-135	172	1:12	19, 20
126	269	1:13	19, 20
127	171	1:13-14	18, 20
128	171	1:15	18, 19, 22
129:5	25	1:16-17	21
130	168	1:18	21
131	171	4:5	149
132:7-8	137	4:6-12	17
132:8, 14	267	5, 26-27	98
135	166, 172	6:1	145
135:1, 21	166	6:2	146
135:5	162	6:4	149
136	67, 167, 172	6:5	150
136:1, 26	167	6:6-7	151
136:1-26	67	6:8	152
136:26	167	6:9-13	153
137	169, 269	6:10	153
138:5	162	6:13	153
139:21-22	170	8:3	201
141:2	83, 136	42:1	207
143	168	42:5-7	271
145-150	166	42:8	34, 53
150:2	65, 67	43:1-7	271
		45:5	40
Proverbs		45:12-17	271
29:1	17	53:10	143
		55:7-9	22
Ecclesiastes		58	112, 115
5:1	79, 114	58:1-5	112
5:1-2	4, 160	58:6-12	112
5:2	79	58:13-14	113
12:1-7	51	58:14	115
		61:1	91
		64:1-3	149
Solomon		66:1	146, 267
4:1-7	66		
5:10-16	66	**Jeremiah**	
		2:13	23
Isaiah		3:16	138
1:2	12, 16	3:16-17	137
1:3	12	4:4	29
1:4	13	4:5, 6	29

7	23, 53, 91, 171	**Hosea**	
7:2	24, 30	4:9	188
7:3	7, 24, 29		
7:4	24, 25	**Joel**	
7:4, 8	25	2:28-29	201
7:8	25		
7:9	26, 27	**Amos**	
7:10	26, 27	4	73
7:11	27	4:13	71
7:12, 14	28	5:8	71
7:13	28	5:18-20	194
7:16	30		
7:18	30		
7:21-28	30	**Jonah**	
10:6, 10	45	2	174, 262
15:15	271		
17:18	271	**Micah**	
18:21-23	271	6	10
19:13	30	6:6-7	11
32:17	71		
32:29	30	**Habakkuk**	
44:17	30	3	98
Ezekiel		**Haggai**	
1:28	33, 61, 158	1:13	89
1, 10	137		
2:4	90		
8	32	**Malachi**	
8:3	33	1:2	187
8:3, 5	33, 35	1:2-5	187
8:4	33	1:6	188
8:6	34	1:6-7	18, 188
8:6, 9, 10,		1:7	189
13, 15, 17	35	1:7-13	189
8:8	35	1:13	190
8-10	32, 35	1:14	188, 190
8:12	36	2:1-2	190
8:14	35	2:3	190
8:16	35	2:3, 9	190
8:16-18	35	2:6-7	188
8:18	36	2:10-13	190
10:18	32, 36	2:10-16	190
16:13	214	2:14	190
27:7	214	2:17	191, 194
37:17-22	252	3:1	195, 196
		3:2	193, 196
Daniel		3:5	196
9	67	3:6	197
9:3-19	87	3:7-12	192
11:32	266		

3:8	18
3:13	192
3:14	192, 251
3:16	197. 198
3:17	198
3:18	198
4:1	193
4:1-2	198
4:5-6	196

Matthew

3:1	91
4:4	80
5:14	135
5:17-37	43
5:38-45	170
5-7	49
6:9	55
6:9-13	87
6:10	170
6:19-24	50
10:37	47
11:5	91
11:28-29	105
15:6, 9	10
15:8	10
15:9	9
18:17-20	78
18:20	78
19:16-20	43
28:19	57, 119

Mark

1:22	211
2:27	111
2:27-28	107
7:6	10
7:7	9
7:7-8	10
12:29	46
12:29-30	40
14:36	55

Luke

1:46-55	87, 98
1:67-79	98
2:29-32	98

2:38	267
4:16	79
4:44	91
11:13	135
14:26	47
24:27	163
24:44	163

John

1:1-18	271
1:7	135
1:9	135
1:12	211
1:14	127
2:17	272
4	6
4:23	55
4:24	6, 46, 181
5:23	56
8:12	135
8:58	64
12:41	145
14:6	56
14:15	48
15:3	134
15:16	55
15:25	272
17	87
17:1	55
21:25	68

Acts

1:14, 24	84
1:20	272
2	201
2:15	228
2:25-36	174
2:42	258
2:46	259
3:1	228, 259
4:23-24, 31	84
4:25	174
5:42	91
6:2-4	85
10:9	228
12:5	84
13:14-41	91

14:1	91
17	91
17:11	80
18:4	259
20:7	91
20:27	91
20:36	85
21:9	201
21:26	259

Romans

1:18-32	35
2:28-29	29
3:23	15
3:24-25	138
4:25	140
5:1, 10	142
5:6	140
6:23	140
7:12	43
8:3	130
10:13-17	93
11:36	250
12:1	134, 258
14:5-6	266
15:3	272
15:16	258
16:1, 3, 6, 7, 13, 15	200

1 Corinthians

1:18	92
1:21	92
1:29	214
3:16-17	127
4:9	211
6:19	57
6:20	57
10	28
10:6, 11	172
10:31	250
11	200, 202, 205, 206
11:2, 16	206
11:3	207
11:4-5	212
11:4-6	208
11:5, 6	214
11:6	213

11:7	210, 213
11:7-15	210
11:10	210, 211
11:11-12	211
11:12	212
11:13	212
11:14, 15	212
11:15	210, 213
11:23-26	119
11:26	120
11:29	118, 121
12:28-29	204
14	203
14:4	208
14:15-19	261
14:21	202
14:24	208
14:26	261
14:29-40	202
14:34	199
14:34-35	202
14:40	78
15:3-4	263

2 Corinthians

1:3	55
1:20	197
2:17	93
3:18	134
4:4	135
4:6	271
5:14	105
5:14-15	44
5:21	140
6:16	127
13:14	57

Galatians

1:8-9	271
3:28	211
4:10-11	266

Ephesians

1:7, 12	73
1:15-23	87
1:22	207
3:10	311
3:14	55

3:16   253
4:11   204
4:11-12   93
5:2   141
5:18-19   98
5:19   173, 208, 248
5:26-2   134

Philippians
2:6-11   99
2:10-11   56, 154

Colossians
1:13-20   271
1:16   69
1:27   253
2:16-17   266
3:1-2   52
3:16   98, 173, 208,
                248, 258

1 Thessalonians
2:13   96

1 Timothy
1:17   66
2:1   87
2:5   56
2:8   203
2:9   203
2:11-12   199, 208
3:16   99
4:6, 13   90
4:13   79
5:21   211

2 Timothy
3:5   25
4:2   90, 95
4:10   54
4:14   271
4:18   56
Titus
3:5   134

Hebrews
1:6   56

1:6-7, 14   151
1:12   214
3:3b-4   69
4:9   107
4:13   27
4:15   130
8:2   258
9:8, 9   132
9:12   132, 141
9:23-24   127
10   30
10:19   141
10:22   34
11:6   61
12:19-20   82
12:26   82
13:12   143

James
1:22-25   261
1:23-25   134
1:27   21, 112
4:4   31
5:13   173

1 Peter
1:3   55
1:15-16   105
1:19   139
2:5   74
2:9   73
4:11   56, 94

2 Peter
1:20-21   160
3:18   56

1 John
1:6   26
1:7, 9   143
1:9   167
1:9, 7   152
2:1-2   143
3:20   151
4:19   47
5:3   48, 105

Revelation

1:1	154
1:3	79
1:6	56, 158
1:8, 11, 17	157
1:12, 20	156
1:13	78, 156
1:13, 20	127
1:14	157
1:15	157
1:16	157
1:17	61, 158
1:18	157
1:20	157
2:1	127
2, 3	211
3:20	31
4	155
4:8-11	99
4:11	68, 155
5	155
5:5	155
5:9	75
5:9-13	99
5:11	155
5:12	75
5:13	75, 154
7:10-12	156
7:12	154
11	196
13:8	139
19:10	39, 40
21:22	103
22:3	103